Red Hat® Linux® 7

Install, Configure, and Customize

Send Us Your Comments

To comment on this book or any other PRIMA TECH title, visit our reader response page on the Web at **www.prima-tech.com/comments**.

How to Order

For information on quantity discounts, contact the publisher: Prima Publishing, P.O. Box 1260BK, Rocklin, CA 95677-1260; (916) 787-7000. On your letterhead include information concerning the intended use of the books and the number of books you wish to purchase. For individual orders, visit PRIMA TECH's Web site at **www.prima-tech.com**.

Red Hat Linux 7

Install, Configure, and Customize

Brian Proffitt

A Division of Prima Publishing

A Division of Prima Publishing

Prima Publishing and colophon are registered trademarks of Prima Communications, Inc. PRIMA TECH is a trademark of Prima Communications, Inc., Roseville, California 95661.

Linux is a registered trademark of Linus Torvalds. The Linux penguin, Tux, is used with permission from Larry Ewing (**lewing@isc.tamu.edu**). Ewing created this image using The GIMP (**www.gimp.org**). Modifications to Tux were made by Jim Thompson.

Red Hat, the Red Hat "Shadow Man" logo, RPM, Maximum RPM, the RPM logo, Linux Library, PowerTools, Linux Undercover, Rhmember, Rhmember More, Rough Cuts, Rawhide, and all Red Hat-based trademarks and logos are trademarks or registered trademarks of Red Hat software, Inc. in the United States and other countries.

Microsoft and Windows are registered trademarks of Microsoft Corporation. Mac and Macintosh are trademarks or registered trademarks of Apple Computer, Inc.

Netscape is a registered trademark of Netscape Communications Corporation.

Sun, Sun Microsystems, and StarOffice are trademarks or registered trademarks of Sun Microsystems, Inc.

Prima Publishing and the authors have attempted throughout this book to distinguish proprietary trademarks from descriptive terms by following the capitalization style used by the manufacturers.

Important: If you experience problems running or installing Red Hat Linux 7, go to Red Hat's Web site at **www.redhat.com** for support and technical information. Prima Publishing cannot provide software support.

Information contained in this book has been obtained by Prima Publishing from sources believed to be reliable. However, because of the possibility of human or mechanical error by our sources, Prima Publishing, or others, the Publisher does not guarantee the accuracy, adequacy, or completeness of any information and is not responsible for any errors or omissions or the results obtained from use of such information. Readers should be particularly aware of the fact that the Internet is an ever-changing entity. Some facts may have changed since this book went to press.

ISBN: 0-7615-3150-5

Library of Congress Catalog Card Number: 00-108122

Printed in the United States of America

00 01 02 03 04 II 10 9 8 7 6 5 4 3 2 1

Publisher
Stacy L. Hiquet

Marketing Manager
Judi Taylor

Associate Marketing Manager
Jody Kennen

Managing Editor
Sandy Doell

Acquisitions Editor
Lynette Quinn

Project Editor
Kelly Talbot

Editorial Assistant
Cathleen D. Snyder

Technical Reviewers
Charles Coffing
David Fields

Copy Editor
Kate Shoup Welsh

Interior Layout
Scribe Tribe

Cover Design
Prima Design Team

Indexer
Johnna VanHoose Dinse

*To 10 years of marriage to
the best friend I'll ever have.*

Acknowledgments

It goes without saying that you would not be holding this book in your hands had not some very talented and creative people lent their skills to help me get this done in what may be record time.

I can never express enough gratitude to my editors. For those of you who think this brilliant writing is the sole product of my fevered work (all two of you), you would be wrong. And I thank them all profusely!

This is the second edition of this book, and I must thank the previous authors whose work I expanded upon to cover Red Hat Linux 7: Randal G. Nelson, Duane Evenson, Charles Coffing, Patrick Lambert, and Zonker Brockmeier.

They say no man is an island. I am fortunate enough to have three spectacular women in my life who know how to treat me right (or drive me insane, depending on the time of day). My wife and two wonderful daughters get the big thanks and smooches for putting up with me squirreled away in the office for days at a stretch.

Brian Proffitt lives and works deep in the booming metropolis known as Indianapolis, where three times a year race fans swoop in and drive like maniacs—in RVs, no less. Otherwise, a nice place to live. When he's not writing books like *Sun StarOffice for Linux* (Prima, 2000) or *XHTML Web Development Fast & Easy* (Prima, 2000), Brian loves being a dad and husband.

In his very limited spare time, Brian does some swooping of his own as a soloing student pilot, trying to get his private pilot's license before it starts snowing—which in Indiana means October.

Contents at a Glance

Contents

Part II:
Configuring Red Hat Linux 7 69

Chapter 3: Configuring the X Window System 71

Chapter 4: Configuring Your Environment 93

Chapter 10: Installing Software 237

Chapter 11: Adding New Hardware 253

Chapter 12: Compiling a Kernel 271

Chapter 13: Troubleshooting 299

Part IV:
Appendixes 323

Suddenly, Linux is a hot property in the world of business. In late 1999, Linux companies who ventured out onto the stock market with their initial public offerings found their stock snapped up and the prices for it skyrocketing. Now in mid-2000, this buying seems to have slowed down a bit, but the Linux world is still growing at a fantastic rate.

I tend to think that there may be some validity to this growth and, since I'm writing this book, I'll tell you why. It has finally gotten across to business people that there is more to Linux than just a desktop operating system.

If you were to look for Linux PCs in the business environment, you would be hard-pressed to locate such machines. The common misperception that there are "no good Linux applications" (a point of view, I often notice, is endorsed highly by a Redmond, Washington company) has not been shaken in corporate America. Minds are getting changed, but its slow going.

Where Linux is really making big waves is in the embedded systems market. *Embedded systems*, for those who are not familiar with the term, are the programming commands that run within many of today's modern electronic devices. Set-top computers, microwaves, digital cameras—all have embedded systems. And in this arena, Linux is king.

Why is this so? Size. While hardware is always striving to be bigger and faster, software strives to be smaller and faster. The bigger the code, the slower the application, and the more chances it has to break. Linux, as an unadorned operating system, is very small and stable compared to Windows or Mac OS. It is also a lot smaller and faster than Windows CE, one of Linux's competitors in embedded systems. Even running on a PC with a window manager and a desktop environment's graphic user interface, Linux still outperforms its competitors.

Linux's success in embedded systems is finally turning enough heads and gotten people to wonder if its stability and speed can be reflected on the PC. The answer is, of course, it can!

Where Linux has its greatest strength is also one of its major weaknesses. Linux has been lovingly crafted and added upon by programmers and developers since its creation in 1991. Code was written for efficiency, with user needs coming in second or even third. After all, initial users of Linux were typically fellow programmers who loved to play with the code just as much as the designer.

Now that Linux is making headway in the PC arena, many changes are being made to some of these troublesome areas. With Red Hat Linux 7, no longer is it necessary to use strange, arcane rituals to install the OS on your PC. Installing software and hardware, while still sticky, is becoming easier as well.

Linux is not perfect; nothing ever is. Red Hat Linux can be characterized as being in its adolescent phase, awkward with great potential. Which is why this book has been written—to show you the ins and outs of working with one of the hottest operating systems today.

Is This Book for You?

Oh sure, we could lie to you and say "yes" no matter what. But, to be honest, this book is not for everyone. Much of the book focuses on customization and configuration issues with X Window and Red Hat Linux—something that will rankle "pure" Linux enthusiasts who prefer to use the console all the time. To those advanced users, I might suggest getting another book that suits your needs.

This book is geared more for new Linux users, especially those of you who possessed any skill level in the Microsoft Windows arena and are now wondering what the heck this whole Linux thing is about. There are parts of Linux that will seem nice and familiar to Windows users, and parts that will seem like an alien landscape.

Linux users with a moderate amount of experience will also benefit from this book, as several powerful configuration methods will be revealed.

How This Book Is Organized

Like the title says, this book is designed to help you install, configure, and customize Red Hat Linux 7. For that purpose, the chapters of the book are organized in these three major sections:

- Installing Red Hat 7
- Configuring Red Hat 7
- Customizing Your Red Hat 7 System

Finally, an extensive appendix section will provide a Linux primer, online resources, and a hardware configuration journal template.

Conventions Used in This Book

When you need to hold down the first key while you press a second key, a plus sign (+) is used to show this combination (such as Alt+F or Ctrl+Z).

The quickest way to access a feature is often by clicking a button on a toolbar. In this case, the appropriate toolbar button is mentioned in the text after the menu choice (for example, "Choose File, Open, or click the Open button").

Bold text indicates text you should type; ~~monospace~~ text indicates commands.

Special Elements in This Book

You will find several special elements that will make using this book easier as you read each chapter.

BUZZWORD

Terms and phrases that geek-like people toss around. Great for understanding this book, bad for use at parties and other social functions.

Tasks

TASK

This book contains dozens of tasks, each designed to walk you right through the most commonly performed functions in Red Hat Linux. This approach gets you on the way to using the application in the most efficient manner.

Tips tell you about new and faster ways to accomplish a goal.

TIP

Notes delve into background information regarding a given topic.

NOTE

Cautions warn about pitfalls and glitches in the application or procedures.

CAUTION

PART I

Installing Red Hat Linux 7

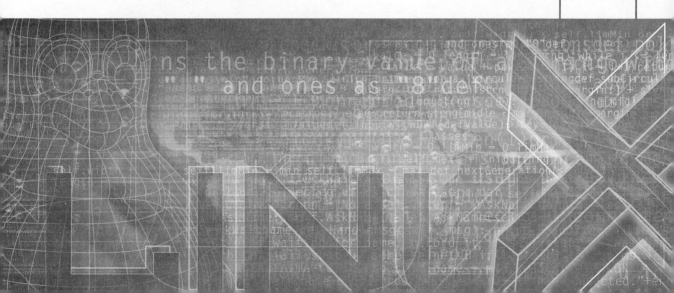

Chapter 1: Before You Install Red Hat Linux 7

Gathering Information About Your System

Checking for Hardware Compatibility

Backing Up Your Old Data

To Dual Boot or Not to Dual Boot——That Is the Question

L et's start by dispelling a common myth: Red Hat Linux 7 is not an exceptionally hard operating system to install. Nor, truth to tell, is it exceptionally easy as compared to, say, Microsoft Windows.

Since the inception of Microsoft Windows 95, users have become accustomed to relying on its ubiquitous SETUP.EXE file, designed to automatically identify your computer's components. It then attempts to match the components with their appropriate files and places those files in the proper locations on your computer (you hope).

Windows users can get away with this simply because Microsoft, with its very pervasiveness, has managed to keep hardware systems within a certain "compatibility window." For example, each PC manufacturer logically attempts to make small improvements over its competitors, changing and enhancing various component parts and then competitively marketing those enhancements. However, if each wants to include Windows with its products, thus taking advantage of the huge Microsoft following, each will adhere to Microsoft's specifications despite fierce competition. This way, any enhancements can, in theory, be reasonably identified by the Windows SETUP.EXE program.

Critics of Linux have said that Linux is too rigid and inflexible and thus is it too difficult to use. Although Linux does indeed have its problems, inflexibility is certainly not one of them. Windows only *appears* to be more flexible, but that's because its installation path to a given PC has already been paved by hardware manufacturers whose components conform to Windows' suggested standards. Linux, on the other hand, does not have cooperative agreements with PC and hardware manufacturers (although some have come into existence very recently). So, like Scarlett O'Hara, Linux too must "depend on the kindness of strangers" to find its way onto different systems. It is partly through the efforts of talented and dedicated volunteers that hardware support is accomplished.

During installation, Linux distributions will typically ignore any unrecognizable hardware device, indifferently continuing its installation process. Linux may also incorrectly identify the hardware. As you can imagine, this can be a problem if the device in question is your PC's video card and you can't see anything on the screen, or worse, the video card has been misidentified and you are left with a miasma displayed on the monitor. Luckily, the number of devices that Linux cannot work with is decreasing rapidly, and this trend is expected to continue. Linux programmers continue to add hardware drivers to the Linux kernel, including Plug and Play technology—Windows' method to configure new hardware devices.

Until the majority of common devices are automatically recognized by the Linux kernel, you'll need to first determine whether Linux will run on your computer. To do so, you will need to know where to locate the hardware information about your PC.

Gathering Information About Your System

How well do you really know your PC? *Really* know it? Are you just passing acquaintances, or do you know it down to its very soul (or at least the jumper settings on your sound card)? To find out just how well Linux will run on your PC, you need to know the workings of your machine fairly well.

Don't worry, you will not have to open your computer. In fact, I strongly recommend against this. Your Windows machine has a tool that enables you to see into the inner mechanics of your PC.

Checking Your Device Manager in Windows

As you begin examining your computer, notice that a lot of the information you need to know is right there in front of you. Your monitor, for instance, is sitting on your table or desk with its brand name and model displayed on the front or back. The same is probably true for your printer and any other external devices you might have. You'll want to take note of both the brand name and model as they appear on the device.

In addition to identifying external devices, you'll need to determine what's actually inside your computer. One place to start is by displaying a list of devices as identified by your existing operating system. Windows 95, 98, and 2000 use a built-in applet called the Device Manager to list known devices. In Windows NT, perhaps the best place to view installed devices is the Windows NT Diagnostics applet, located in the Administrative Tools menu.

In Windows 95 and 98, open the Device Manager by clicking the Start button on the Windows taskbar and then choosing Settings, Control Panel. When the Control Panel window appears, double-click the System icon to open the System Properties dialog box, shown in Figure 1.1.

Click the Device Manager tab to list the inner workings of your computer, as shown in Figure 1.2.

Now you need to do some old-fashioned detective footwork. Your computer may (or may not) actually use a device for each of the device types listed in the Device

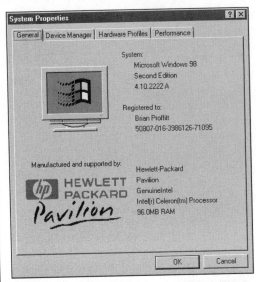

Figure 1.1   *The System Properties dialog box is the home of the Device Manager.*

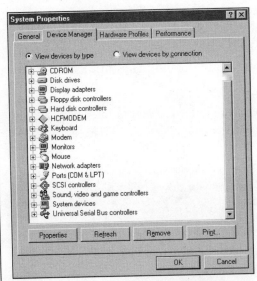

Figure 1.2   *The Device Manager will show you nearly every hardware device used by your computer (at least as identified by your current operating system).*

Manager. For example, to determine whether you have a CD-ROM drive installed in your computer and to list its brand, first expand the CD-ROM list by clicking its expansion control—the little plus sign (see Figure 1.3).

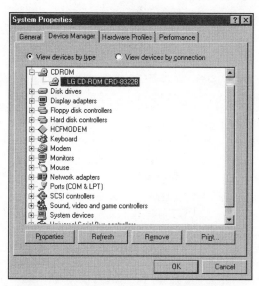

Figure 1.3   *Open a list of devices by clicking the expansion box.*

As you can see in Figure 1.3, this computer has one CD-ROM drive, with a rather cryptic label. To find out more about a device, select it and then click the Properties button. (Alternatively, double-click the selected device.) For example, click the listed CD-ROM device and then click Properties. The Properties dialog box for the CD-ROM drive appears (see Figure 1.4).

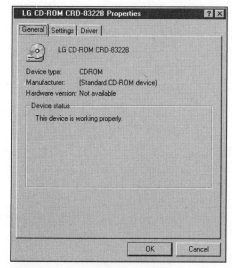

Figure 1.4   *Not too much information here, but every little bit helps.*

This is a classic example of a device that has been made to conform to Windows' standards—so much so that Windows does not care who manufactured it. As far as Windows is concerned, this is just a CD-ROM drive that follows Western Digital's ATAPI standard. Even so, it is still a good idea to record the information so that it can be checked against Red Hat Linux's hardware-compatibility list.

You may find that other books urge readers to keep a Linux Journal to track and record all of their PC's hardware along with any other issues that may arise while installing Linux. I agree with this approach, to the point that I've included a working form in Appendix C, "Hardware Compatibility Journal," to use as you gather hardware data. Some sort of journal is a good idea. Jotting down all of this information with a pencil and paper, however, can be an onerous job. Follow these steps to simplify the task and print all of your PC's hardware information in one fell swoop:

1. In the System Properties dialog box, click the Print button. The Print dialog box will appear, as shown in Figure 1.5.

2. Select All Devices and System Summary and then click OK. All of the information available to the Device Manager will be printed.

You will find this information to be very technical—most of which you will not need. To successfully install Red Hat Linux, the most important information you need is for those devices that make your computer operable, as listed in Table 1.1.

In addition to the critical hardware, other hardware types that may be part of your computer system should also be recorded in your journal. These hardware types are listed in Table 1.2.

Most of the information you require is included in the Device Manager output you printed, but not all. For example, you can locate information on the amount of RAM installed on your computer by clicking the Performance tab in the System Properties dialog box. Another option might be to right-click on your hard drive

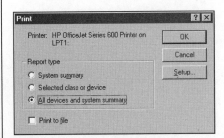

Figure 1.5 *Getting your device information on paper*

Table 1.1 Primary Hardware Information Needed for Red Hat Linux Installation

Hardware	Information Needed
CPU	Manufacturer, model, speed
Motherboard	Manufacturer, model
Buses	Manufacturer, model
Memory (RAM)	Size
Video card	Manufacturer, model, video RAM size
Monitor	Manufacturer, model, horizontal and vertical synchronization rates
Hard drive	Manufacturer, model, size, type (SCSI versus IDE)
Network card	Manufacturer, model
CD-ROM drive	Manufacturer, model, size
Floppy drive	Manufacturer, model, size
Modem	Manufacturer, model, transmission speed
Printer	Manufacturer, model
Mouse	Manufacturer, model, type (PS/2 versus serial)
Keyboard	Manufacturer, model, number of keys, language
SCSI card and devices	Manufacturer, model, type of device controlled
IDE adapters	Manufacturer, model, type of device controlled

Table 1.2 Secondary Hardware Information Needed for Red Hat Linux Installation

Hardware	Information Needed
ZIP/JAZ drive	Manufacturer, model, size
Tape drive	Manufacturer, model, size
Sound card	Manufacturer, model
Scanner	Manufacturer, model
Infrared device	Manufacturer, model, type of device controlled
Joystick	Manufacturer, model
Serial device	Manufacturer, model, type of device controlled
Parallel device	Manufacturer, model, type of device controlled
PCMCIA	Manufacturer, model, card type

letter as listed in My Computer or Windows Explorer, checking the Properties option to see how large your drive space is. A little detective work will go a long way toward making your Red Hat Linux installation easier.

Checking Your BIOS for Information

The type of BIOS used by your PC presents another potential compatibility issue when you are installing Red Hat 7. The Basic Input Output System (BIOS) is firmware that exists on your PC regardless of what operating system you're using. It exists primarily to take care of the really basic housekeeping functions of your PC. For instance, the BIOS controls which drive boots up first and how power is managed on your PC.

The BIOS may have issues with Red Hat Linux's Linux Loader (LILO). The LILO starts to load Linux (hence the name) after the BIOS is finished with its boot process. When Linux is loaded, LILO first looks for the boot partition, which is whatever partition you define to be booted first. Usually, this is the /boot partition, but it does not have to be. If the /boot directory is somewhere where the BIOS and LILO can't find it, you'll have a problem.

NOTE

> The setup of the boot partition (and other partitions) of Red Hat Linux 7 will be discussed in the "Partitions Required by Linux During Installation" section later in this chapter.

Most older BIOSes can't handle more than two hard drives. They may not be able to locate data stored above cylinder 1,023 of any drive. New BIOSes have different, less stringent limitations, but these restrictions are still very prevalent. If you have an older computer, you will want to be sure you have the latest BIOS available for it. This will certainly ease your installation of Red Hat 7.

To examine the BIOS settings for your computer, simply restart your system. Then watch closely. Before your operating system begins to load, you will typically see a line that says `Press F2 for Setup`, or something similar. Sometimes the message passes quickly as your computer steps through its boot-up sequence. Before your operating system beings to load, press the specified key to be taken into the BIOS setup program.

Unless you are very confident about what you are doing, you should follow a strict "look but don't touch" policy when changing BIOS settings. One wrong move and you could have major system problems.

Once inside the BIOS setup program, you should record information relating to your hard drives. Specifically, you are looking for how many and how large the hard drives are on your PC and whether they are IDE- or SCSI-type drives.

Be careful not to confuse the appearance of multiple drive letters on a directory list with the true physical presence of multiple drives. Partitioning software can divide one real (physical) hard drive into a number of virtual (logical) hard drives that operating systems treat as separate entities. The BIOS will list information about your physical drives and information regarding logical drives can be viewed through any directory utility such as Windows Explorer.

Once you've noted your drive information in your Linux journal, exit the BIOS setup program as described by your PC's program, discarding any inadvertent changes you may have made. The computer will then continue to load your primary operating system.

Checking for Network Information

Checking for network information now will save you time as you actually perform your Linux installation. When you install Red Hat Linux, you will be quizzed on various settings, such as how your PC is connected to its network. Even if your PC is not on a physical network, perhaps you connect to the Internet or some other system using a dial-up connection. Therefore, if you'll want to access the Internet using that connection, it is a good idea to write down some important settings so that you can refer to them during Linux installation.

If you typically use a dial-up connection to access the Internet via one of the national service providers such as America Online or CompuServe, be aware that Linux does not provide connection protocols to these services. AT&T Global Network Services is the only Internet service provider (ISP) with a proprietary connection format to which Linux will connect at this time. If you connect to the Internet via an ISP with the more universal PPP connection format, and then you will be all set.

Figure 1.6   *Exploring your computer's connections.*

To check your dial-up settings, click the Start button on the Windows taskbar. Then choose Programs, Accessories, Communications, Dial-Up Networking. This will open the Dial-Up Networking window, shown in Figure 1.6.

If you have any existing dial-up connections, they will appear in this window. Right-click your connection's icon to open the shortcut menu; then select Properties from the menu to open the dialog box for your dial-up connection (see Figure 1.7).

Click the Server Types tab. Note the Type of Dial-Up Server setting in your journal, as well as any other settings on this page of the dialog box. When you're ready,

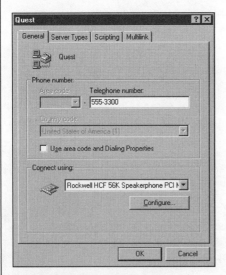

Figure 1.7   *The properties of a dial-up networking connection.*

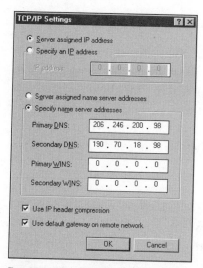

Figure 1.8   *TCP/IP settings are the heart of most Internet connection settings.*

click the TCP/IP Settings button. The TCP/IP Settings dialog box will appear (see Figure 1.8).

The information contained in this dialog box is essential to any connection to the Internet. These settings dictate how your computer talks to other computers on the network once you have dialed in. Every connection is different, so you will want to record these settings exactly.

When finished, click the Cancel button to close the TCP/IP Settings dialog box. Then click Cancel once more to leave the connection dialog box.

> Don't forget to record your user name and password for the connection! You can usually find these in the Network settings in your Windows Control Panel.

If you have any other connections in the Dial-Up Networking window that you'll want to retain in Linux, repeat the procedures in this section for each of them to determine their settings.

Checking for Hardware Compatibility

Now that you have a record of the different pieces of hardware that make up your computer, it's time to start checking whether that hardware is compatible with Red Hat Linux 7.

Resources for Checking Compatibility

When purchasing software at the store, you can flip the box over to read its system requirements. For the most part, the listed requirements are usually complete. Alas, Red Hat Linux's requirements are woefully generalized. Only broad parameters are detailed on the side of the box and with good reason: The hardware-compatibility lists available for Red Hat Linux are pages and pages long. Where do these famed lists exist? Fire up your computer, because you're going surfing on the Web.

Red Hat Hardware

It only makes sense that the best place to locate information about Red Hat Linux 7 is on the Red Hat Web site. The hardware-compatibility lists (HCLs) for all of the major releases of Red Hat Linux are gathered at **www.redhat.com/support/hardware/**.

Before you click the Intel Hardware link to begin examining the HCL for Red Hat Linux 7, allow me to say a few words about the different levels of compatibility in the list: Red Hat supports a very finite set of hardware. That does not mean that other hardware will not work with Red Hat—just that it is not directly supported.

Red Hat divides these differing levels of compatibility into tiers: Tier 1, Tier 2, Tier 3, and Incompatible. Each tier represents the level of compatibility or *comfort* Red Hat will have with a particular piece of hardware. Table 1.3 defines these levels.

Table 1.3 Hardware Compatibility Tiers

Tier	Definition
Tier 1	Fully supported hardware. Red Hat tested, used and approved. Go crazy.
Tier 2	Compatible and supported, but occasional problems have occurred. Red Hat support is limited. Proceed with caution.
Tier 3	Compatible and unsupported. Devices in this category may or may not work. Red Hat will provide very limited support, primarily pointing you to other potential sources for help. Danger, Will Robinson.
Incompatible	Very little chance of this working with Linux. Other daredevil users may have found workarounds, but don't count on it. Here there be dragons.

Despite the fact that the Red Hat HCL is constantly evolving as more solutions to hardware-compatibility issues are discovered, the HCL is very well organized. Each section focuses on a particular type of hardware and includes a definition of the compatibility levels. There is also an important warning about hardware names that bears repeating here.

In the hardware world, the *branding* of a given product occurs by keeping a popular name associated with what may be a completely different product. To provide you with a rather simplified example, a Pentium processor is very different from a Pentium II processor or a Pentium III. Even though the name Pentium is prevalent throughout, these are not the same products. Other brand name differences are much more subtle and the product differences far more drastic. The point here is that if the exact model name or number is not listed in the HCL, the safest assumption is that the hardware is incompatible.

> Later in this chapter, some of the highlights of the Red Hat HCL are discussed.

Linux Hardware Database

Unlike the Red Hat Web site, the Linux Hardware Database Web site (**lhd.datapower.com**) does not offer a comprehensive look at all the hardware that can work with Red Hat Linux. It does, however, offer something the HCL does not: user-written ratings of how hardware really worked with Linux and tips on how to get around some of the sticky issues that can crop up. As shown in Figure 1.9, the Linux Hardware Database Web site contains links to hardware organized by category types.

Clicking on a category link reveals a tabular listing of all the tested hardware types for that category. The hardware is sorted by the rating the product has received (see Figure 1.10).

> Hardware in this database is compared on different versions of Linux and different flavors as well. Be sure to read the testing specifications for each product. Hardware that tested well on earlier Linux kernels should work well with later versions.

The rating system used in this site is based on the average of five categories:

- Stability
- Performance

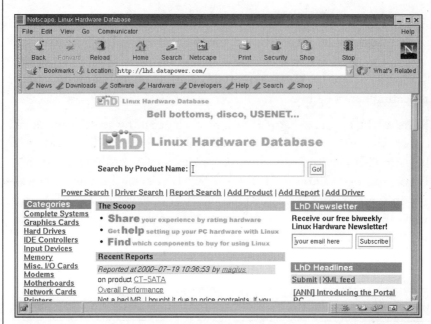

Figure 1.9   *The Linux Hardware Database includes Linux compatibility reviews.*

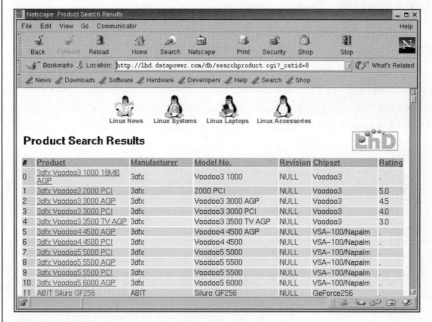

Figure 1.10   *The best hardware to use in a category gets a rating of 5.0.*

- Value
- Ease of setup
- Overall

Each rating category is then based on six rather tongue-in-cheek values—from 0 to 5. The description for the top rating in the Performance category of 5, for example, is "Should be Illegal." (As you've no doubt determined by now, Linux users do not take themselves quite as seriously as do other computer folk.)

Click on the piece of hardware for which you want to view more information. You'll then see a detailed report on the item, including any drivers that can be found for the hardware and user comments or warnings about the item (see Figure 1.11).

As you learn more about Red Hat Linux and become proficient at solving hardware issues, you can come back to this site and enter your own ratings about a product. All you have to do is register, and that's free.

Hardware Supported by Red Hat

Gather your Linux journal and return to the Red Hat Linux Web site so that the HCL is on the screen in front of you. Now it's time to match up your PC's hardware to that on the list. Don't be discouraged if you find that much of your hardware

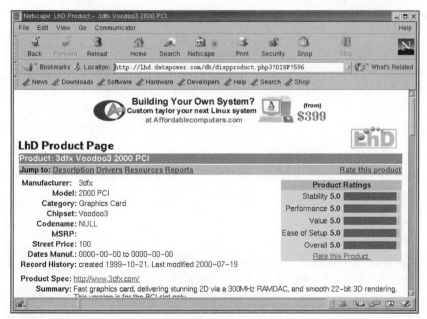

Figure 1.11   *Real, honest opinions really help.*

falls into Tier 2 and Tier 3 categories. Although it may take a bit more effort, it's not the end of the world. There may be a solution that won't involve going to the computer store. (For more information on installing hardware, see Chapter 11, "Adding New Hardware.")

Video Card

Of all of the categories included in the HCL, the section for video cards is probably the most voluminous. That's because the video (or graphics) card could be considered the most important item in a PC, with the exception of the motherboard and CPU. Think about it: If nothing is displayed on the monitor, it's impossible to continue using the operating system. And monitors don't control the video output of the PC—video cards do. Because of this and the vast variations between cards, the HCL devotes a lot of space to listing different video cards.

X Window System

This devotion to detail is a bit ironic when you consider that compatibility with Linux is not the issue; rather, the issue is compatibility with the X Window System. Let me explain: Linux is a text-based, command-line operating system. It's a powerful system to be sure, but really just a collection of command lines much like DOS. To make Linux a more user-friendly system to use, Linux distributors often package a version of the X Window System (also known as *X*) with a release of Linux.

X is the source for all the cool windows and graphical user interfaces (GUIs) that come with today's Linux releases. XFree86 is the most commonly used X server used for Intel-compatible PCs. Because XFree86 is required to display complex screens, XFree86, rather than Linux, is most concerned with video-card compatibility.

Look carefully though the HCL for your video card. Once found, make a note in your journal of which X server will be used. The X server is the specific component of XFree86 used to display the graphics. Since different cards use different versions of X server, you may find it helpful to know this information in case you later have problems with graphic display.

Table 1.4 displays the short list of video cards that are known to be incompatible with XFree86 4.0.1, the release shipped with Red Hat Linux 7.

Table 1.4   Known Incompatible Video Cards

Manufacturer	Product
SiS	530/5591/5596/5511 Pentium PCI/ISA Solution
SiS	600/620/5600 Pentium II multi-function integrated chipsets

Memory (RAM)

As with most operating systems and software, having at least the suggested minimum amount of RAM eliminates most problems. Table 1.5 lists the minimum requirements for RAM for various scenarios, as stated in the HCL.

Table 1.5   Minimum RAM Requirements

RAM	Scenario
16MB	Bare minimum (will need at least 32MB of swap disk space)
24MB	Better performance for the Linux OS
48MB	Recommended to run an X Window manager such as GNOME or KDE

Monitor

As mentioned earlier, the video card performs the lion's share of the work when producing the visual output from your PC. That does not mean, however, that the monitor does not play a role in compatibility with Linux and XFree86. But the place to make sure your monitor can relate well to XFree86 is not here in the pre-installation stage. Monitor compatibility is settled during the installation itself.

To be sure that you are ready for installation, note in your journal the settings for your monitor's synchronization rates. During installation, those settings will be matched to the X server component of XFree86.

For more information on monitor compatibility, visit the FAQ section of the XFree86 Web site at **www.xfree.org/FAQ/#MONITORS**.

Hard Drive

Two types of hard drives are used in PCs: IDE and SCSI. If you haven't already, you can identify the type you have by examining your system BIOS (refer to the section titled "Checking Your BIOS for Information"). Most hard drives are compatible with Red Hat Linux.

Generally, if you have an internal IDE drive, your drive is okay by Red Hat Linux. Because Linux looks at the drive's SCSI controller, the same holds true for any SCSI drive, either internal or external. If the controller is supported, all of the drives connected to it are supported by default.

> External IDE drives, such as Syquest's removable drives, are the one incompatible type of drive mentioned in the HCL, but there is a workaround. Surf to the Linux Parallel Port Home Page (**www.torque.net/linux-pp.html**) to learn how to use this device.

Ethernet Card

During the installation of Red Hat Linux, the presence of a network card is typically detected. Linux will then ask you for your network settings. This section of the HCL reveals that many cards fall into Tier 1 and Tier 2 compatibility categories.

Given the history of Linux and its grandparent UNIX, this makes sense. After all, UNIX was initially designed to work on networks. Therefore, it's logical that network devices are largely compatible. Further, the communications protocols of the Internet are based on UNIX.

You should make sure your card is listed and find out where it falls in the compatibility tiers. Most of the big-name cards fall into Tier 1, which is good. There are even token ring cards that have Tier 2 compatibility—very useful in today's mix-and-match corporate environments.

Table 1.6 lists the Ethernet cards that are known to be incompatible with Red Hat Linux 7.

Table 1.6   Known Incompatible Ethernet Cards

Manufacturer	Product
Intel	EtherExpress Pro/10 PCI
Xircom	Ethernet adapters

While Xircom cards are listed as incompatible, there are workarounds to be found. Try the Xircom Ethernet Issues page at **pcmcia.sourceforge.org/cgi-bin/ HyperNews/get/pcmcia/xircom.html**.

Sound Card

Of all of the devices people will likely add to or upgrade on their computer, the sound card is likely to be near, or at, the top of the list. But sound cards, even in the Windows environment, can be difficult to install and configure. Maybe that's why the HCL lists no sound cards in the Tier 1 category.

It should be noted that even if you have a compatible sound card, it may not be used by Red Hat Linux until you set it up through the sndconfig program. This is rapidly becoming unnecessary as Red Hat is updated, but it is still a prevalent issue. More information on sound cards can be found in Chapter 7, "Configuring Printers, Sound, and Other Devices."

CD-ROM and DVD-ROM

Because hard drives are easy for Red Hat to utilize, you might think CD-ROM drives would be equally accessible. But Red Hat is more picky about what CD-ROM drives it will and will not use.

On the one hand, all 100% ATAPI-compliant CD-ROMs and SCSI CD-ROMs are Tier 1 compatible. Deviations from these, however, can get a little tricky. This is one section of the HCL that you will want to review carefully.

Table 1.7 lists the CD-ROMs that are known to be incompatible with Red Hat Linux 7.

Table 1.7   Known Incompatible CD-ROMs

Manufacturer	Product	Notes
Varied	Parallel-port CD-ROMs	Some BackPacks are Tier 3
LMS/Phillips	Drive 206/cm260	Includes all clones
Liteon	All models	

Unfortunately, DVD players are not yet supported on Red Hat systems. Although progress is being made, for now you're just going to have to watch your favorite movie some other way.

> Your DVD drive is not completely useless. Red Hat Linux will still be able to use it as an extra CD-ROM drive.

Zip/Jaz Drive

It's not immediately obvious where to find Zip drive compatibility listings in the HCL; you'll need to look in Section 3.5, "SCSI Drives." Once you find the listing, however, you'll discover that external Zip and Jaz drives will work, including parallel port Zip drives.

Tape Drive

Most SCSI tape drives are likely to be Tier 2 supported. Remember that if the SCSI controller is supported, any SCSI device attached to it will be supported as well. There is an exception to this rule in this device class, which is listed in Table 1.8.

Table 1.8   Known Incompatible Tape Drives

Manufacturer	Product	Notes
Varied	Non ATAPI parallel-port drives	
Onstream	30GB drive	Includes *all* types (IDE, SCSI, and parallel)

Modem

This is the device you will most likely have trouble with. Simply put, if your computer has an internal modem, it probably won't work. This is because most internal modems use Windows-specific drivers and won't work in other operating systems.

> There is one internal modem, for instance, that will work under Red Hat: the Lucent Venus PCI modem. If you are lucky enough to have this internal modem, return to the Modem section of the HCL after you have installed Red Hat to learn how to tweak your system to use the device. To find more internal modems compatible with Linux, surf to **www.o2.net/~gromitkc/winmodem.html**.

There is a flip side to this bad news. If you have an external modem, it will work. Modems that talk to the PC through a serial port rather than internally do not need Windows drivers to work. Even though I have recommended that you try to find workarounds to other device issues, this is one instance where you should just make life easier and purchase an inexpensive external modem.

Other types of external communications devices work under Red Hat Linux as well. ISDN routers, if they are external and can emulate a modem, will usually work, although Linux does classify them as Tier 3.

If you are lucky enough to live in an area of the nation that has cable Internet access, you may have a cable modem. Cable modems that connect to a supported Ethernet interface are Tier 3 supported.

Printer

Setting up a printer in Red Hat Linux has a Windows-like feel to it. Basically, Red Hat Linux does not care what type of printer you have at installation. Setting up your printer is something you will do after installation (see "Printers" in Chapter 7).

The HCL has a good list of the printer filters contained within this version of Red Hat. These filters are directly analogous to the Windows printer drivers. Check the list to see if your printer is there, but don't worry if it isn't. There will be ways of getting the printer installed even if it is not on the compatibility list.

Mouse

The second thing Linux configures during its installation is the mouse. There are four types of mice: PS/2, serial, bus, and USB. The most common types are the PS/2 and serial mice, which are Tier 1 compatible. Bus mice fall into the Tier 2 category, and USB mice are classified as Tier 3.

Since your mouse will very likely fall into either a Tier 1 or Tier 2 category, this device doesn't require much concern. If you have a USB mouse, however, you should be aware that Linux is still in the experimental stages where USB is concerned. You might want to consider getting a new mouse type or not getting a USB mouse in the first place.

For more information on USB devices in Linux, visit **www.linux-usb.org/**.

Keyboard

No keyboard section exists in the HCL. Keyboards are universal to PCs (if any device can truly be called *universal*). Keyboards have long been held to the ANSI standard, which uses a specific code for every character the keyboard can create, no matter what operating system is being used. This standard makes it very easy for Linux to access any keyboard, including the new natural keyboards and those keyboards with pointing devices contained within. USB keyboards, however, like their mice counterparts, should be utilized with caution.

Notebook Computers

A laptop or notebook computer is no more a single device any more than your desktop PC is. There is no one notebook PC that is compatible with Linux as a whole.

A section for notebook computers is included in the HCL, but it is a bit different, containing a great link to the Linux Laptop Web pages. You should follow this link if you are thinking about installing Linux on your laptop PC.

SCSI Adapters

Finally, the section on SCSI cards bears a close look, if only because so many other devices could depend on the compatibility of the primary SCSI card.

This is a large section of the HCL, and you should take the time to find your PC's SCSI adapter. Although there are no incompatible SCSI cards, you will need to use some caution if your card falls into the Tier 3 category.

Backing Up Your Old Data

After you have ascertained your hardware compatibility with Red Hat Linux, you will need to get your computer ready for the installation. One of the first things you should do is back up the data on your PC.

It is always a good idea to back up your valuable data, thus guarding against system catastrophe. At the very least, you'll want your data protected from power surges, virus attacks, computer theft, or anything else that can affect your ability to access the data on your machine.

Installing Linux certainly can't be classified as a catastrophic event. But you are going to be changing your hard drive's partitions or perhaps even formatting your hard drive. These events can and will erase data completely.

The first thing you should decide is what data should be backed up. That really depends on what you want to do in your Linux installation. If you plan to dual boot (running Windows and Linux on the same PC), you will need to make sure you've safeguarded most of your Windows data. More information about dual booting can be found in the section titled "To Dual Boot or Not to Dual Boot—That Is the Question" later in this chapter.

Even if you plan to completely remove Windows, there is still merit to saving your data files. You'll be able to open many of them even after you change to Linux, such as graphic files (GIFs and JPEGs, among others). In addition, Microsoft Office files can even be opened, compliments of a great office suite application called StarOffice, which is fully Office compatible. You'll need to save, not back up, these files if you plan to use them on your Linux machine, though. Linux will not be able to read a Windows backup file.

Most computer applications these days use huge amounts of disk space, primarily because today's big hard drives enable them to do so. Backing up your data and your application files is a big job. If you have sufficient storage capacity (such as a tape or Jaz drive), I recommend that you back up your entire hard drive. Those of you who do not have a sufficient large-capacity device to hold an entire drive's worth of data should just back up your data files—that is, the documents, spreadsheets, drawings, and other files that you have created over time on your computer. If you do run into trouble, you can restore your system by first re-installing your operating system and your applications using your original disks and then restoring your archived personal data files.

If you have never used a backup program, you will find them easy to use. Many backup programs are available, including an excellent one found with Norton System Utilities. The principles for backup utilities are pretty much the same: Locate and identify the files you wish to archive, specify the location of the new archive file, and then create the file. Restoration is simply the reverse of this action.

Microsoft Windows has its own utility for backup that can be used to archive your data. The next few paragraphs describe how to work with the Windows Backup utility.

From the Windows 98 taskbar, click the Start button. Then choose Programs, Accessories, System Tools, Backup. The Microsoft Backup application will start with the Welcome to Microsoft Backup dialog box open (see Figure 1.12). You can now choose to create a new backup file, open an existing backup job, or restore archived data.

The Backup application in Windows 95 is similar to that in Windows 98, except for the lack of a wizard to step you through operations.

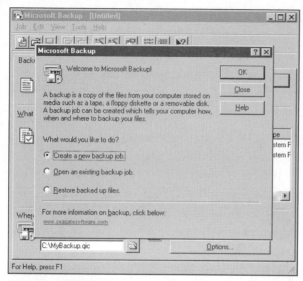

Figure 1.12   *Microsoft's Backup utility.*

Select Create a New Backup Job, and then click OK. The Backup wizard will appear, as shown in Figure 1.13.

Here you can choose either to back up your entire set of computer files or to back up only selected files. If you have the storage space and the time, go ahead and archive your entire PC. If not, select the Backup Selected Files, Folders, and Drives option, and then click Next. The second dialog box of the Backup wizard will open.

On the left side of the dialog box, select the check boxes for the drives and folders you want to back up. As necessary, use the expansion icons in the directory listing

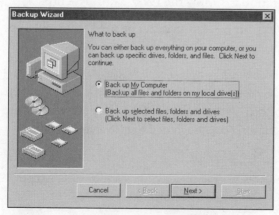

Figure 1.13   *The first step in the Backup process.*

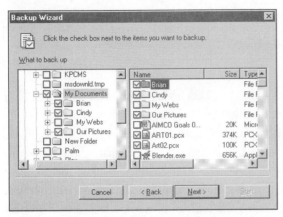

Figure 1.14   *You can select all or part of a folder's contents.*

to view subfolders. Note that selecting a folder automatically selects all of the files within the folder. Alternatively, select or clear the check boxes for the specific files you want to include or exclude from the file list on the right side of the dialog box. Figure 1.14 shows an example of selected files in the My Documents folder.

When you've selected all the files you want to include in your backup job, click Next to continue to the next dialog box of the Backup wizard. You are asked whether you want to back up all the selected files or just the ones that have changed since a prior backup. Since this is likely your first backup, select the All Selected Files option and click Next to continue.

In the fourth dialog box (see Figure 1.15) you are asked where you want to store the backup file. Choose your preferred location and type a file name for your backup file. When complete, click Next to continue.

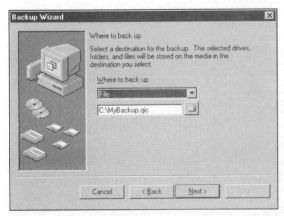

Figure 1.15   *Where do you want to store your backup file?*

> **TIP**
>
> Make sure you save this information on a drive other than your hard drive. Zip, Jaz, or tape drives are good places.

The fifth dialog box gives you two choices on how to back up your data. The first specifies that you want your data to be double-checked to make sure it was successfully archived. Double-checking your data as it's being archived will slow the process down, but I recommend that you do so. After all, what's the point of backing up erroneous data? The second option asks whether you want to compress the backup data. Unless you have virtually unlimited space to store your backup, you'll want this option checked, even though doing so will also slow down the backup process. Choose your preferences, and then click Next to continue to the final dialog box of the Backup wizard.

In the last dialog box (see Figure 1.16), you provide a descriptive name for your backup file. This is different from the file name you previously selected. Use a name to help you remember the contents of the backup archive file.

After you confirm the choices you have made, simply click the Start button to begin the backup process. The Backup Progress window will appear to display the process's progress (see Figure 1.17).

When completed, the backup file will be verified (if you chose to do this), and you will be notified that the operation is complete. Click OK to acknowledge the notification, and then click OK again to close the Backup Progress window.

Make sure the file is stored away from your hard drive (that is, in a Jaz or Zip drive, a CD, or a tape drive). As you will see in the next section, big changes may be coming to your drive.

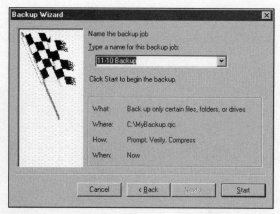

Figure 1.16   *Confirm your backup choices in this dialog box.*

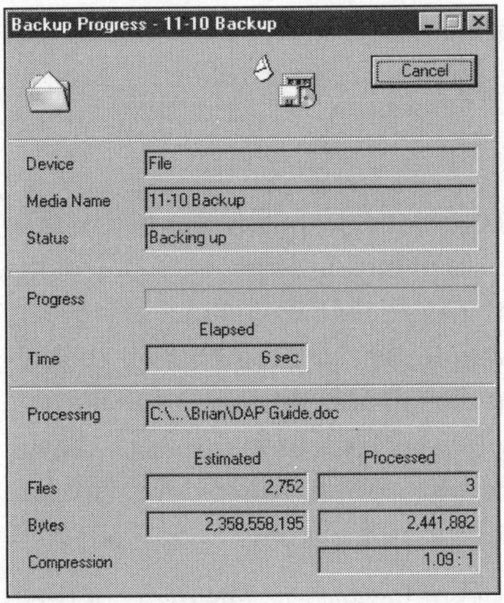

Figure 1.17   *The backup process in action.*

To Dual Boot or Not to Dual Boot—That Is the Question

Now comes the time where you have a really important decision to make. As with all important decisions, you should weigh your options carefully. You must now decide whether you are going to run Red Hat Linux alone on your PC or whether you want to retain your existing operating system and add Linux.

There are several pros and cons for using multiple operating systems on one computer. The cons include the headaches of installing two or more operating systems on a machine, resulting in more limited memory available for each of the operating systems. But the benefits of using multiple operating systems are huge. For instance, you will have the ability to run all of the programs available for each of the operating systems. You will also be able to use all the hardware your PC has. Finally, you'll save money by not needing to buy another PC.

I think dual booting is the way you should go—especially if you are just trying Linux out. This option gives you the benefits of using Linux without a lot of investment in time or money.

Making Room for Multiple Operating Systems

If you decide to include Linux on your PC in addition to Windows, you will need to make room for it on your hard drive. Making room on your hard drive for Red Hat Linux is a far different operation from making room for the latest computer game; you must create a brand new *partition* from which Linux will operate.

This is the part of the book where you get a crash course in disk partitions and why you can't write data to a disk without them, so hang on to your collective hats.

Why Partition?

Imagine the bee, buzzing around your garden. If you were to follow this bee back to its home, you would find a seemingly chaotic mass of buzzing insects, each looking as if it aimlessly wanders about with nothing better to do than hang out and buzz. As we all know, however, bees all have a specific purpose, working together for the collective benefit of the hive. One group of bees has the job of taking care of all the cute little baby bees after the queen lays her eggs. Now, think back to your science classes: Where are the baby bees raised? If you said the honeycomb, you're right. If you're wondering what the heck this has to do with partitions, hang on.

The honeycomb is an ingenious device composed of hexagonal cells made of beeswax, where honey and bee larvae are stored for safekeeping. Now, ponder this: How would the bees get by if they did not have honeycombs? The answer is they wouldn't.

Keeping the honeycombs in mind, consider how data is stored on a disk drive. Data, you see, cannot be stored on a drive without some sort of structure already in place for the data to be organized. When data is placed on a drive, it is written into this structure, called a *file system* in the Linux community. A file system is the format in which data is stored—a honeycomb of cells if you will, where each little piece of data gets placed.

Computers being computers, it's a little more complicated than that. Data for a single file, for example, does not get stored in data blocks that sit right next to each other. The data may be stored in data blocks 456, 457, and 458, and then block 6,134, then block 7,111, and so on. (This is an oversimplification, but you get the idea.) It's the job of the file system to track where every part of a file resides. When you send a command to work with a file, the file system knows all of the separate blocks where the file is stored.

Because of all this file tracking and retrieving, computer engineers came up with the idea of keeping the file systems small, even on large hard drives. In this way, the idea of partitions came into play. Basically, the *partition* is a virtual barrier that tells the file system: "You used to be able to write to blocks 1–25,000 all over the disk, but now you're only allowed to write to blocks 1–17,500. A second file system will write to blocks 17,501–25,000, so hands off!"

Thus, you have partitions, and each partition can use a different file system. As an analogy, honeycombs created by honeybees are different than those created by wasps—similar structures but different outcomes.

There are six major types of file systems used on Intel-compatible PCs today, as seen in Table 1.9.

Table 1.9   File System Types (Intel PCs)

File System	Used By
FAT	Windows 95, Windows 98, Windows NT
FAT32	Windows 95b, Windows 98, Windows NT, Windows 2000
NTFS	Windows NT, Windows 2000
ext2	Linux
os2	OS/2
swap	All operating systems

Different types of partitions typically do not work with other operating systems. Thus, in order to install Linux on your PC, you will need to create an ext2 partition on your hard drive. Unfortunately, if your PC contains a typical installation of Windows, your Windows file system is contained within one big partition that covers your entire hard drive. This leaves no room for a partition and a new file system. Remember, even if you have gigabytes of empty space on your drive, this space, like files and directories, may be scattered throughout the drive.

The easiest way to add a partition to your existing hard drive file system is to use a third-party application. This shoves all your data into a single collection of data blocks, leaving truly contiguous empty and unstructured (unformatted) space elsewhere in the drive where you can install a partition.

> Before you use any tool to manipulate and/or create partitions, back up or save your data to an alternate physical drive.

PartitionMagic 5.0

Of all of the partitioning software out on the market today, PartitionMagic is arguably the easiest to use and certainly the most time-tested. PartitionMagic enables you to create partitions on your hard drives with ease. It even comes with BootMagic, a multi–operating system boot utility.

BUZZWORD

Swap partition: A section of space on a hard drive used by the computer as auxiliary RAM. When a program or process uses more memory than RAM exists on the computer, the swap partition provides additional memory for the process to use.

CAUTION

What makes PartitionMagic so great to use is that it actually creates a Linux ext2 partition without potential loss of data. Using PartitionMagic to create a native Linux partition saves you a lot of steps in installation.

For more information on PartitionMagic, surf to **www.powerquest.com/ partitionmagic**. There you will find detailed product information. I heartily recommend this product for your use.

> If you run a search for "linux" on the PartitionMagic Web site, you will find detailed instructions on how to install Linux partitions and mount points. You will learn about mounts points later in this chapter.

fips

If you do not want to plunk down the cash for PartitionMagic, never fear. Red Hat Linux has thoughtfully provided fips, a utility that can resize and create FAT (either FAT16 or FAT32) partitions in Windows systems.

The fips utility reduces the size of your current FAT partition and creates a new FAT partition. Because Linux will only sit inside an ext2 file system, created only from unformatted space during the installation process, you'll need to run the DOS fdisk utility to remove the new FAT partition.

> The fips utility is located in the \dosutils directory on the Red Hat Linux/Intel CD 1. Documentation for fips is located in the \dosutils\fipsdocs directory on the same CD. I strongly agree with Red Hat, which urges you to read the fips documentation before using the application.

When to Use fdisk

You may have heard in computer legend and lore that eventually you will have to use the DOS utility fdisk on your PC. This utility is used when you have to completely wipe the data from your hard drive.

> This section is referring to the DOS fdisk utility, not the Linux version of fdisk, which sometimes has trouble with Windows partitions.

All kidding aside, be very careful when you use fdisk. One wrong move and you *will* lose all of your data.

For the purposes of Linux installation, there are really two instances where you will need to use fdisk. The first instance is if you plan to install Red Hat Linux by itself on the PC. The fdisk utility may be the preferred method should you want to completely wipe the slate clean and install Linux. The second instance is to eliminate any partitions a third-party partitioning utility (such as fips) might have created for you. The fdisk utility can wipe these non-ext2 partitions from the hard drive.

Here's how to use fdisk to remove partitions on your hard drive:

1. Using Windows Explorer, format a floppy disk. Make sure the Create System Disk option is checked.

2. Copy the fdisk.exe file from the \Windows\Commands folder to the floppy disk.

3. Reboot your computer, leaving the floppy disk in the drive. The floppy disk is bootable because you copied the system files to it.

4. When the DOS prompt appears, type **fdisk**, and then press Enter. A message regarding large disk drives will appear (see Figure 1.18).

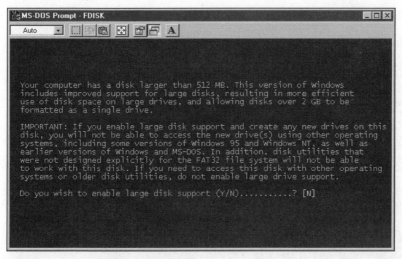

Figure 1.18 *Starting fdisk will display important information about large disk drives.*

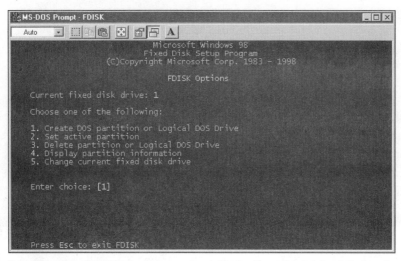

Figure 1.19 *Your FDISK Options—potentially deadly unless in the right hands.*

5. Press N so that large drive support is not enabled.

6. In the FDISK Options screen (see Figure 1.19), press 3 to start the Delete Partition or Logical DOS Drive option.

7. In the Delete DOS Partition or Logical DOS Drive screen (see Figure 1.20), press 1 to activate the Delete Primary DOS Partition option.

8. In the Delete Primary DOS Partition screen, type the number that identifies the partition you want to delete (see Figure 1.21). Refer to the memory listings and file system types to help you identify which partition number you want to remove, if there is more than one.

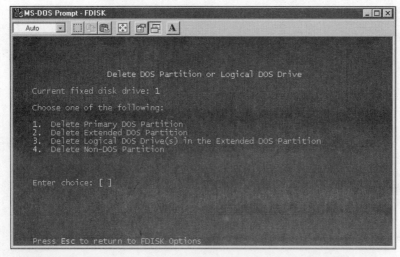

Figure 1.20 *Choose which partition you want to delete in this screen.*

```
MS-DOS Prompt - FDISK                                          _ □ ✕
Auto        🔲 📋 🔳 📂📄 A

                     Delete Primary DOS Partition

        Current fixed disk drive: 1

        Partition  Status   Type   Volume Label  Mbytes  System   Usage
          C: 1       A     PRI DOS  HP_PAVILION    9177   FAT32     100%




        Total disk space is  9177 Mbytes (1 Mbyte = 1048576 bytes)



        WARNING! Data in the deleted Primary DOS Partition will be lost.
        What primary partition do you want to delete..? [1]


        Press Esc to return to FDISK Options
```

Figure 1.21   *The last step before the partition deletion occurs.*

9. Type the volume label of the partition you are deleting. A confirmation line will appear.

10. Verify that you do want to delete the partition, and then press Y in the confirmation line. The partition you chose will be deleted.

11. When complete, press the Esc key until you return to the DOS prompt.

If you're wondering why the deletion of the partition only took a second or two when it seems to take longer to erase just a portion of the hard drive, it's because only the *partition definition* is deleted, not the data within. Without the partition and its file system, however, the data within is a jumbled and worthless mass of data blocks—like honey and bee larvae would be if the honeycomb suddenly vanished. Eliminating this partition essentially erases the data, since you'll never get to it again.

NOTE

Now that you have an idea of how to make room for a Linux partition, it's time to examine just how to set up your Linux partitions. That's right: partitions—plural.

Partitions Required by Linux During Installation

On a Windows PC, you may see that you have multiple hard drives. When Windows sees a new partition, it automatically assigns a drive letter to the drive. This is a pretty simple system.

This is not what happens in Linux, however. Linux needs at least three partitions to work. But if you were to open the File Manager in Linux, you would see the appearance of a single drive's directory tree. So what gives?

Linux manages its files in a completely different way than does Windows. Rather than using drive letters to refer to a partition and its corresponding file system, Linux separates the files and directories needed to compose its single file directory. In truth, this "single" file directory is really composed of separate directory trees that are seamlessly connected across partitions. Where these sub-trees connect or break from the main directory tree are called *mount points*.

Rather than using drive letters to denote partitions, Linux uses a different naming convention:

`/dev/[Drive Type][Device Where Partition Resides][Partition Number]`

Table 1.10 explains the variables used in this naming convention.

Table 1.10   Partition Naming Convention

Variable	Definition
/dev/	All devices in Linux are managed in the /dev/ directory, in-cluding hard drives and their partitions.
Drive Type	This is a two-letter indicator of the hard drive type. Possible values are hd (IDE disk) and sd (SCSI disk).
Device Where Partition Resides	This is the device the partition is on. Possible values are /dev/sda (first SCSI disk) and /dev/hdc (third IDE disk).
Partition Number	This denotes the partition. Possible values are 1–4 (primary or extended partitions) and 5+ (logical partitions).

Within Linux, this division of directories among partitions will be seamless. But when installing Linux, you'll need to think through what partitions you want, what the mount points will be, and how much memory you'll allot to each partition.

What You'll Need

Red Hat Linux recommends that you have three partitions for optimal performance. You can have more, but not fewer. Table 1.11 lists the desired partitions, their space, and their mount points.

Table 1.11   Recommended Linux Partitions for Intel PCs

Partition	Mount Point	Memory Allotment
Boot partition	/boot	No more than 16MB
Root partition	/	A minimum of 600MB for minimal install, 1.5GB to install all packages
Swap partition	None	Equal to your PC's RAM, a minimum of 32MB

You do not have to use these settings, but they are reasonably straightforward and will enable Linux to run at peak performance.

Swap Partitions and You

The swap partition is not a new concept for those of you coming from a Windows background. In that environment, the swap partition was called a *swap file* or *virtual memory*.

What the swap partition does, simply, is to act as extra memory beyond that found in RAM for your applications to run. You see, applications, especially graphic interface applications such as X, use RAM as "workspace." If applications require and use a lot of RAM, they may have to slow down or pause while waiting for other applications to finish and free up RAM.

To help counteract this slow-down, swap partitions use hard disk space that emulates operating memory for greedy applications. Granted, swapping information into and out of hard drive space is slower than RAM, but it can be faster than waiting to share a finite amount of available RAM.

The swap partition gets no mount point, because there is generally no need for the user to access what's transpiring.

It is a common misconception that the upper limit of the swap partition is 128MB. Since Linux kernel release 2.2.0, that limit is no longer a factor.

Partitioning Strategies with Disk Druid

The place where you will actually apply your partition strategy is Disk Druid. Disk Druid is either first seen in the Installation program (if you have any existing partitions on your PC) or during the Custom installation path.

> Disk Druid is also a partitioning utility, but it is not recommended that you create a disk partition from scratch with it. Such partitions may become unreadable to other operating systems on your PC. You will have better results using a third-party utility as suggested earlier in this chapter and then using Disk Druid to change partition types and set partition mount points. This process will be described in Chapter 2, "Installing Red Hat Linux 7."

The most crucial part of your partition strategy is where you decide to put your /boot partition. If you recall, many BIOSes have limitations as to where they can refer to find the Linux Loader (LILO) that resides in the /boot partition. If you put your /boot partition somewhere your BIOS can't access, you will not be able to start Red Hat Linux.

Positioning the /boot Partition on Large Drives

Hard drives are physically divided into cylinders. Because of BIOS limitations, it is vital that the /boot partition sits completely below cylinder 1,023, without any portion of the partition overlapping cylinder 1,023. Keep the whole partition under this cylinder to avoid massive headaches, whether you are using single- or multiple-drive strategies.

Multiple Drives

You may remember that when you checked the BIOS for information, you recorded how many physical drives you had and what kind they were. Here's where that information comes into play.

The BIOS on many PCs has trouble booting to certain types of drives. Therefore it is imperative that you place the /boot partition on the correct hard drive. Table 1.12 illustrates different hard drive scenarios and recommends /boot partition locations.

Table 1.12 Recommended /boot Partition Locations

Partition	Solution
Multiple IDE drives	/boot should be mounted on one of the first two hard drives connected to your *primary* IDE controller.
IDE and SCSI drives	/boot should be mounted on the first IDE drive or the ID 0 SCSI drive.
Multiple SCSI drives	/boot should be mounted on the ID 0 or ID 1 SCSI drives.

Conclusion

This chapter delves into some of the major considerations and information you need to gather prior to installing Red Hat Linux 7 on your system. In Chapter 2, this preparation will be put to work while you install Red Hat Linux 7 on your PC.

Chapter 2: Installing Red Hat Linux 7

Starting the Red Hat Installer

Running Your Installation

Other Installation Concerns

By the end of this chapter, you should have Red Hat Linux 7 installed on your PC.

Bold statement? Hardly. The plain fact is that installation is not that big of a deal any more—*if* you did your preparation in Chapter 1, "Before You Install Red Hat Linux 7." It is important that you gathered all the information specified in Chapter 1 because you are going to need it to double-check what the installation program does, entering the information yourself if need be.

Three words of advice before you begin: do not panic. If you read the instructions carefully and have the right information, little can go wrong.

Starting the Red Hat Installer

There are various ways to install Red Hat Linux 7. The easiest way is to use the official Red Hat 7 CD-ROMs that you can buy with the official boxed sets in most software stores.

Red Hat Linux 7 can be purchased in three flavors: The Standard, Deluxe, and Professional editions. The Standard edition contains the *Red Hat Linux Installation Guide and Reference Guide*, as well as a boot disk. You'll find out more about this important disk in the next section, "Creating a Boot Disk." In the Deluxe and Professional editions, a CD-ROM set of Linux workstation applications, PowerTools, and a CD-ROM with Sun StarOffice 5.1 are included for your use. The Professional edition also includes a bonus pack of server applications and additional Web building tools.

If you can't get a boxed copy of Red Hat Linux or don't want to lay out the cash, you can always download the software yourself, as well as all the tools you need. A quick check of Linux-related Web sites will point you to these tools and more. For example, StarOffice, a very robust office suite application that's fully compatible with Microsoft Office, can be found at **www.sun.com/staroffice**. The documentation included in the boxed set is freely available in HTML or Acrobat PDF format on the Web at **www.redhat.com/support/manuals/**.

If you do download the Red Hat Linux software, I strongly recommend burning the material to your own set of CD-ROMs. Not only is installation a lot easier from a CD-ROM, but you will also have a permanently stored set of Red Hat 7 software.

The final component needed to duplicate any of the boxed sets is the boot disk, the creation of which is detailed in the next section.

> A great place to learn about downloading Red Hat Linux is **www.redhat.com/ download/howto_download.html**.

> Shameless plug: For more information on Sun StarOffice, read *Sun StarOffice 5.2 for Linux* (Prima, 2000), written by yours truly.

Creating a Boot Disk

The most important resource you'll need besides the Linux program is the boot disk. Without your own copy of the boot disk, you may have difficulty installing the software.

A boot disk is required because Linux cannot be installed from within another operating system. The installation process must begin right after a PC starts, before any operating system loads. Many older PCs cannot start directly from a CD-ROM drive, but they can start from the floppy drive. Have you ever noticed the sound of the floppy drive rattling when your computer is turned on? That's the BIOS looking for a boot disk in the drive.

BUZZWORD

Boot disk: A floppy disk containing Linux system files that allow users access the Red Hat Linux CD-ROM *before* the operating system is loaded.

> If you are fortunate enough to have a bootable CD-ROM drive, you will not need a boot disk. You can simply insert the Red Hat Linux CD 1 into your CD-ROM drive and restart the computer. The installation program will then begin automatically.

The boot disk contains just enough Linux commands to start a mini-version of Linux, including the instructions that enable Linux to recognize and run your CD-ROM drive. At that point, you can "jumpstart" the full installation program into action.

Use this procedure to make your own boot disk:

Creating a Linux Boot Disk

This task demonstrates how to create a Linux boot disk.

1. Format a 3.5-inch disk and leave it in the floppy drive.
2. Insert the Red Hat Linux CD 1 into the CD-ROM drive.
3. Start an MS-DOS window by selecting Programs, MS-DOS Prompt on the Start menu.
4. Type ***<drive letter>:***, where *<drive letter>* is the letter of your CD-ROM drive.
5. Type **cd \dosutils**. You should now be in the dosutils directory on the CD.
6. Type **rawrite**. The rawrite application will start.
7. When prompted for a disk image source, type **..\images\boot.img**.
8. When prompted for the target diskette drive, type ***<drive letter>:***, where *<drive letter>* is the letter of your floppy drive.
9. Press the Enter key when prompted. The Red Hat Linux boot instructions will be copied to your floppy disk.

If you later choose to use the Custom installation path, you will be prompted to create another copy of the boot disk. Since having more boot disks is safer, you'll want to go ahead and make one at that time too.

Navigating the Installer

You're ready to begin now. You have all your information, disks ready, and a cute stuffed penguin for luck sitting on your desk. It's time.

Insert the Red Hat CD-ROM 1 into your CD-ROM drive and then shut down your computer. While the computer is off, insert the boot disk into the floppy drive. Then turn your computer on again. Your computer will begin the boot process, starting from your floppy drive. It will then use the instructions on the floppy drive rather than continuing to your hard drive and consequently loading your other operating system.

Remember that if you have a bootable CD-ROM drive, you will not need a boot disk. Your computer will read the boot instructions from the installation CD-ROM disk.

Once the computer recognizes the bootstrap code from the floppy disk or CD-ROM drive, it will then start Anaconda, the Red Hat installation program. The very first screen of Anaconda is shown in Figure 2.1. As you can see, it's rather plain, but it prompts you to make a significant decision.

There are three installation options (sometimes termed "installation classes") from which you can choose when installing Red Hat Linux 7. The first is the graphical mode, which is a Windows-like installation that is certainly the easiest to use. The second option, text mode, is slightly less robust than the graphical mode. It will also get the job done.

The final option is the expert mode. For now, I suggest that you stay away from this one. You should only use expert mode if Linux has trouble detecting the hardware you need to run the installation program, such as the CD-ROM drive and the hard drive. Such an event is rather rare.

Press Enter at the screen shown in Figure 2.1 to start the graphical installation mode.

> After leaving the first screen, more hardware detections will occur. If Red Hat's installation program does not recognize your video card, your screen may appear all white or black. If this happens, restart the PC, this time typing **text** at the opening installation prompt. Text installation mode is less picky about display drivers. You can configure the graphic display once Linux is installed.

TIP

The graphical mode of installation will begin. The next sections of this chapter detail each step of a typical workstation installation.

```
              Welcome to Red Hat Linux 7.0!

o  To install or upgrade a system running Red Hat Linux 3.0.1
   or later in graphical mode, press the <ENTER> key.

o  To install or upgrade a system running Red Hat Linux 3.0.1
   or later in text mode, type: text <ENTER>.

o  To enable expert mode, type: expert <ENTER>.  Press <F3> for
   more information about expert mode.

o  To enable rescue mode, type: linux rescue <ENTER>.  Press <F5>
   for more information about rescue mode.

o  If you have a driver disk, type: linux dd <ENTER>.

o  Use the function keys listed below for more information.




[F1-Main] [F2-General] [F3-Expert] [F4-Kernel] [F5-Rescue]
boot: _
```

Figure 2.1   *Choose the type of installation program to use.*

Running Your Installation

As the installation progresses, you will see a sequence of installation screens that present choices to you based on the type of installation class you chose. These screens are organized in the same manner throughout the entire installation process, as shown in Figure 2.2.

On the left side of the screen, you will see the Online Help pane. This pane contains general help pertinent to the current installation screen. Although it takes up some screen space, I recommend that you leave it on throughout the installation process. This enables you to quickly find help for a term or option you may not understand. If you really think you don't need the Online Help, you can turn it off by clicking the Hide Help button.

The pane on the right side of the screen is where all the action happens. The action pane displays the options appropriate to the current task from which you make your installation choices. Each time you complete a selection, click the Next button to move to the next screen. Conversely, if you need to reverse a decision you made, you can click the Back button and return to the screen you want to change.

In some cases, the Next button is disabled (indicated by its gray appearance) until you have made all the necessary choices—a helpful safety feature.

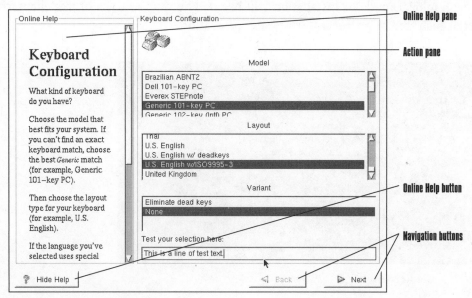

Figure 2.2 *A typical installation screen.*

You can step backward through the Anaconda screens until you reach the About to Install screen. Once you pass this point of no return, you cannot change your mind.

Determining Language, Keyboard, and Mouse Settings

Early in the installation process, Red Hat Linux gathers important information so that its installation can continue smoothly. This information is centered around input—specifically, how you will input data into both Anaconda and, later, Linux. You'll need to select the language, keyboard, and mouse device you want to use.

The very first screen of the installation path requires you to select the language you will use. This will be the language used during the installation process, not necessarily within Red Hat Linux. From the list of languages, select your preferred language and then click the Next button.

The Keyboard Configuration screen, shown in Figure 2.2, appears. There are three categories here used to define your keyboard: Model, Layout, and Variant.

While keyboard models are currently fairly ubiquitous, there are some variations among styles. One example many Americans will recognize is the difference between "natural" (ergonomically designed) keyboards and the more standard (flat) 101-key keyboards. Check for your keyboard model and style in the Model list. If you do not see your specific keyboard model, select Generic 101-key PC.

Layout refers to the alphanumeric characters used by the selected keyboard. For example, someone using the German language will need characters such as ü, and if you live in Great Britain you might require characters such as £. In the United States, one of the U.S. English choices will be appropriate.

The Dead Keys option should be selected if you want an English layout but you also use alternate characters that require the creation of dead keys. If you have a newer computer, choose the ISO-9995-3 option, as it will enable your keyboard to adhere to an international standard.

Dead keys: Keys that allow the quick creation of non-English characters on an English keyboard.

The options in the Variant category will change based on the Layout selected. Typically, the option is to have no variants on your keyboard model and layout versus one or more different variants, such as using dead keys. See your keyboard's documentation for help if you have an unusual typing situation. Once you have completed all your selections, click the Next button.

In the Mouse Configuration screen (see Figure 2.3), you have the option to choose the type of mouse you use. As you can see when you go to the local computer store,

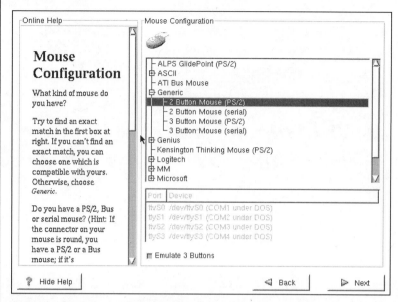

Figure 2.3 *The Mouse Configuration screen.*

not all mice are created alike—but they all have to perform the same task: move the mouse pointer across the screen.

There are three types of mice that can be used: bus, serial, and PS/2. Bus and serial mice are not as popular in the PC world, as most PC makers recognize that users want to use their bus and serial ports for something other than a mouse. So most PCs use a PS/2 port mouse. The latest PCs have USB-supported mice, which are still rather unstable when used with Linux.

If you are not certain what type of mouse you have, refer to the documentation for your mouse to determine its connection. Again, if you cannot locate the specific type of mouse you own, choose one of the generic options.

> What? You don't religiously save the documentation for every piece of hardware you own? In that case, check the back of your PC. If the mouse is plugged into a little round 6-pin port, it's PS/2. If it's plugged into a trapezoidal 9-pin port, it's a serial port. Anything else is a bus port.

You will notice that there are options for three-button mice in the list. These types of mice are used primarily by UNIX users rather than Windows users; many UNIX and Linux X applications make use of the center button found on three-button mice, while Windows applications do not. Because Linux applications often use the center button, Linux can configure a two-button mouse to emulate a three-button mouse (you click both mouse buttons at once to simulate pressing the center button). I recommend that you select the Emulate 3 Buttons option because you will likely run across the need to have a center button in Red Hat Linux—and it's less expensive than going out and buying a new mouse.

Use the expansion icons to explore the mouse options, select the mouse you need, and click the Next button to continue.

Choosing the Installation Class

Before you move into the more critical areas of the installation process, you will get a brief break with the Red Hat Welcome screen, shown in Figure 2.4. This screen is more than the official beginning of the System Installer; the Online Help pane contains some helpful information about where you can get the *Red Hat Linux Installation Guide* and other manuals.

Click the Next button to move to the Install Type screen. You must now decide what you are going to install. There are three primary installation options that you can select; these options are each discussed in more detail throughout this section.

- **Workstation**. This automatically installs Linux with X and either the KDE or GNOME desktop environments, or both, should you so choose. (You decide on desktop environments later.) This installation option includes the packages needed to run a standard PC workstation.

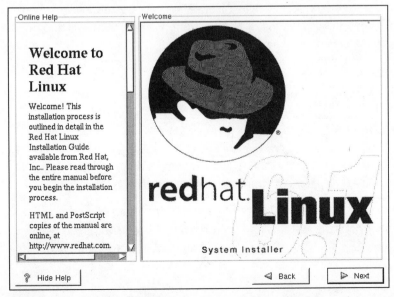

Figure 2.4   *The Welcome screen is the real start of the installation process.*

- **Server System**. This automatically installs Linux with additional server packages, including the Apache Web server, perhaps the most-used Web server. With this choice, X is not automatically installed.
- **Custom System**. Custom enables you to select exactly which packages will be installed. You are also given the opportunity to configure settings that might otherwise be automatic in the other installation paths, such as placement of LILO and partitioning of the hard drive.

There is a fourth option on the screen, but it is does not actually affect what is installed. Upgrade will let you keep your current Linux installation on your hard drive and will simply upgrade your current version of Red Hat Linux to 7.

CAUTION

> You should be very clear on one thing: With the exception of the Upgrade option, all of the Installation options will remove *at least* all of the Linux data and partitions on your hard drive. A Server installation will remove *all data and partitions on your hard drive*—DOS, Windows, anything.

When should you use each of these options? Well, like most computer-related installations, your specific situation will very likely differ from any scenario I could present here. Table 2.1 lists some basic guidelines you can follow when deciding which installation path to choose.

TIP

> Make sure that you not only select each installation option's button, but that you also select (click and highlight) the Install option. Otherwise, nothing will happen when it comes time to install packages.

When you finish selecting all installation options, click Next to continue.

Selecting Your Partition Options

The Automatic Partitioning screen is the next to appear in the installation process. Here, you decide whether to partition your hard drive yourself or to have Linux do it.

If Red Hat Linux will be the only operating system on your PC and you have eliminated all other operating systems and their partitions, you should allow Linux to perform the partition for you. Choose the Automatically partition and RE-MOVE DATA option.

Table 2.1 Installation Path Guidelines

Path	Issues
Workstation	This is the simplest path to take. It's good for a home PC with a single operating system. It automatically installs X Window and can be used if you are setting up a dual boot system with Windows 95/98, but *not* Windows NT or OS/2.
Server	This is good for the more advanced user, particularly someone looking to create a network or Web server. It can be used if you are setting up a dual boot system with Windows 95/98, but *not* Windows NT or OS/2.
Custom	This option must be used to install on a PC that will be shared with Windows NT or OS/2, so that LILO will be placed in the correct place on the hard drive. It is not very complicated, and it gives users the ability to pick and choose between every application package, not just what Linux supplies in the other two installation paths.

You can also allow automatic partitioning if you plan to dual boot with Windows 95 or 98. In the Workgroup installation, only existing Linux partitions are replaced with new partition settings for Red Hat Linux 7. The existing DOS partition used by the Windows operating system remains unaffected.

Table 2.2 lists the partition settings you will have if you allow Red Hat to partition for you using either the Workgroup or Server installation choices.

If you want to manually partition the Linux portion of the hard drive yourself, you can use one of two tools: Disk Druid and Linux fdisk. Of the two, I *strongly* recommend that you choose the Disk Druid option. Although Linux fdisk (quite different from DOS fdisk used in Chapter 1) is very capable of partitioning the hard drive, it is not a very intuitive application and therefore could irreparably harm your drive's partitioning.

When you select the Manually partition with Disk Druid option and click Next, you will see the Disk Druid screen, as shown in Figure 2.5.

The fundamental operation of the Disk Druid tool is simple. You are given a list of existing drive partitions, either Linux or DOS. Below the Partition list is the Drive Summary list, which gives the details of the hard drives on your PC. Watch the

Table 2.2   Linux Installation Partitions

Partition	Mount Point	Memory Allotment
Workstation		
Boot partition	/boot	16MB
Swap partition	None	64MB
Root partition	/	The remainder of any unpartitioned space on the disk
Server		
Boot partition	/boot	16MB
Swap partition	None	64MB
Root partition	/	256MB
Var partition	/var	256MB
Usr partition	/usr	Half of remaining unpartitioned space on the disk
Home partition	/home	Half of remaining unpartitioned space on the disk

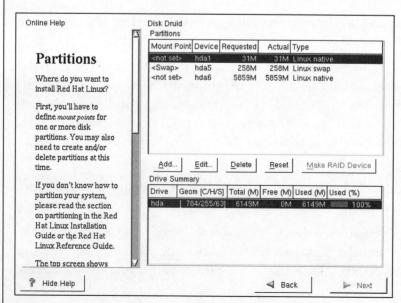

Figure 2.5   *Manual partitioning is controlled in the Disk Druid tool.*

Used (M) and Used (%) fields as you add or delete partitions. The percentage of used disk space will approach or move away from 100%. As long as the field displays less than 100%, unpartitioned space remains on the drive for you to use. Conversely, if the Used (%) field displays 100% usage and you still need to add partitions, you will have to delete some existing partitions to make room.

The following steps are used to manually create a workstation partition set on your PC. I recommend that you add the partitions in the following order: boot, swap, and root (/). Since the root partition will be set to fill all the remaining space on the hard drive, you'll first want to specify exactly what share the other partitions will require.

Partitioning with Disk Druid

If all existing partitions were removed by DOS fdisk prior to the installation process, use the Disk Druid screen to create partitions for a workstation PC.

First, create the /boot partition using these steps:

1. Click the Add button in the Partitions section. The Add dialog box will appear.
2. In the Mount Point field, type **/boot**.
3. In the Size (Megs) field, type **16** (16MB is the recommended size for the boot partition on an Intel-compatible PC).
4. Confirm that the Partition Type is Linux native.
5. Select the hard drive where you want to place the boot partition (refer to Table 1.12 in Chapter 1 to make sure the selected drive is acceptable).
6. Click OK. The Add dialog box will close.

Now, create the swap partition:

1. Click the Add button again so that you can create the swap partition. The Add dialog box will appear.
2. Leave the Mount Point field blank.
3. In the Size (Megs) field, type **94**.

> The value of the swap disk should be at least the number of MB of RAM memory you have on your PC. In this example, 94MB of RAM suggests a 94MB swap disk size.

4. Click the Partition Type list control and select Linux swap.
5. Select the hard drive where you want to place the swap partition.
6. Click OK. The Add dialog box will close.

Finally, create the root (/) partition:

1. Click the Add button again to create the root partition. The Add dialog box will appear.
2. In the Mount Point field, type /.
3. Leave the Size (Megs) field setting as 1MB.
4. Click the Grow to fill disk? option.
5. Confirm that the Partition Type is Linux native.
6. Select the hard drive where you want to place the root partition.
7. Click OK. The Add dialog box will close.

You will now see the new partitions displayed in the Partitions list on the Disk Druid screen. The Used (%) value should be 100%.

If you want to change any of these values, simply select the partition to be modified and click the Edit button. The Edit Partition dialog will appear. If the partition was pre-existing on your PC, you can only change its mount point. To make other changes, delete the partition by selecting it and then pressing the Delete key. You can then create a new one to your specifications.

> The Next button on the Disk Druid screen will not activate until there is a Linux-compatible partitioning scheme set up, which is a handy way of knowing your settings are okay.

After partitioning is complete (using either the automatic or manual choices), click the Next button to advance to the Choose Partitions to Format screen. This screen lets you decide which of the new Linux partitions that you just created in Disk Druid will be formatted. The default option is for all of them to be formatted, and I suggest you let that stand. I also recommend that you select the Check for bad blocks while formatting option, which allows Anaconda to scan your hard drive for physical defects on your hard drive while the partitions are formatted. This is a good idea even though many people don't do this very often because every little bit of disk maintenance helps.

Click the Next button to advance to the next screen, which could be the Network information screen or the Time Zone Selection screen.

Networking Your Computer

If the installation program detects that you have a network card, you will need to provide the pertinent information about your computer.

If you are on a large network, it's a good idea to get the requested data from your network administrator. If that's you, you should have the information from the data-gathering process you performed before installation.

For more information on network settings, see Chapter 6, "Configuring a Network Connection."

Setting the Time Zone

You might think the subject of time zones would not be rocket science. 24-hour day, divide the Earth into 24 parts, and there you have it, right?

Wrong. Several nations around the world have set their clocks based on reasons that are more political than geophysical. Even here in the United States, there are a couple of states that don't adjust their clocks when daylight savings time is in effect. So time settings get tricky. Looking at Figure 2.6, it's clear that the Red Hat developers have taken this into account.

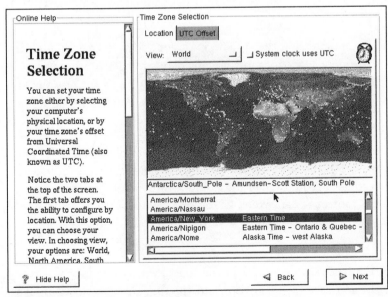

Figure 2.6   *Does anyone have the time?*

Dominating the screen is a map of the world with several areas highlighted. Since the cities are so small at this scale, click the View drop-down list, and select the region where you live. A larger scale map of your region will appear.

To set your time zone, simply click the city/region closest to you on the map. Alternately, you can select your city/region from the list that appears below the map. Your choice then appears in the field immediately below the map.

If you wish, you can set the time based on the Universal Time Clock (UTC) (an unchanging standard time based on the Greenwich Mean Time). To do so, click the option labeled System Clock Uses UTC, entering your time based on the number of hours offset from UTC.

When complete, click the Next button.

Configuring Your Accounts

Whenever a Linux system is created, the root account must be created as well. The root account is the administrator account for the Linux PC. Because the root account is used when modifications are made to the operating system settings, it is the most powerful account on the system. All you need to do to set up the root account is to enter the same password in both the Root Password and Confirm fields. The Confirm field entry ensures that you have not made a typographical error in the password.

If you will have additional users on the system, it's a good idea to create additional user accounts for them now. User accounts are analogous to user profiles found in Windows. They allow certain users to have customized access to a Linux system and provide the additional security of letting you know who's doing what on the system.

> Even if you are the sole user on the PC, it's a good idea to make a regular account for yourself. Using the root account all of the time can lead to errors, whereas using a regular account limits the amount of damage you can cause. The powers of the root user can wreak havoc on a Linux system, up to and including the destruction of every file on your partitions.

As you can see in Figure 2.7, to create a user account, you type a user ID in the Account Name field and supply a password and the user's full name. Similar to creating the root account, you'll need to type the password twice to ensure that no typos are made. Clicking the Add button will finish the process.

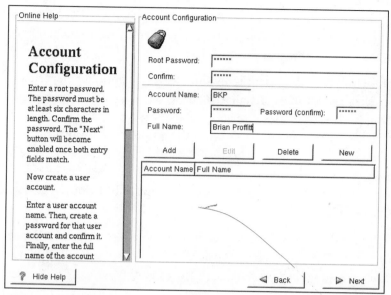

Figure 2.7 *Adding users to your Linux system.*

Passwords within Red Hat Linux are case sensitive.

After you have added users to the system, click the Next button to continue.

Selecting Package Groups

At this point in Anaconda, you get to decide what packages will be installed on your Linux machine. It's like a birthday celebration!

Packages in Red Hat Linux are synonymous with application installation programs. Inside each software package are most or all of the files a given application needs to run. Opening a package will automatically install the application within onto your PC.

The first package selection screen, and really the only one you need, gives you what appears to be three measly choices: GNOME, KDE, and Games. But what choices they are!

GNOME and KDE are different desktop environments that run on top of X. Truthfully, there are few operational differences between the two, just different approaches in the interface. If you have a lot of space on your hard drive, I recommend that you select both and see for yourself. If you have a preference, just select the one you like. (I chose GNOME for this example.) Whether you select Games is up to you, of course, but if you have the room, go ahead and yield to the temptation. Everyone needs a break now and then.

On the bottom of the screen is the Select individual packages option. Select this if there is a certain package you want to install that you know is not part of one of the three predetermined package sets. Because you will likely get everything you need from the default package sets, I suggest you skip this option. If you want to really delve into the various package choices, however, go ahead and click the Select Individual Packages option at the bottom of the Package Group Selection screen. Once you've selected this, clicking Next will take you to the Individual Package Selection screen.

On the left side of the Individual Package Selection screen is a structure similar to a directory tree that lists all the package groups. Selecting any group will display a list of its individual packages on the right side of the screen.

To select a package for installation, double-click the package name. A red check mark appears on the package icon, indicating its readiness for installation.

Click Next to continue to the Unresolved Dependencies screen. This screen addresses packages that may need additional files within other packages in order to work. Recall that some packages don't always contain every file an application needs for installation. Many times, they rely on the presence of other packages to work correctly. That's what a dependency is. An *unresolved dependency* is when a needed package is absent. Anaconda checks all the package sets you selected in the previous screen and makes sure that every package in the sets has all of its dependencies resolved.

If a few unresolved packages appear in the screen, don't worry. Click the Install packages to satisfy dependencies option and then click Next. All the needed files will be added to the installation set automatically.

Configuring the X Window System

In the Workstation installation path, the next two screens are the X Configuration screens. These screens are important because they determine how X coordinates with your graphics card and monitor to generate graphic displays. (Recall that the Linux OS is based on textual command lines and requires X server to run graphic-based interfaces.)

Unlike Microsoft Windows, X must be carefully configured to work with your video hardware. Does this mean that Windows is more flexible? Not at all. It's just that monitors and graphics cards in recent years have been made to comply with Windows. Linux is a relative newcomer to hardware vendors, so manual configuration is still required.

Before you even get to the first X Configuration screen, the Linux tool, Autoprobe, has attempted to identify the type of monitor you have. If Autoprobe finds it, the monitor's identity will appear at the top of the first screen, Anaconda's Monitor Configuration screen. Check this very carefully because Autoprobe could guess wrong. If it's correct, click Next to continue.

If Autoprobe can't decide what monitor type you have, it selects the Unprobed Monitor category. At this point, you will need to make sure you have the right values in the Horizontal and Vertical Sync fields at the bottom of the screen. Be careful here. You don't want to use a monitor setting that will damage your monitor. Erroneous sync rate settings can lead to *overclocking* of the monitor, a fancy term that basically means making the monitor run beyond its display tolerances.

The best place to locate your monitor's sync rates is in the manual that came with the monitor. Barring that, try the monitor manufacturer's Web site. After you get your sync rate values entered, click Next to continue.

In the next screen, Anaconda reveals what video card Autoprobe has found. The video card is important because it will determine what X Window server will be used to run X later. Confirm the card selected, or, if need be, select a value that better matches your card. Just below the video card list are eight options for the amount of video memory your card has, in kilobytes. Click the appropriate value.

When the video hardware has been determined, click the Test This Configuration button. The screen will then flicker on and off. If all goes well, you should see a blue-green screen with a small dialog box asking if you can see the message on the dialog box. Click Yes. If you cannot see the message, you will need to change the settings for the graphics card and monitor. You will be returned to the X Configuration screen to re-enter new settings for your video equipment.

The X Configuration screen may also harbor a list box that allows you to choose which desktop environment you want to be the default during your work with Red Hat. I say "may" because it appears only if you selected both the GNOME and KDE packages groups to install. It will not appear if you selected only one of these desktop environments. Select the environment you wish to be the default.

Just below the Test button are three options. If you select Customize X Configuration and then click Next, you will be taken to a screen where you can try out different color depths (the number of colors on the screen) and screen resolutions.

The Use Graphical Login option is very important for new users to select, as it enables the appearance of the X login each time you start Linux.

CAUTION

> There appears to be a glitch in the Linux program at this point. If you select the Customize option and go to that screen, the Use Graphical Login option (even if you selected it) will be cleared and X will not load on boot. For this reason, I suggest that you wait until later to change your video settings.

An expert who wants to set up X manually should be the only person to click the Skip X Configuration option. New users should stay away from this option.

For maximum ease, I recommend that you click the Use Graphical Login option and then click Next to continue.

Finishing the Installation

All the pertinent installation information has now been gathered by Linux, and the installation program is ready to copy files to your computer. Figure 2.8 shows the About to Install screen, which warns you that this is about to happen.

Remember, after this point you will not be able to click the Back button to make changes to your chosen installation settings. Don't worry, though; if you have made

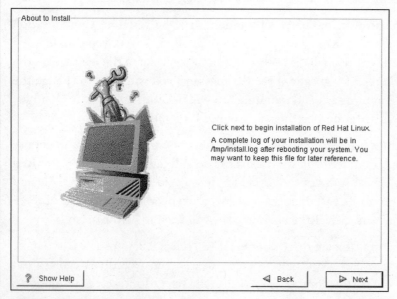

Figure 2.8   *Ready to begin?*

it this far, you are probably okay. The hardware configuration to display graphics was the trickiest part of the installation. So take a deep breath and click the Next button to continue.

You will see the Installing Packages screen. Before any packages are actually installed, however, the partitions you have set up will be formatted. You'll know this is happening by the appearance of a progress message (see Figure 2.9).

Formatting the partitions can take anywhere from 5 to 15 minutes, depending on the amount of formatting required. If you had selected the option to check for bad blocks while formatting, the formatting will take longer. The Linux installation will then gather all the information obtained in the first part of the installation program and build its file copy list. A progress bar appears on the screen (see Figure 2.10) so that you can monitor the process.

Now the bulk of the installation occurs. As seen in Figure 2.11, the Installing Packages screen displays the progress of the installation as it proceeds. The top progress bar indicates the status of the package being currently installed. The bottom bar shows the cumulative installation progress of all packages. There is also a time remaining value displayed that will let you know if you have time to go grab a sandwich.

When everything is finished, the Boot Disk Creation screen appears. You may not have created a boot disk before installing Red Hat Linux 7, particularly if you have a bootable CD-ROM drive. If you did not, now's your chance to make one—and I

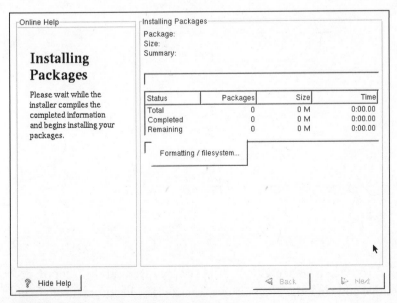

Figure 2.9 *Formatting your Linux partitions.*

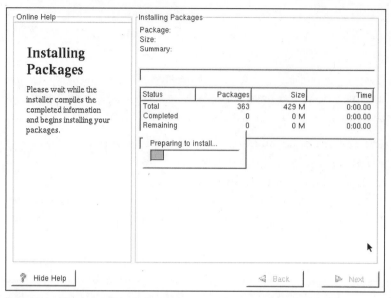

Figure 2.10   *Getting ready to copy files.*

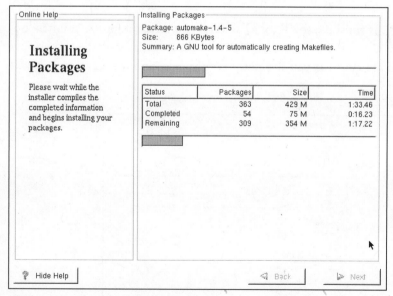

Figure 2.11   *The package installation process.*

highly recommend you do. To make a boot disk, simply insert a blank floppy disk into your floppy drive and click the Next button. Anaconda will automatically build a boot disk that is completely up-to-date with your Linux installation.

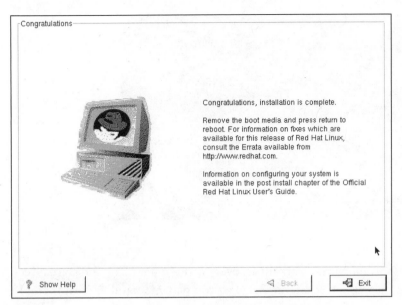

Congratulations

Congratulations, installation is complete.

Remove the boot media and press return to reboot. For information on fixes which are available for this release of Red Hat Linux, consult the Errata available from http://www.redhat.com.

Information on configuring your system is available in the post install chapter of the Official Red Hat Linux User's Guide.

Show Help   Back   Exit

Figure 2.12 *You have now arrived in the strange world of Linux.*

When the boot disk is complete, the Congratulations screen will appear, as shown in Figure 2.12. Remove the boot disk from the drive now.

Clicking the Exit button will close the installation program and restart your machine. Make sure you have removed the boot disk from the floppy drive (or the installation CD-ROM if you have a bootable CD-ROM drive) before clicking Exit.

Once the PC has restarted, you will see a bright blue screen that contains a list of all the operating systems on your PC. This screen, the graphical LILO screen, appears each time Linux begins to load. Use the arrow keys to select the operating system you want to boot up, and press the Enter key to continue. If you want Linux to load, you don't have to do anything; LILO defaults to loading it first.

If you see "DOS" in the LILO list, and not Windows, don't worry. LILO recognizes operating systems; on a Windows PC, DOS is the true operating system, while Windows is just the graphical interface. Selecting DOS will start Windows...if you have to.

You can increase the amount of time the LILO prompt stays on the screen using the linuxconf utility, which is explored in Chapter 3, "Configuring the X Window System."

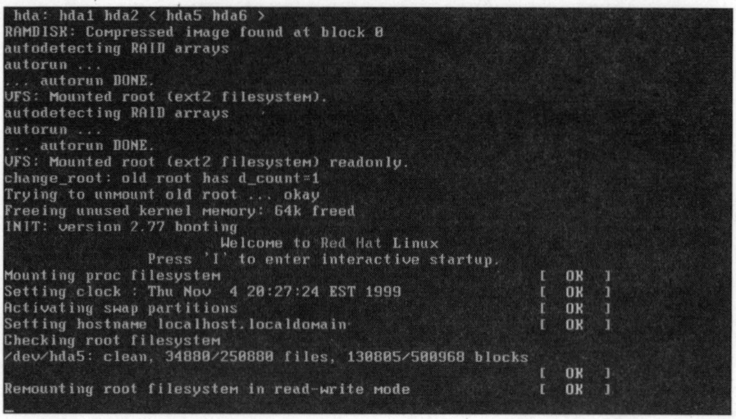

```
hda: hda1 hda2 < hda5 hda6 >
RAMDISK: Compressed image found at block 0
autodetecting RAID arrays
autorun ...
... autorun DONE.
VFS: Mounted root (ext2 filesystem).
autodetecting RAID arrays
autorun ...
... autorun DONE.
VFS: Mounted root (ext2 filesystem) readonly.
change_root: old root has d_count=1
Trying to unmount old root ... okay
Freeing unused kernel memory: 64k freed
INIT: version 2.77 booting
                    Welcome to Red Hat Linux
              Press 'I' to enter interactive startup.
Mounting proc filesystem                              [  OK  ]
Setting clock : Thu Nov  4 20:27:24 EST 1999          [  OK  ]
Activating swap partitions                            [  OK  ]
Setting hostname localhost.localdomain                [  OK  ]
Checking root filesystem
/dev/hda5: clean, 34880/250880 files, 130805/500968 blocks
                                                      [  OK  ]
Remounting root filesystem in read-write mode         [  OK  ]
```

Figure 2.13 *Watching Linux start up.*

Unlike Windows, Linux likes to broadcast every little step it takes as it starts. Keep an eye on these messages (see Figure 2.13) so you become familiar with them. In time, this familiarity will enable you to identify any problems that occur as Linux loads just because you recognize a message that is out of the ordinary.

In a moment, you will arrive at the login screen for the desktop environment you selected in the X Configuration screen. Type the account login name and password you created during the installation process. You'll then enter the desktop environment and begin your Red Hat Linux journey.

Other Installation Concerns

If you've successfully installed and started Red Hat Linux 7, you can skip ahead to Chapter 3. Some of you, though, may need additional information about other installation modes and paths. Text installations, custom install options, and dual booting are examined in the remainder of this chapter.

Text Installation

If you had trouble with the graphical mode of installation, you should now use the text installation mode. While not pretty, the text mode is just as effective as the graphical mode. The text installation mode is a great fallback to use if you experience initial display problems.

Navigating the text screens is done without a mouse, but it is fairly simple. You move between objects on the screen by pressing the Tab key (or Alt+Tab to move backward). You can select or clear check box options by pressing the spacebar. Pressing Enter activates a selected function. Not too hard, right?

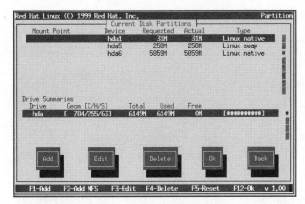

Figure 2.14 *The text version of Disk Druid.*

All the same installation information is gathered during text installation as was done during graphical installation. One exception occurs, however, in that text installation asks for permission before starting to probe your system's video hardware (which you should grant).

By comparing Figure 2.14 to Figure 2.4, you can see that, other than mere aesthetics, not many differences exist between the two interfaces.

Configuring LILO

If you plan to use more than one operating system on your Red Hat Linux PC, you will need to make sure Linux Loader (LILO) is installed in the correct location. If it isn't, you may run into trouble.

Dual Booting Explained

When a system with a single operating system boots, the BIOS looks at a special section of the hard drive called the *master boot record* (*MBR* or *boot sector*) to see what operating system will be loaded.

When a PC has two or more operating systems, a special multi-boot application must reside in the boot sector that temporarily halts the boot process and allows the user to choose which operating system to load. LILO is just such a program.

How to Dual Boot with Windows 95/98

To configure LILO to run Linux and another operating system, you will need to use the Custom installation path. If you are installing Linux on a system preconfigured with Windows 95 or 98, however, you can just run the Workstation installation path. This is because the default LILO settings provide all you need to run both operating systems.

LILO is then installed in the MBR and the Linux boot sector is given the default priority to load. You can change these settings later from within Linux using a utility called linuxconf; for now, use the Workstation settings.

How to Dual Boot with Windows NT

Quite simply, the easiest way to get Linux and Windows NT to work together is to install NT first on your machine. Then, when you install Linux, make LILO boot to the Master Boot Record (MBR). Finally, edit your /etc/lilo.conf file, and add an "nt" option that points to the device NT resides on (for example, /dev/hda1).

If you want to run Linux with Windows NT or Windows 2000 installed later, you will need to take some special steps during the installation. Of primary importance is that you *must* run the Custom installation path, as it is the only method that enables you to configure LILO to meet your needs.

Basically, the problem is this: The Windows NT OS Loader does not recognize Linux as a valid operating system (imagine that) because Linux does not produce the type of file the NT OS Loader needs to read before starting an operating system. In addition, the NT OS Loader will not function from anywhere other than the boot sector. Since only one boot loader can be in the boot sector at a time, you will have a problem if LILO sits in the MBR.

The Custom install path gives you access to the LILO Configuration screen, where you can elect to have LILO either installed on the MBR (the default setting) or on the first sector of the Linux boot partition. If you select the latter option, there will be no conflict between LILO and the NT OS Loader. Unfortunately, the NT OS Loader will still not see Linux, and it won't present Linux as a boot choice. Now comes the chicanery.

There is a way to create a file in Linux that the NT OS Loader *can* use to boot Linux, but creating it takes a bit of time. I recommend that you obtain a little third-party program called Bootpart, available at **www.winimage.com/bootpart.htm**. This program quickly creates the Linux boot file for NT OS Loader and places it where NT OS Loader can use it. I highly recommend this application if you plan to use either Windows NT or Windows 2000 with Linux.

For more information about configuring Windows NT and Linux, read the mini-HOWTO document at **www.linuxdoc.org/HOWTO/mini/Linux+NT-Loader.html**.

Conclusion

This chapter got you where you wanted to be: the owner of a PC running Red Hat Linux 7. Now that you have completed this task, it's time to configure and customize your newly installed OS to meet your needs. In Chapter 3, you'll learn about the underpinnings of the graphical interface: configuring the X Window System.

PART II

Configuring Red Hat Linux 7

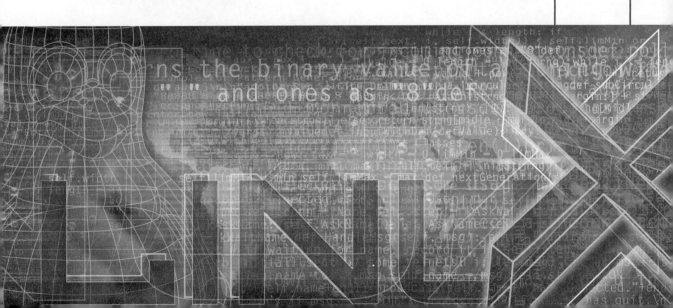

Chapter 3: Configuring the X Window System

Take an onion. Peel away the brown, crinkly stuff on the outside. What are you left with? A peeled onion. If you pull off another layer, you are left with…? That's right, a smaller peeled onion.

While not exactly the most stunning comparison, in some ways it's applicable to the relationship between Linux, X server, and a window manager on a Linux system. They are all layers of a big onion of an operating system—except they don't make you cry.

In this chapter, the layers of the Red Hat Linux 7 OS are examined, followed by a look at how the deepest layer of the graphical interface, X server, can be configured.

What Is X?

Non–Linux users are often a bit confused about which components make up X . In the Microsoft Windows environment, you have the DOS operating system with the Windows operating system interface running on top of it, as illustrated in Figure 3.1. "Running on top" means that Windows is essentially one big program that runs from the DOS platform, essentially no different from running a program like Doom. The upshot of this is that you must have DOS running in order to run Windows.

For Windows NT users, it's a bit more simplified. Windows NT (like Windows 2000) is a true graphical user interface that runs on its own. The advantage here is that you really do get what you see. You can still run DOS when you have to, but in Windows NT, a DOS emulator runs within Windows. One disadvantage to Windows NT is that your PC must have a lot more memory and speed to run as efficiently as a comparable Win98 system.

The Linux system you have just installed is most analogous to the DOS/Windows system. Like DOS, Linux is a text-based, command-line operating system (albeit a *much* more sophisticated one). You can perform many functions using just the Linux operating system, and many people do. Many more people, however, have been bitten by the GUI bug and are accustomed to using windows, menus, and dialog boxes to get things done.

BUZZWORD

Graphical user interface (GUI): Any computer interface that uses visual rather than textual information to convey information and accept commands.

BUZZWORD

Emulator: A program that can mimic the look and feel of another operating system.

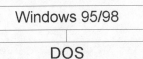

Figure 3.1   *The DOS/Windows relationship.*

In 1986, an international consortium of UNIX programmers began putting together a graphical operating system based on the GUI research done by the Xerox Palo Alto Research Center. Thus was X born. After Linux was introduced in 1991, X soon found its way to the Linux desktop. When Linux began appearing on Intel-based PCs, a new version of X, XFree86, helped make the transition.

XFree86 is the heart of any GUI that runs on Red Hat Linux. Also referred to as the *X server*, XFree86 is where video output and PC input are brought together to form one cohesive interface. PC input is obtained from two basic input devices: the keyboard and the mouse. Video output is then sent through the graphics card to the monitor.

Although this sounds like the entirety of the GUI, it's not. That's because the X server is only a network-transparent display layer that provides the "home" for the GUI to operate. To generate the actual windows and menus that make up what is traditionally considered a GUI, you need a window manager running on the X server display layer.

Several window managers can be used with Red Hat Linux: AfterStep, AnotherLevel, Enlightenment, fvwm, fvwm95, KWM, olvm, Sawfish, and tvm, to name a few. However, the two big ones you may have heard of are GNOME and KDE.

KDE is the K Desktop Environment—an award-winning environment that is packaged with Red Hat Linux 7. Often referred to as a *window manager*, in fact it is not. KDE usually runs over a window manager called KWM (K Window Manager). As KWM enhances the look and feel of XFree86, so KDE enhances the look and toolsets of KWM.

A similar relationship exists when running the GNOME (GNU Network Object Model Environment) desktop. GNOME is not a true window manager, either. GNOME is an enhancement for a window manager running on XFree86. By default, Red Hat 7 installs the Sawfish window manager with GNOME. Confused yet? Take a look at Figure 3.2, which displays a simplified representation of the relationship between all of these components.

It should be noted that just because a certain combination of window managers and desktop environments has been installed, it does not mean that you must lock yourself into that combination. For example, you can run GNOME on top of fvm95 if you want to. That's one of the great things about Linux's open platform philosophy: You have real choices on how to run your PC.

A big question that's often asked, though, is what do all these choices mean? What is each of these components responsible for? In the installation performed in Chapter 2, "Installing Red Hat Linux 7," it was recommended that you install both desktop

BUZZWORD

Window manager: The application that gives X server its "look" and determines how graphical applications will be displayed.

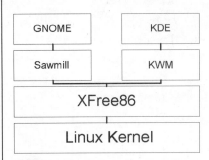

Figure 3.2   *The components of a Linux GUI system.*

environments. Table 3.1 breaks down the different responsibilities of each of the Linux components in the GNOME environment.

Table 3.1   Components of a Linux/GNOME System

Component	Responsibilities
Linux	This is the base on which everything runs, and it handles all basic file system and device tasks, as well as translating commands into the PC's rudimentary machine language.
XFree86	This is the heart of the GUI. It generates a display layer that allows the creation of graphics and then marries those graphics to input from the keyboard and mouse.
Sawfish	This, the window manager, is responsible for the look of all windows, dialog boxes, and menus that are generated from the applications being used.
GNOME	This enhances the Sawfish window manager by providing additional interface tools and appearance. Additional controls are provided for input device configuration.

Notice in Table 3.1 that certain components of X have different responsibilities; the remainder of this chapter focuses on XFree86's video output, keyboard, and mouse responsibilities.

Using Xconfigurator

Within Red Hat Linux 7, there are two tools designed to manage XFree86: Xconfigurator and xf86config. Each tool focuses on a different aspect of XFree86 and should be used accordingly. Table 3.2 reveals the capabilities of each tool.

Table 3.2   Comparison of XFree86 Configuration Tools

Xconfigurator	xf86config
Video monitor	Video monitor
Video card	Video card
Video resolution	Keyboard
	Mouse

Although xf86config appears to be the best program to use because of its greater capabilities, in actuality I recommend that you split the usage of these programs. Xconfigurator has an easier-to-use interface for making changes to your display parameters, while xf86config uses a multiple choice linear interface that's a bit more difficult to follow.

One great use for Xconfigurator is changing the video resolution of your display. When Red Hat first installs, it may default to a resolution you don't like, such as the 640×480 resolution shown in Figure 3.3.

Xconfigurator is a text-based application, so to use it you need to use the command-line interface after logging in using the root account. The command line can

BUZZWORD

Video resolution: The number of pixels arranged across a display. The smaller the resolution, the larger the pixels, and the less information that can be displayed on a screen.

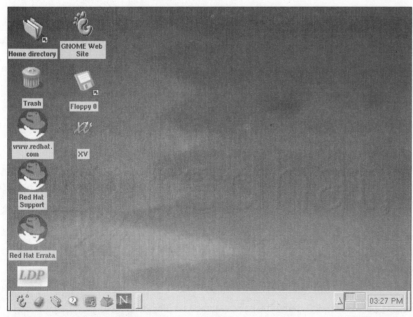

Figure 3.3   *There's not a lot of real estate in this screen resolution.*

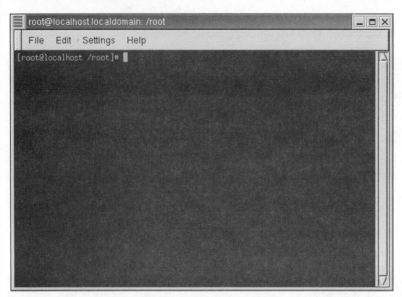

Figure 3.4   *The terminal emulation program is a gateway to the Linux operating system.*

be accessed with a terminal emulation window (*terminal* for short). A terminal is not the real Linux interface, but it can be used as such for most operations. To start the terminal, click the Terminal icon on the GNOME panel. This opens the terminal window (see Figure 3.4).

Now that the terminal is up and running, the following steps will guide you through the use of Xconfigurator to modify your video resolution.

Changing Video Resolution

1. In the terminal, type **Xconfigurator**. The Xconfigurator tool will start in the terminal window (see Figure 3.5).

No, I wasn't fibbing when I said Xconfigurator was text-based. All the color and lines are just individual text characters put together to give the appearance of a graphic interface.

2. By default, the OK control on the Welcome screen of Xconfigurator is selected. Press the Enter key to accept the OK selection and continue.

3. The next screen (see Figure 3.6) shows the results of the PCI Probe, which Xconfigurator started when the second screen was reached. PCI is a type

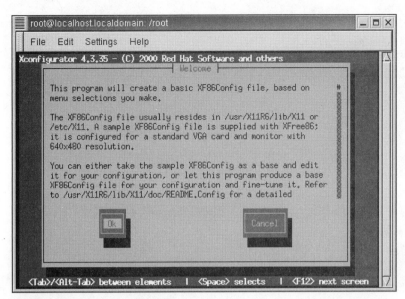

Figure 3.5 *Running Xconfigurator.*

of add-on card for PCs, a category into which graphics cards sometimes fall. If the result matches the card you have (and it should), press the Enter key.

If the PCI Probe is unsuccessful, a screen displaying a list of graphics card choices will appear from which you can make an alternate choice.

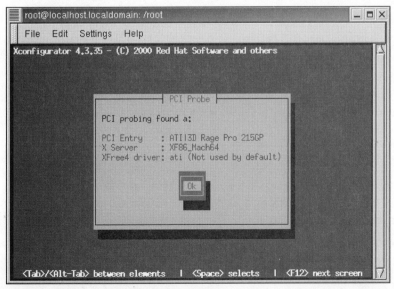

Figure 3.6 *Confirming the graphics card on your machine.*

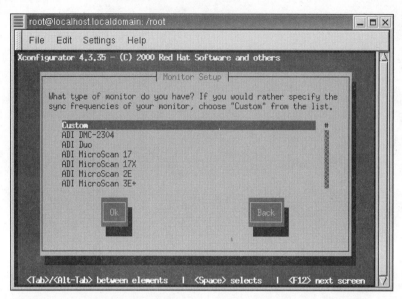

root@localhost.localdomain: /root

File   Edit   Settings   Help

Xconfigurator 4.3.35 - (C) 2000 Red Hat Software and others

┤ Monitor Setup ├

What type of monitor do you have? If you would rather specify the
sync frequencies of your monitor, choose "Custom" from the list.

```
Custom
ADI DMC-2304
ADI Duo
ADI MicroScan 17
ADI MicroScan 17X
ADI MicroScan 2E
ADI MicroScan 3E+
```

Ok   Back

<Tab>/<Alt-Tab> between elements | <Space> selects | <F12> next screen

Figure 3.7   *Choosing your monitor.*

4. The Monitor Setup screen appears next (see Figure 3.7). Select your monitor from the list using the up and down arrow keys.

> If you cannot locate your monitor, select the Custom option that appears at the top of the list. You should also choose Custom if you want to verify the synchronization (sync) rates with your monitor's settings.

5. Press the Tab key to select the OK control and then press Enter. If you selected Custom, proceed to Step 6. If you selected any monitor, skip ahead to Step 15.

6. In the Custom Monitor Setup screen, you should read the lengthy message that describes the importance of the horizontal and vertical refresh rates. Make sure you know this data for your own monitor (ideally obtained when you went through the steps in Chapter 1, "Before You Install Red Hat Linux 7") and then press Enter to continue to the next screen.

7. The second Custom Monitor Setup screen (shown in Figure 3.8) lets you set the type of monitor based on a horizontal sync rate. Select a monitor type that has a higher resolution (such as 800×600) and still has a sync rate within your monitor's horizontal sync rate parameters.

8. Press the Tab key to select the OK control and then press Enter.

9. The third Custom Monitor Setup screen requires you to specify the vertical sync range of your monitor (see Figure 3.9). Select the appropriate range using the up and down arrow keys.

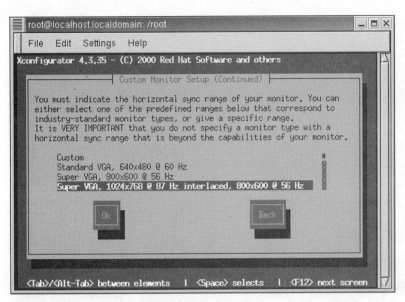

Figure 3.8 *Choosing the horizontal sync rate.*

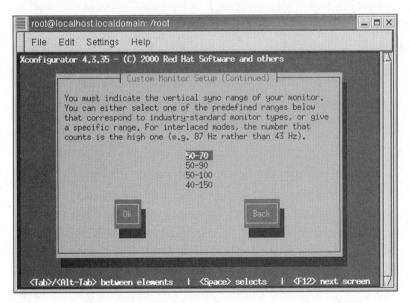

Figure 3.9 *Selecting the vertical sync rate.*

10. Press the Tab key to select the OK control and then press Enter.

11. In the Video Memory screen, shown in Figure 3.10, select the amount of video memory your video card has using the up and down arrow keys.

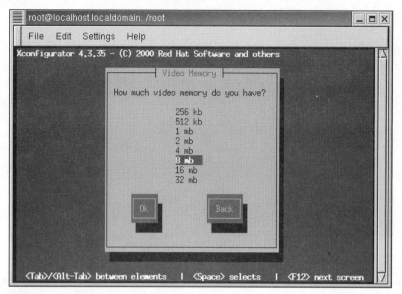

Figure 3.10 *Choosing the amount of video memory.*

NOTE

This is information you should have obtained in Chapter 1.

12. Press the Tab key to select the OK control and then press Enter.

13. Many older video cards have specific clockchip settings, which are displayed in the Clockchip Configuration screen (see Figure 3.11). On the off chance your card has an active clockchip, select the type of clockchip using the arrow keys. Since most newer cards do not have clockchips, you will likely need to select the No Clockchip Setting.

14. Press the Tab key to select the OK control and then press Enter.

15. You will now see the Select Video Mode screen (shown in Figure 3.12). Use the Tab key to navigate to the appropriate column and the up and down arrow keys to move within the color depth columns, and then press the spacebar to select any option. You should choose resolutions you know your card can handle.

TIP

Select more than one resolution in this screen. If they are all successful, you will be able to quickly cycle through each configured resolution by pressing Ctrl+Alt++ within X. This will save you from using Xconfigurator every time you want to change screen resolutions.

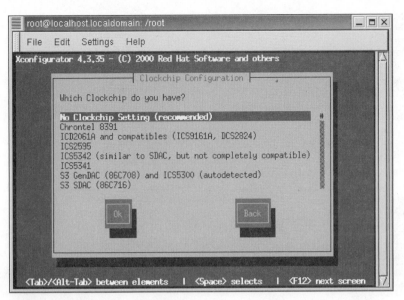

Figure 3.11 *Setting up the clockchip.*

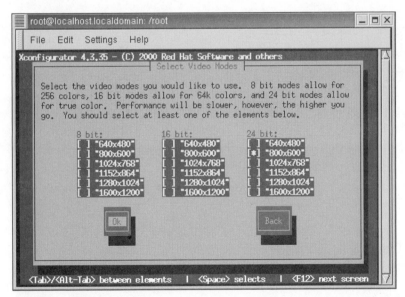

Figure 3.12 *Selecting a video resolution for your monitor and card.*

16. Press the Tab key to select the OK control and then press Enter.

17. You will arrive at the Starting X screen (see Figure 3.13), which simply informs you that another session of X will be started to test your settings. Press Enter to continue.

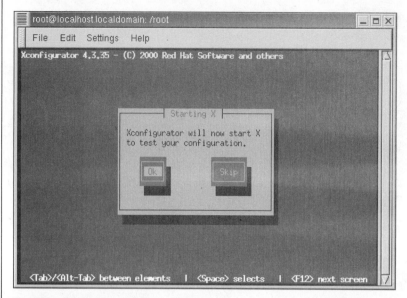

Figure 3.13 *Preparing to test your settings.*

BUZZWORD

Color depth: Expressed in bits per pixel, color depth can be translated into the number of available colors by raising 2 to the power of n, where n is the number of bits per pixel. Thus, an 8 bits per pixel color depth would have 2^8, or 256 colors; 16 bits per pixel equals 65,536 colors; and 24 bits per pixel equals 16,777,216 colors.

18. If your settings are okay, your will see a message on screen indicating your success. Click Yes to continue.

    If you see any other kind of message, or if no message is displayed, use the Back controls to move back to the previous screens, where you can change your settings.

19. A message will appear, asking you if you want to start X when you reboot. Click Yes.

20. Yet another message will appear, informing you where the changes to your system were recorded. Click OK to continue.

21. Xconfigurator will close. Restart your X Window session by clicking Log Out on the GNOME Control Menu.

22. Select the Logout option in the Really Log Out dialog box and then click Yes.

    Upon returning to the graphical login screen, the new default video resolution will be set. You will see this most dramatically after logging into X again (see Figure 3.14).

Starting Up the xf86config Tool

When you have significant changes to make to your system's input devices, you should use xf86config to reconfigure X. You can also use it to make monitor and

Figure 3.14   *A higher resolution gives you more screen real estate.*

display setting changes; if that's all you need to do, however, I suggest that you use Xconfigurator.

> Be sure you're logged in using the root account screen when you make any configuration changes to XFree86.

Like Xconfigurator, xf86config is located in the /usr/X11R6/bin directory. But all you need to do to start xf86config is type **xf86config** in a terminal window.

> If at any point you need to leave xf86config, press Ctrl+C.

Configuring the Mouse

In the first xf86config screen, you will see a text message detailing what changes will be made to your system (see Figure 3.15). Press Enter to continue to the next screen.

The second screen reveals a list of nine possible mouse types. To select an option, type its number and then press Enter (see Figure 3.16).

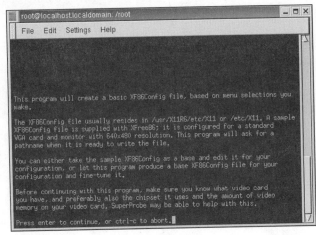

Figure 3.15 *The opening message for xf86config.*

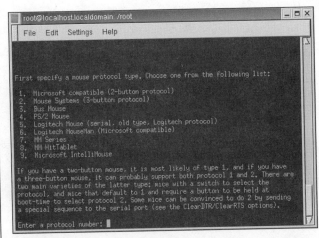

Figure 3.16 *Selecting a mouse type.*

If you selected a mouse type other than Mouse Systems (3-button protocol), you will be asked whether you want to activate the Emulate3Buttons option. Because a number of Linux programs use three buttons, I recommend that you press Y and then press Enter to continue.

Next, you will be asked the device name of the port to which the mouse is connected. Unless you are using a non-standard port, press Enter to accept the default.

The mouse portion of xf86config is now complete, and you are ready to answer questions about your keyboard.

Configuring the Keyboard

Once your mouse type is selected, you will see a list of keymaps, which apply to different types of keyboards.

This keymap list is nothing overly dramatic, as you can see in Figure 3.17; it's just a list of twelve keymaps. Most keyboards in the United States fall into the first keymap category. Type the number associated with your keyboard, and press Enter to continue to the next screen.

After you select the keymap for your keyboard, you will see a list of languages that can be used in X. As shown in Figure 3.18, only 18 are listed at first; if the language

BUZZWORD

Keymap: A configuration setting designed to match the keys of a keyboard to the correct electronic characters. Each type of keyboard has a different keymap.

Figure 3.17 *A dozen of the most commonly used keymaps.*

Figure 3.18 *Sprechen sie Deutsch? Get X to speak your language, too.*

you need is not shown, just press the Enter key to see more options. After you locate the language you want, simply type the number that corresponds to the language and press Enter to continue.

Configuring the Monitor

After the keyboard and mouse are configured, xf86config moves into the video settings. Because of the importance of these settings, xf86config spends a lot of time and screen space working with every aspect of video configuration, beginning with the monitor.

As you might expect, the first screen of the monitor section (shown in Figure 3.19) warns you about the importance of having the correct horizontal and vertical synchronization rates for your monitor.

> The monitor information you gathered in Chapter 1 will be used repeatedly. Be sure to save it where you can easily refer to it.

Press Enter to continue to the monitor section, which displays a list of the possible horizontal sync ranges for a monitor. There is also an option to enter a custom range, as shown in Figure 3.20. Type the number of the range category you want and press Enter to continue.

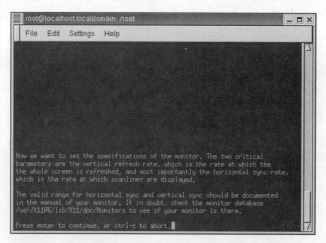

Figure 3.19   *Make sure you know your monitor's sync rates.*

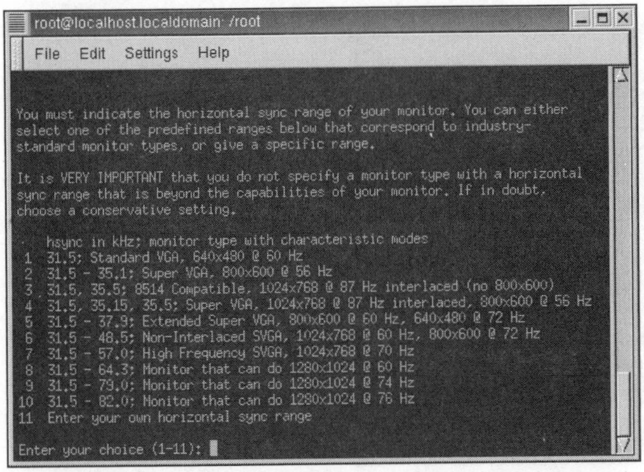

Figure 3.20 *Choose the horizontal sync rate range very carefully.*

After entering the range, a smaller list of vertical sync rates is displayed (see Figure 3.21). Again, use care in selecting your range to avoid overclocking and damaging your monitor.

Unlike the installation program and Xconfigurator, xf86config gives you a chance to assign a name to your monitor. You can type a proper name, the vendor name, and the model to this monitor configuration. Type the designation you want to use and press Enter, as shown in Figure 3.22.

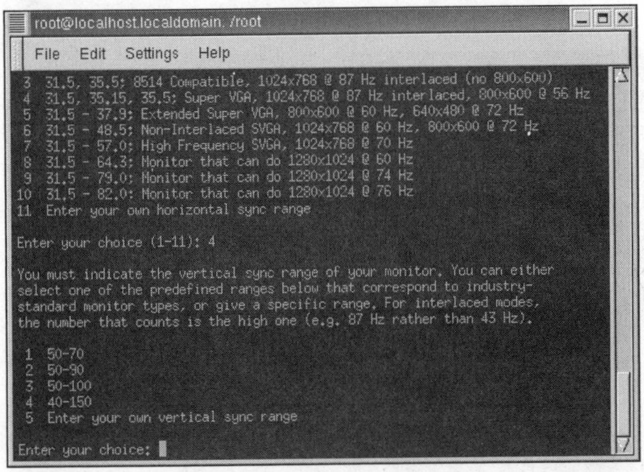

Figure 3.21 *Choose the vertical sync rate range with equal care.*

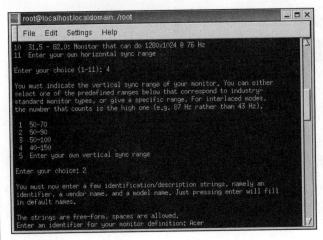

Figure 3.22   *Assign a name to your monitor settings.*

Once the monitor settings are complete, xf86config will move to the graphics card section—the last, and most detailed, portion of xf86config.

Configuring the Graphics Card

If you ever need to modify your graphics card settings, you can use xf86config to do so. You must first navigate through the entirety of the program to get to this point.

The first screen (see Figure 3.23) discusses the value of using the current database of graphics cards that are accessible by xf86config. I recommend that you try to find your card in this database, but like the message says, you must be very careful

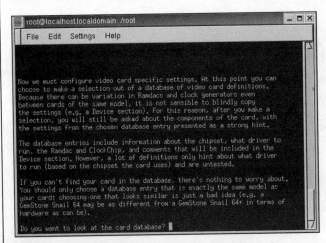

Figure 3.23   *Take the time to read this message about the graphics card database.*

about selecting your card. Similarly named cards may not be compatible with each other. If you try to fake it with a card that looks close to yours, you might inadvertently damage your monitor.

If you choose to check out the database (and you should), press Y and press Enter to continue. The beginning of a lengthy list of graphics card models and manufacturers, complete with chipset information, is displayed (see Figure 3.24). Scroll though the list by pressing Enter to see the next batch, but be careful not to scroll past your card, since there is no "back" option. When you locate your card, type the number of the card and press Enter.

Whether you use the card database or not, the next screen will be the video RAM settings screen. Here, you are asked how much video RAM memory your card has. It's important to get this right, since you will be cheating yourself out of all of your card's capabilities if you underestimate your VRAM. Type the size of your video RAM and press Enter.

The program will now ask you to supply a plain English designation for your card's configuration just as you did for the monitor. Type the name you want to use. Then, in the next screen, specify the color depth you want the X server to use, as shown in Figure 3.25. I recommend that you use at least 16-bit color depth to get a good range of colors on your screen.

Finally, you are informed that xf86config is about to save your settings to the all-important XF86config file. If you are in any way unsure of any settings you have made, you should press N, because there is no way to back up and fix a particular setting. If you think everything is in order, press Y and then Enter to finish the program.

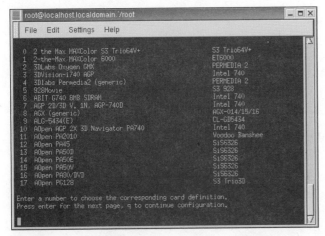

Figure 3.24 *The list of graphics cards.*

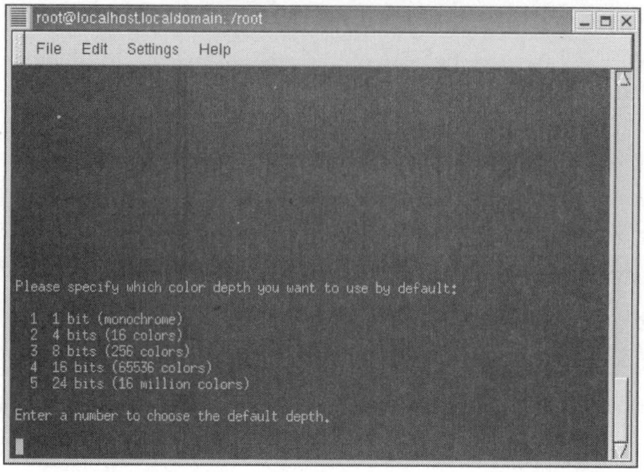

Figure 3.25   *From 2 to 16,000,000 colors!*

Using the Control Panel

Although configuring the settings for the keyboard and mouse is primarily the function of the X server, it is possible to make certain settings changes from the window manager, too. These changes are accomplished from the Control Center. While these settings are not major, they are little things that can make your life easier.

You can use either the GNOME or KDE control panels to make these settings. Just remember that any changes you make will be exclusive to the environment you are configuring.

Configuring the Keyboard

To access the Control Center application in the GNOME environment, click the GNOME control menu and choose Settings, Peripherals, Keyboard (or Mouse). Choosing the Keyboard option will open the Control Center directly at the Keyboard settings pane, shown in Figure 3.26.

If you are not satisfied with the performance of your keyboard, you can adjust the slider controls to change the values of repeating keys or keyboard clicking. You can also change the tone of the keyboard bell, something that in past versions of GNOME was handled in the Sound section of the Control Center. After making a change, click the Try button and then test your new settings in the Test setting field near the bottom of the dialog.

Once the settings are to your liking, click OK to close the Control Center window.

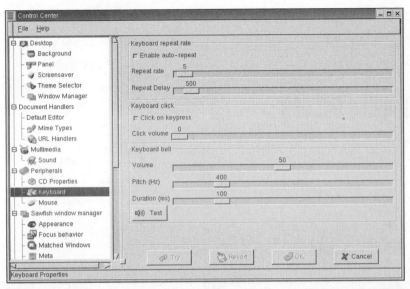

Figure 3.26 *Keyboard user settings can be modified from the GNOME environment.*

Configuring the Mouse

As noted in the previous section, you can also tweak your mouse settings in the Control Center. Again, these are not earth-shattering changes, but sometimes these little things really matter. Start by clicking the Mouse category in the Peripherals section of the GNOME Control Center. In the screen shown in Figure 3.27, you

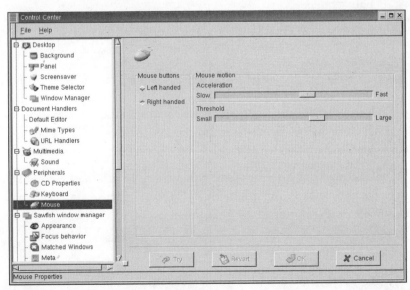

Figure 3.27 *Lefty? You'll love this pane of the Control Center.*

can change the button orientation on your mouse as well as the mouse's responsiveness to motion, both very handy features.

When you're finished experimenting with the settings, click OK to close the window.

Properly Logging Out of X

Windows and Mac users are accustomed to the fact that they simply can't just turn off their PCs. Instead, they must shut down first. Because most people are comfortable with this action, the steps necessary to leave X should feel familiar. Like its sister operating systems, X likes an orderly departure, not an abrupt power outage.

To leave X, you must first log out and close your account. In GNOME, click the Main Menu icon and select Log Out. A message box will ask you whether you want to log out, halt, or reboot.

If you want to log out leaving the computer on for the next user, click the Logout option and then click Yes. The X session closes and the screen returns to the graphical login screen if the Workstation installation was the option you selected. If you installed Red Hat as a server, you are returned to the command-line interface.

If you want to reboot the system, click Reboot, then Yes. X closes, and the Linux system halts your PC and then reboots itself, returning to the graphical login screen.

Finally, if you just want to turn the computer off and go watch TV, click the Halt option before clicking Yes. X Window closes, and Linux closes all running processes as part of its halt sequence.

If you change your mind, simply click No to resume your X Window session.

Conclusion

In this chapter, you learned about the components that make up the X environment and found out which components handle specific aspects of your PC. The procedures to configure video and input devices at the X server level were also reviewed.

In Chapter 4, "Configuring Your Environment," you will explore X even further at the window-manager and desktop-environment levels. You will also start to learn the ways you can make configuration settings at those levels.

Chapter 4: Configuring Your Environment

With apologies to my fellow countrymen: Americans are obsessed with choices. I mean crazy. For example, the average supermarket has an entire aisle devoted solely to breakfast cereal. Boxes and boxes of breakfast cereal. Americans revel in having the ability to choose between brands, cereal types, packaging…don't believe me? Ask yourself what would happen if the breakfast cereal fairy came down one night and reduced all of the different brands of cereal to just one generic brand.

Imagine: one kind of corn flakes, one kind of raisin bran, and one kind of sugary popped oats. No big deal, right? How many ways can you make a corn flake, anyway?

Wrong. The resulting revolt would make the worst Y2K scenario look like a picnic.

America's obsessive need for choices, ironically, has not been extended to the PC very well. After all, for the last decade or so, PC users have (for the most part) accepted one operating system—no substitutes allowed.

That's because, unlike the mass marketing of breakfast cereal, many consumers really did not even know that they had a choice of operating systems. OS/2 and the Mac were for those odd people who never fit in at a party. UNIX and Linux? Those users were perceived as strange, geeky people who weren't even *invited* to the party.

I'm exaggerating, of course, but only to a point. Events in late 1999 and early 2000 have raised public awareness about life outside of Redmond, Washington (home of Microsoft). It turns out that there are other choices for operating systems, and you don't have to be a geek to use them.

To which our friends in Europe reply: "What took you so long?"

Choosing a Desktop Environment

Not only is Linux a viable alternative to Microsoft Windows as a workstation platform, the operating system itself contains several graphical interfaces you can use.

For example, with Microsoft Windows you can change the look of the desktop by manipulating the colors and fonts of the menus and windows. There are even pre-packaged themes available to unify the desktop into a cohesive look. You can accomplish the same thing in X Window and even go way beyond that point. Not only can you manipulate the look of a desktop environment such as GNOME, you can also change the entire desktop environment to something else entirely! This complete ability to customize your system makes X Window a much friendlier tool to use than the static Microsoft Windows.

There are two other advantages to moving across desktop environments: You have the ability to access environment-specific tools you might not otherwise see; and you can decide which desktop approach you prefer to use, since each environment has a different presentation and work method.

But enough discussion, let's get to the tour!

Login Options

The first place you can choose which environment you will use occurs at the login screen. You now have the ability to pick the environment for the account you're logging in to. For instance, if I log into KDE as root and set KDE as the default, KDE will only be set as the default for the root account. Any other accounts into which I may log will use their own default environment.

The Session menu command appears in the login screen. When this command is clicked, the menu opens to reveal the available environment options. If you originally installed using the KDE Workstation path, your options will be

- **Default**. The default environment is set by either the original installation or the GNOME Desktop Switching application.
- **Failsafe**. The Failsafe command-line interface is used when there is difficulty getting an environment to run, as might occur when an incorrect video setting was made in Xconfigurator or xf86config that needs to be adjusted.
- **GNOME**. The GNOME desktop environment.

If you have added any other Linux desktop environments to your system, they will appear here as environment options as well. Once selected, the choice is confirmed by a message just below the Login field. After you complete your login procedure, the environment of your choice will appear.

Switching Desktop Environments

Once inside your environment (let's assume it's GNOME for now), you can quickly switch to another environment, as you will discover in the following task.

In Chapter 10, "Installing Software," you will learn how to install multiple desktop environments on your machine if for some reason you just installed either GNOME or KDE singly. For the remainder of this chapter, we'll be working with a PC that has both GNOME and KDE installed.

Switching Desktop Environments

This task explains how to move between desktop environments.

1. Click the Main Menu icon to open the Main menu.

2. Choose Programs, System, Desktop Switching Tool. The Desktop Switcher window will open, as shown in Figure 4.1.

> If you're wondering where the tvm window manager option came from, it is installed by default in a workstation installation.

3. Click the KDE option. The KDE logo appears (see Figure 4.2).

Figure 4.1 *The Desktop Switching tool.*

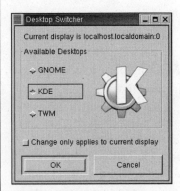

Figure 4.2 *Picking the KDE environment.*

You should click the Change Only Applies to Current Display option if your Linux PC is networked to other PCs and you want to make changes to only your own workstation.

4. Click OK. A message will remind you that these changes will not take effect until you log back in to the X Window system (see Figure 4.3).

5. Log out of the environment and return to the graphical login screen.

6. Log in using the same account. You will see the new default environment, KDE. (See Figure 4.4.)

Figure 4.3 *Environment changes occur after you log out of the current environment.*

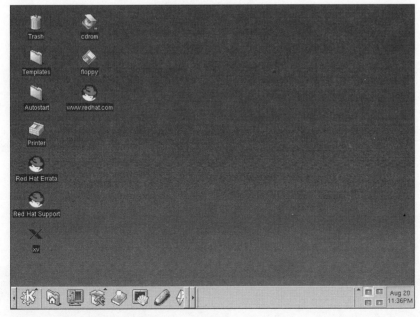

Figure 4.4 *The KDE desktop environment.*

If you want to reset GNOME to be the default environment, simply open the Desktop Switching tool once more. The application can be found on KDE's Application menu (akin to GNOME's Main menu) under Red Hat, System, Desktop Switching Tool.

Understanding the KDE Environment

KDE, like most Linux applications, is maintained with an open-source philosophy in mind. All development is done on a volunteer effort by developers around the world, with the source code being freely distributed to all who want it. The actual version of KDE installed with Red Hat Linux 7 is KDE 1.2.

If you really want to explore the cutting edge, Red Hat has included the pre-release software for the long-awaited KDE2 in this release. Look for the installation packages in the previews directory on Red Hat CD-ROM 2.

At first glance, KDE looks a lot like GNOME. This is because the K window manager's color defaults are similar to the defaults of GNOME's Sawfish window manager. (The K window manager runs beneath KDE.) These defaults are set by Red Hat to maintain a consistent look for the operating system as a whole.

Figure 4.5 shows the various desktop elements of the KDE desktop; these elements are detailed within Table 4.1.

As you can see, there are some subtle differences between KDE and GNOME, but they are not likely to confuse you.

Understanding the GNOME Environment

Similar to the previous section, where some basic elements of KDE were examined, this section takes a quick look at some of the basic elements of the GNOME desktop. This will help further detail some of the differences between these environments.

Figure 4.6 lists the various elements of the GNOME desktop; these elements are briefly explained in Table 4.2.

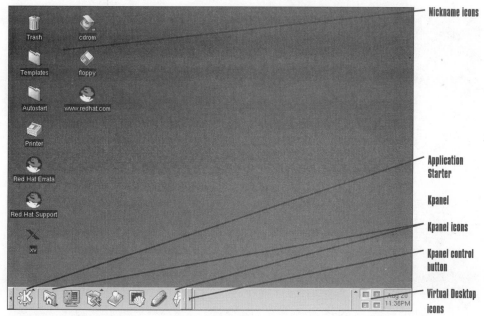

Figure 4.5   *The KDE desktop elements.*

Table 4.1   Elements of the KDE Desktop

Element	Description
Application Starter	This opens the Application menu, where many applications and utilities can be started.
Nickname icons	These can be used to open applications, files, or directories.
Kpanel	This contains several KDE controls, including the Application Starter, Virtual Desktop icons, and other Kpanel icons.
Kpanel icons	These icons can start specific applications from the panel.
Virtual Desktop icons	These display and control which virtual desktop (of four in this case) is open.
Kpanel control button	This control will close or open the Kpanel on demand.

Launcher icons

Main Menu icon

Panel icons

GNOME Panel

GNOME Pager

Panel control button

Figure 4.6   *The GNOME desktop elements.*

Table 4.2   Elements of the GNOME Desktop

Element	Description
Main Menu icon	This opens the Main menu, from which many applications and utilities can be started.
Launcher icons	These can open applications, files, or directories.
GNOME panel	This contains several GNOME controls, including the Main menu, GNOME Pager icons, and other panel icons.
Panel icons	These icons start specific applications from the panel.
GNOME Pager	This displays and controls which virtual desktop (of four in this case) is open, as well as any open applications.
Panel control button	This control will close or open the panel on demand.

Failsafe

In addition to the graphical desktop environments available from the login screen, another option, Failsafe, can be selected. As indicated in the Login section of this chapter, the Failsafe login option is a command-line interface setting. If selected during login, a small terminal emulation window will open in the lower-right corner of the screen.

Note the description of the window in the previous paragraph: This is a terminal *emulation* window. X is still running, even if a desktop environment isn't. This may appear to be a fine point, but the distinction is important. Some programs, such as sndconfig (examined in Chapter 7, "Configuring Printers, Sound, and Other Devices"), are not meant to be run from within X. If you try to run sndconfig in the Failsafe mode thinking it's the true Linux command line (which I actually tried way back in my novice Linux days), bad things may happen to your system, such as a system lockup.

Most applications that can run from the console (the true command-line mode) can also run in Failsafe mode. Any that can't will warn you that they won't run within X. At that point, you should heed the warning and exit the application.

> To access the Linux console while in any X mode, try pressing Ctrl+Alt+F1. To return to X from Linux, press Alt+F7.

The best use I have found for using Failsafe mode occurs when I make a mistake while experimenting with video settings. By logging into X in Failsafe mode, I can start Xconfigurator up and easily repair the error.

Now that you are familiar with the different login modes, a quick examination of the tool sets offered by Red Hat Linux 7 is in order.

X Tools

When you hear people comparing Linux to Windows, one of the big gripes you will hear is the perceived lack of available Linux applications. At the moment, Windows has some 100,000-plus applications available. Although there are not quite that many Linux applications, the number of available applications is nearer than many realize.

Because Linux applications typically are not commercially advertised, they are far less known than their Windows counterparts. Word, WordPerfect, AmiPro—most people have heard of these applications. But how many have heard of StarWriter? Not many. Those who have know that it's a very robust word processor, which is, by the way, compatible with the first three word-processing packages mentioned in this paragraph.

GIMP is another prime example of an application that is just as feature-rich as its Windows counterpart, Adobe PhotoShop. But because GIMP, like most of its Linux brethren, is not on the public radar, it is treated as non-existent—for the time being.

The next five sections of this chapter briefly examine the tools and applications made available by Red Hat with its Linux 7 release. Applications listed are those that were installed by default in the Workstation installation. Any uninstalled applications that are available on the Red Hat distribution CD-ROM will be listed in a separate table.

Editors

Within X are several text editors that can be used for modifying simple text files. Two popular editors, gEdit and gnotepad+, work within the GNOME desktop environment; while kedit and kwrite make their home in the KDE environment. VIM, based on an old UNIX favorite, is a command-line application that is a favorite amongst the console users of Linux.

VIM

Known throughout the UNIX and Linux community as vi, VIM is an improved version of the old vi standby. It cannot be started from a menu (unless a launcher or nickname icon is created) but is run from the command line.

Within a terminal emulator or on the Linux command line, type **vi** to start the VIM editor. As you can see in Figure 4.7, the basic commands are displayed in its opening screen.

One very good use of VIM is to manually edit configuration files. To open a file in VIM, simply type **vi file name** on the command line. To quit VIM and return to the command line, type **:q**.

Before you edit any configuration file, make sure to save a backup copy to which you can revert if an error is made.

gEdit and gnotepad+

The two GNOME applications to use for text editing are gEdit and gnotepad+, both of which are illustrated in Figure 4.8. As you can see from the figure, the

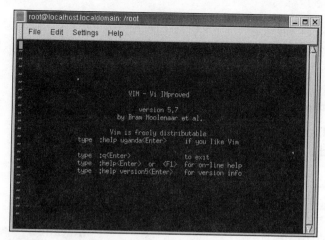

Figure 4.7   *The VIM text editor.*

functionality of these applications is similar, although gnotepad+ has extra tools that enable it to create HTML format commands. This makes sense because an HTML file is merely a text file containing textual codes that enable browsers to display enhancements such as font color and size changes.

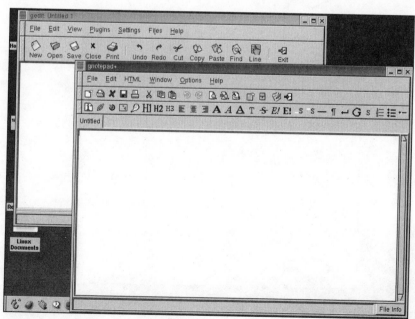

Figure 4.8   *The gEdit and gnotepad+ editors.*

kedit and kwrite

On the other side of the environment street, KDE has its own set of editors for you to make use of. As you can see from Figure 4.9, each of these editors looks remarkably like the other, but kwrite, also known as the Advanced Editor, lives up to its name by providing some sophisticated tools to edit text documents.

Table 4.3 lists additional editors available in Red Hat Linux 7, noting whether they are installed as part of the default package set.

Table 4.3   Additional Available Editors

Application	Description	Installed?
abiword	A full-featured word processor	No
emacs	Another very popular Linux command-line text editor	Yes

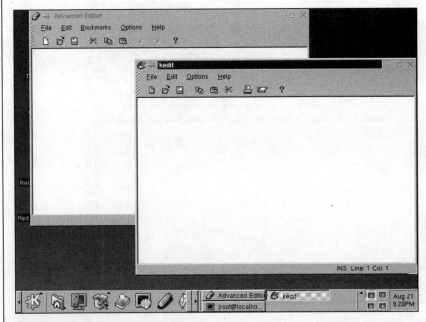

Figure 4.9   *The kwrite and kedit editors.*

Graphics

With the influx of the Internet, the need for applications that can handle graphics with ease has grown tremendously. Linux does not disappoint in this area, giving its users three tools for viewing and editing graphic files: Electric Eyes, GIMP, and Xpaint.

Electric Eyes

Despite the odd name, Electric Eyes is an excellent, simple graphics viewer. Once started, you right-click to open the menu. As with most programs, the File, Open menu selection can be used to open a graphic, just like the example shown in Figure 4.10.

GIMP

If you thought Electric Eyes had a weird name, the GIMP application may set you back a bit. GIMP (short for GNU Image Manipulation Program) is often compared to Adobe PhotoShop because it has many of the same capabilities.

GIMP has some special features that make it necessary to perform a secondary installation when the application is first started. When the GIMP Installation dialog box appears, click Install. When completed successfully, a message box will appear, informing you of the completed installation. Click Continue to open the GIMP interface, shown in Figure 4.11.

Figure 4.10 *Viewing graphics in Electric Eyes.*

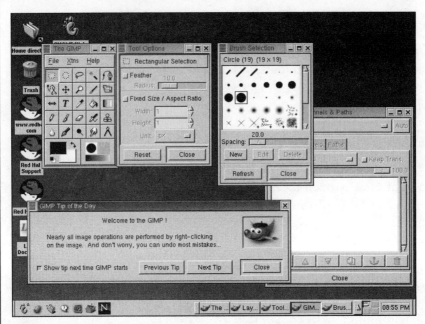

Figure 4.11   *The unusual GIMP interface.*

The GIMP interface is sort of odd, in that there is no "canvas" screen immediately visible—just a toolbar and (if your options are set for it) a Tip of the Day message box. But once you begin working with the program, you will find its capabilities amazing.

An entire book could be written on GIMP alone, so I won't dwell on it here. For further information, I highly suggest that you peruse the *GIMP Manual*, which you can open from the menu bar by choosing Xtns, Web Browser, GIMP Manual.

Xpaint

Unlike GIMP, Xpaint is an application that lets you *create* sharp-looking graphics, not just view them. Found within the Graphics menu option under Paint, Xpaint lets you make your own pictures (such as the hypnotic display shown in Figure 4.12) and save them in a variety of formats.

Certainly, a lot more exploration is possible within these applications, and you are invited to experiment at your leisure

Personal Information Managers

I don't know about you, but my days are hectic. I often find myself going from meeting to meeting, appointment to appointment, until it seems that a 24-hour day is just not long enough. For me, it's just a matter of getting organized.

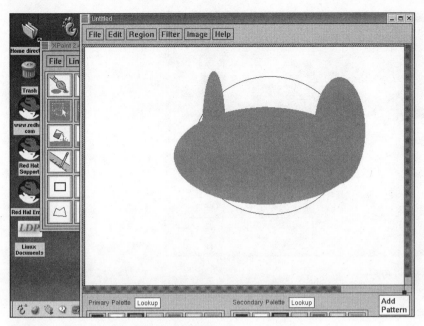

Figure 4.12 *Making your own art in Xpaint.*

This is where having a personal information manager (PIM) comes in handy. The electronic equivalent of a day-planner, a PIM can track appointments and help you avoid scheduling conflicts.

The primary PIM within Red Hat is the Calendar application. This application serves as a scheduler and task manager. Its interface, shown in Figure 4.13, may be very familiar to users of Microsoft Outlook or Symantec Act.

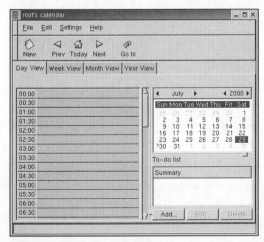

Figure 4.13 *The GNOME Calendar application.*

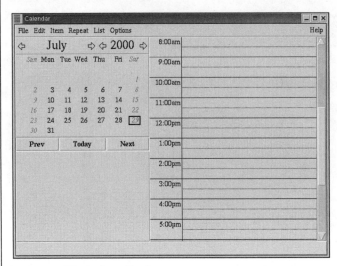

Figure 4.14 *The ical application.*

A more simplified PIM is ical, another application provided in Red Hat Linux 7. As you can see from Figure 4.14, it merely tracks your schedule, not tasks. But if that's all you need, it's a nice little application to use.

Internet Tools

If the previous categories of applications seemed a bit sparse, that's about to change. Linux provides many Internet-based applications, not the least of which is the commercially available Netscape Communicator (see Figure 4.15).

Netscape Communicator is an all-in-one application that provides Web browser, e-mail, and newsgroup-reader capabilities. This one program, which is examined in greater detail in Chapter 5, "Configuring Internet Services," will fill most of your Internet needs.

Even though Netscape provides most of the tools needed for Internet use, Linux provides many more Internet tools for advanced use. Because of the volume of utilities in the tool set, they are listed in Table 4.4. Table 4.4 should give you the idea that Linux wants you to be connected to the Internet.

There are many other types of applications, of course. The number of games alone would fill another book. You should explore the remaining Linux applications available on the CD-ROM. In this way you can see the true power of the operating system: its applications.

Figure 4.15 *Surfing the Internet with Netscape Communicator.*

Configuring Your Desktop

After you have taken the grand tour through the desktop and all that it has to offer, you may find that there are some aspects of the desktop you want to change. Chapter 8, "Customizing Your Desktop's Appearance," and Chapter 9, "Customizing Your Desktop's Usability," explore other aspects of desktop customization, such as color and sound schemes, setup of the startup program, and windows key modifications. The remainder of this chapter discusses the placement of the tools that are available to you within the desktop.

Menu Customization

What if you don't like digging through three or four menu levels to launch one of your most-used applications? In a situation like this, you can place the program's launcher somewhere on the desktop so that you can start that program much more quickly.

The Main menu is a prime place to place your favorite application's launcher. If it's buried four levels down in a tiny little submenu, follow the steps in the next task to place the launcher on the second level of the Main menu, with the Favorites sub-menu.

BUZZWORD

Launcher:
A menu item or icon that starts an application.

Table 4.4   Internet Applications Available in Red Hat Linux 7

Application	Description
elm	A popular e-mail client
exmh	A mail client that can read mh mail folders
fetchmail	Remote mail retrieval and forwarding utility
finger	An Internet tool that obtains information about a specific Internet user
gftp	An FTP application for GNOME
lynx	A text-only Web browser
minicom	An Internet-based remote terminal emulation tool
mutt	A Linux e-mail client
ncftp	A more robust FTP tool
pine	Another popular e-mail client
slrn	A news reader client
talk	An Internet chat tool
telnet	An Internet-based remote terminal emulation tool
tin	A news reader client
trn	A news reader client
whois	An Internet tool that obtains information about a specific Internet domain
xchat	An IRC client
xrn	A news-reader client

TASK

Customizing the Main Menu

This task demonstrates how to customize the Main menu in GNOME.

1. Click the Main Menu icon to open the Main menu.
2. Navigate to the menu launcher you want to relocate (see Figure 4.16).
3. Right-click the menu launcher.
4. Select the Add This to Favorites Menu option.
5. The launcher is copied to the Favorites sub-menu of the Main menu.

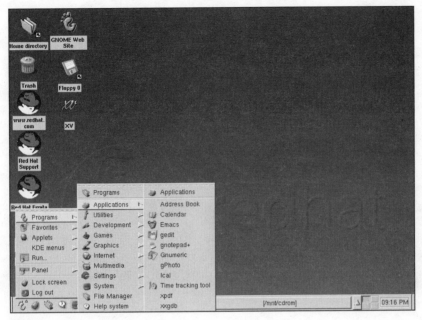

Figure 4.16   *Choosing an application to move.*

Desktop Icons

If you want to place a launcher or nickname on the desktop itself for even faster access, it's a simple drag-and-drop exercise.

Adding a Launcher to the Desktop

This task demonstrates how to place application launchers on the GNOME desktop.

1. Click the Main Menu icon to open the Main menu.
2. Navigate to the launcher icon to be moved.
3. Select the application launcher icon, and then drag the icon out to the desktop area.
4. Release the mouse button. A copy of the launcher icon is placed on the desktop (see Figure 4.17).
5. You can drag the icon to another location for aesthetics, if need be.

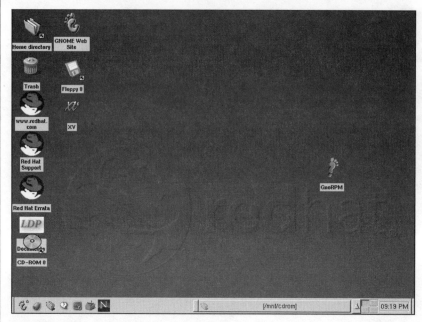

Figure 4.17   *Placing a launcher on the desktop.*

You can automatically arrange icons on the desktop by right-clicking any blank area of the desktop and selecting one of the Arrange Icons options.

6. To remove the icon, right-click it and choose Delete from the control menu. Click Yes when asked to confirm.

TASK

Adding a Nickname to the Desktop

This task demonstrates how to place application nicknames on the KDE desktop.

1. Right-click on the desktop. The control menu for the KDE desktop appears.
2. Select New, Application. The krootwm dialog box opens (see Figure 4.18).

Figure 4.18   *Choosing a name for your new nickname icon.*

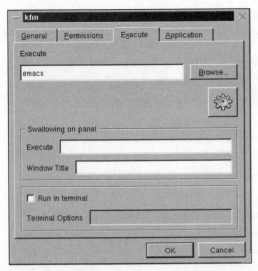

Figure 4.19 *Setting the properties for the new nickname.*

3. Substitute the name of the application you want to link to for "Program" in the New Application field and click OK. The kfm dialog box opens.

4. Click on the Execute tab (see Figure 4.19).

5. Type the program's command in the Execute field. Click on OK to place the new icon on the desktop.

You can change the icon for the nickname by clicking the icon graphic in the Execute pane and selecting from a library of icon art in KDE.

6. To remove the icon, right-click it and choose Delete or Move to Trash from the control menu. Click Yes when asked to confirm.

Panel Icons

A launcher can also reside on the GNOME panel, and a nickname can be created on the Kpanel, too. The next tasks detail how to accomplish this.

Adding a Launcher to the Panel

This task demonstrates how to place application launchers on the GNOME panel.

1. Click the Main Menu icon to open the Main menu.

2. Navigate to the launcher icon to be moved.

3. Right-click the application launcher.

4. Select the Add This Launcher to Panel option.

5. The launcher is copied to the GNOME panel (see Figure 4.20).

6. If you want to move the icon's position on the panel, right-click the icon and select Move Applet.

7. Without clicking the icon, move the multi-directional pointer along the panel. The selected launcher icon will follow.

8. When the icon is in the appropriate position, single-click the icon to lock its position.

9. To remove the icon from the panel, right-click the icon to open the control menu. Then choose Remove From Panel.

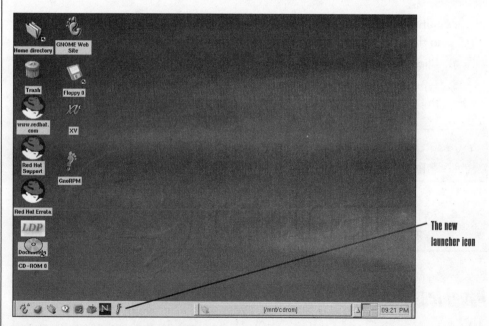

The new launcher icon

Figure 4.20   *A new GNOME panel launcher icon.*

Adding a Nickname to the Kpanel

This task demonstrates how to place nicknames on the Kpanel.

1. Create a new nickname on the KDE desktop as illustrated in the previous section "Desktop Icons."

2. Click and drag the nickname to a blank area of the Kpanel.

3. Release the mouse button. The nickname is copied to the Kpanel.

Conclusion

This chapter introduced you to the desktop environments that ship with Red Hat Linux 7 and the tools that each environment contains. You'll certainly want to do more exploring of whichever environment you like the best; but that's the fun part, isn't it?

Chapter 5 continues discussing the fun part of using a PC at the turn of the century: getting on the Internet and exploring the biggest network of all.

Chapter 5: Configuring Internet Services

Setting Up Your Internet Account

Using Netscape Communicator

Much has been said about the Internet this past decade. Although much hoopla and hype has been associated with this—the largest of all public computer networks—it should be noted that the Internet is not even close to being finished.

The growth of the Internet (thus far) is in many ways similar to the growth of the telephone in the United States in the late 19th century. For the first five years of its commercial existence, the telephone was in about 10 percent of U.S. households. In five more years, it was in 50 percent of American homes. Within another five years, it was in 90 percent of all U.S. homes.

The Internet matches this growth pattern fairly closely. By 1994, five years after the Internet broke out of its pure academic setting, connection to the Internet could be found in about 10 percent of U.S. homes. Now, over six years later, the pervasiveness of Internet access in the United States has reached nearly 50 percent. Incredible as it may seem, the United States is only at about its halfway mark toward full Internet usage. (The Internet's presence in other nations is behind in terms of percentages, but perhaps only because the U.S. had a head start; the pattern of the growth remains the same.)

Whether you are one of the new kids on the Internet block or you have been surfing since the days of Lynx, you will find that the Internet is becoming less of a place to play and more of a place to work. More and more people are turning to the Internet to handle banking needs, shop for holiday gifts, and even check up on their kids at daycare via Web cameras.

The history of Linux and the Internet is an intertwined one. Linux's predecessor, UNIX, was *the* operating system upon which the Internet was built. In fact, much of the syntax of the Internet ("http://," FTP commands, forward slashes for directory separators, and so on) is directly derived from UNIX line commands. So it should come as no surprise that Red Hat Linux 7 provides a rich set of Internet tools for access. All you have to do is get yourself connected.

Setting Up Your Internet Account

These days, getting an Internet account is fairly simple. I know I seem to get a CD-ROM in the mail with connectivity software almost once a month. But with Linux, you will need to make sure you are using the right type of account and speaking the right language.

The "language" of the Internet is called TCP/IP. This language (called a protocol) is how data is sent from your computer to a Web server computer in, say, Durham, North Carolina.

BUZZWORD

TCP/IP (Transmission Control Protocol/Internet Protocol): A suite of communications protocols used to connect hosts on the Internet. TCP/IP is a product of the UNIX operating system and is used by the Internet.

Even though TCP/IP is a UNIX-based product, Red Hat Linux needs additional protocol help connecting to the Internet through a dial-up connection. TCP/IP, after all, does not transmit the IP (Internet Protocol) data packets through serial lines very well—serial lines like those in modems, for example.

To get all of the data packets through a modem, an additional protocol, PPP, is used. The irony of this is that PPP is not a UNIX invention—it and its predecessor, SLIP, was developed to connect Windows computers to the Internet.

PPP can be used on Linux systems—Red Hat (RH) being no exception. The RH PPP Dialer program manages connection of your PC to the Internet. You must first configure the Dialer so that it can communicate properly to the computers at your Internet service provider (ISP).

Configure the PPP Dialer

Red Hat Linux 7 comes with the Dialup Configuration tool, an automated method of setting up your Internet connection. For most ISPs, using this application is enough to create a routine connection. There may be instances where more control over a connection's configuration is needed—which is why this section also examines the manual editing of a connection using the Dialup Connection tool.

Using the Dialup Connection tool is directly analogous to using the Internet Connection wizard within Microsoft Windows. The idea is to step though the application, providing the snippets of information needed by Red Hat to create a new PPP connection.

Before you begin the next task, which will demonstrate the creation of a connection, you should gather the following information:

- The domain name of the ISP (for example, earthlink.net)
- The user name of your account
- The password for your account
- The phone number for the ISP

You should also confirm what communications protocol your ISP requires. A vast majority of the ISPs will require PPP; some may use alternate protocols, such as SLIP or PLIP.

BUZZWORD

PPP (Point-to-Point Protocol): A communication protocol used to deliver data packets through modem lines during a dial-up call to the Internet.

BUZZWORD

Domain Name Service (DNS): A network of specialized servers within the Internet that translates alphabetic domain names into IP addresses. All Internet servers have a unique IP address, such as 198.105.232.95. Since these are more difficult to remember than plain-language host names, the DNS service translates domain names into their corresponding IP addresses. Many ISPs have a default DNS that gets queried first when a request to connect to a Web server is made.

> Many ISPs provide connection information in a single Web page or Web-accessible document. If you have access to the Internet from another PC or a Windows partition, visit the Web site of your ISP to see if yours has provided this information. A good place to check can be the "technical support" or "FAQ" sections.

Once this information is gathered, it is a simple matter to enter it into the Dialup Configuration tool.

Configuring an Internet Connection with the Dialup Connection Tool

This task shows how to use the automated Dialup Connection tool to establish an Internet connection.

> You will use the same connection tool in both the KDE and GNOME environments. This task highlights the setup in GNOME, but the steps are the same in either environment.

1. Click the Main Menu icon to open the Main menu.
2. Choose Programs, Internet, Dialup Configuration Tool. The application window will open in the foreground, with a window of existing Internet connections visible in the background (see Figure 5.1).

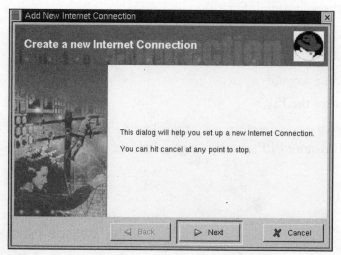

Figure 5.1 *Starting your new Internet connection setup.*

3. The first window is an introductory message. Click Next to continue.

4. Typically, you will have set up your modem during the initial installation of Red Hat. If you have not yet configured your modem, the Select Modem screen will appear (see Figure 5.2). Click Next to have the application automatically search for all modems connected to your PC.

Be sure you have turned your external modem on and that it is properly connected to the computer before the application searches for the device.

5. A list of modems connected to your PC will appear, as displayed in Figure 5.3. If the list of modem(s) is correct, click the modem you want to use. Then click the Keep This Modem option. Finally, click Next to continue.

6. In the Phone Number and Name screen (displayed in Figure 5.4), type a descriptive name for the connection, as well as the phone number your modem will need to dial. Click Next when finished.

Don't enter prefix or area/country code data in their respective fields unless needed. The RH PPP Dialer does not have a setting to turn off area code dialing.

7. Every ISP account includes a user ID and a password. Input this data on the next screen (see Figure 5.5). Click Next to continue.

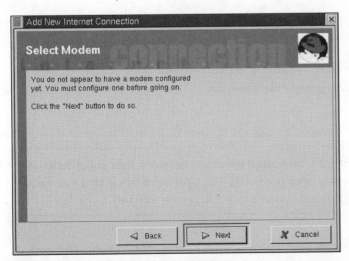

Figure 5.2 *If the Dialup Connection tool does not have a record of your modem, it will ask to configure it for you.*

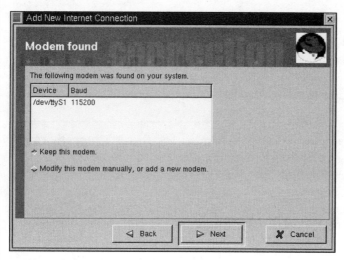

Figure 5.3   *Confirming the found modem choice.*

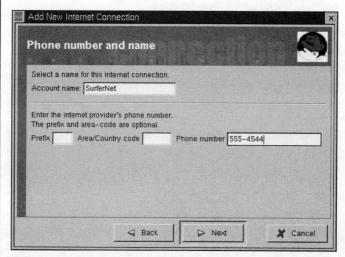

Figure 5.4   *Enter telephone information for the connection.*

> To protect your account from unwanted use, the password field substitutes asterisks for each character in your password. The upshot of this is that you need to use care while typing your password to avoid typing miscues.

8. Red Hat Linux can access two types of ISPs: the AT&T Global Network Services and regular non-proprietary ISPs. Select from one of these two categories (see Figure 5.6) and click Next to continue.

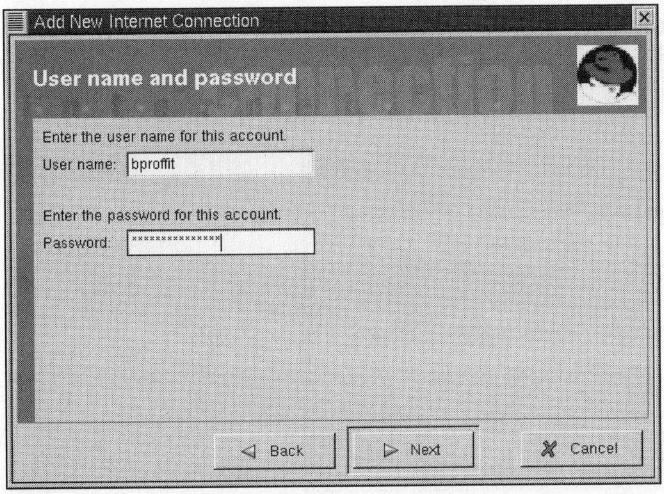

Add New Internet Connection ⊠

User name and password

Enter the user name for this account.

User name: bproffit

Enter the password for this account.

Password: ***************

◁ Back ▷ Next ✗ Cancel

Figure 5.5 *The user name and password screen.*

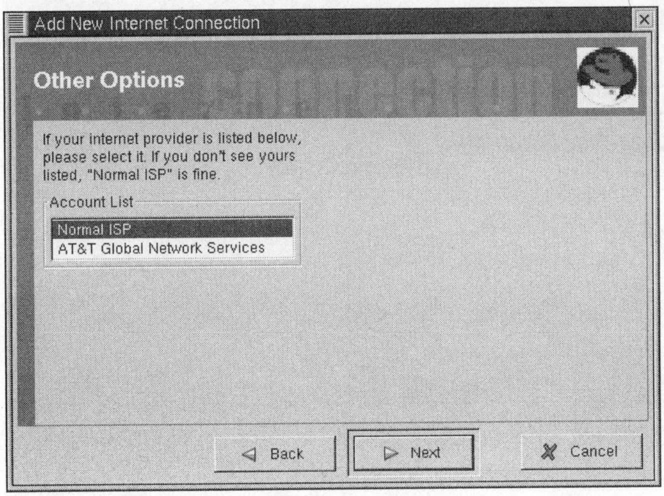

Add New Internet Connection ⊠

Other Options

If your internet provider is listed below, please select it. If you don't see yours listed, "Normal ISP" is fine.

Account List
Normal ISP
AT&T Global Network Services

◁ Back ▷ Next ✗ Cancel

Figure 5.6 *Choosing your ISP type.*

"Proprietary" ISPs are those online services that use their own communications protocols. They also typically provide their own content over and above Internet access. These services include America Online, CompuServe, and Prodigy, to name a few.

9. The final screen of the application is shown in Figure 5.7; it summarizes the information entered in the previous screens. If it is correct, click Finish to end the program.

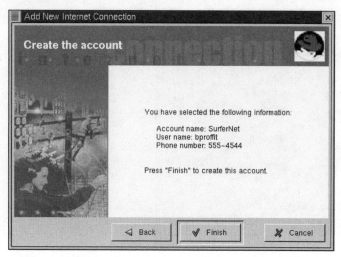

Figure 5.7 *Wrapping up the Dialup Connection tool process.*

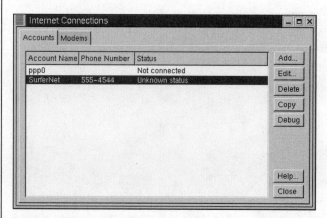

Figure 5.8 *The new Internet connection.*

The Add New Internet Connection dialog box will close, and you will be returned to the Internet Connections window. Your new connection will appear in this screen, as shown in Figure 5.8.

Though the Dialup Connection tool is by far the most intuitive method of creating Internet connections, there may be times that you will need a bit more control over your connection. For example, your ISP may require you to enter Domain Name Service (DNS) information. For this type of detail, you will need to use the Dialup Connection tool again to manually fine-tune a connection.

In the following task, you will learn to add or confirm the modem port for your modem device. Similar to hard drives, modems are also mounted on the Linux file system. Modems are, after all, just another type of device with which Linux exchanges data. Like other PC devices, modems appear in the /dev directory of the file system. Table 5.1 lists the available modem ports and their DOS equivalents.

Table 5.1   Modem File System Paths

Path	DOS Equivalent Port
/dev/ttyS0	COM1
/dev/ttyS1	COM2
/dev/ttyS2	COM3
/dev/ttyS3	COM4
/dev/modem	The link for any configured modem

TASK

Manually Configuring an Internet Connection with the Dialup Connection Tool

This task illustrates how to use the Dialup Connection tool to edit an Internet connection.

NOTE

Be sure you are logged in as root for this task.

1. Click the Main Menu icon to open the Main menu.
2. Choose Programs, Internet, Dialup Configuration Tool. The Internet Connections window will open.
3. Click on the Modems tab. The Modems pane will appear in the window, as shown in Figure 5.9.
4. Click Add to start the process of configuring a new modem. The Edit Modem Properties dialog box will open (see Figure 5.10).

TIP

To save some time, click the Auto Configure button and have Red Hat get the correct settings for you.

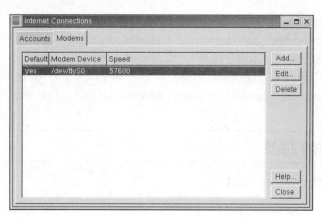

Figure 5.9 *Configured modems are listed in this pane.*

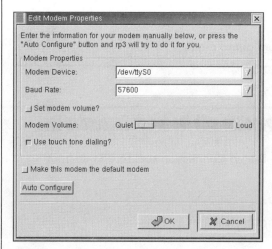

Figure 5.10 *You can change your modem options in this dialog box.*

5. Change the properties you need to change and then click OK. The settings will be saved and the Edit Modem Properties dialog box will close.

6. Click on the Accounts tab. The Accounts pane will appear.

7. Select an account to fine-tune and click on Edit. The Edit Internet Connection dialog box will appear, as shown in Figure 5.11.

8. Click the Advanced tab. The Advanced pane will appear (see Figure 5.12).

9. To enter the DNS information, type the IP address sections in each of the four First DNS Server fields. Use the Tab key to quickly navigate the fields.

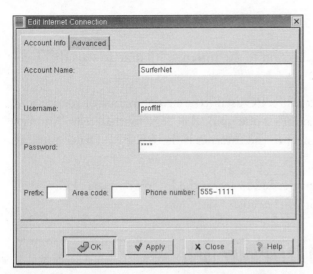

Figure 5.11 *This dialog box allows you to modify your connection settings.*

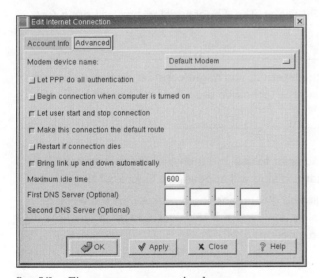

Figure 5.12 *Fine-tune your connection here.*

10. Prevent some hang-ups by setting the Maximum idle time value to more than the default 600 seconds. Try 1,200 seconds, which will give you 10 minutes.

11. Click on OK. The Edit Internet Connection dialog box will close.

12. Click on Close. The Internet Connections dialog box will close and your new setting will be saved.

Connect to the Internet

Now that you have set up a connection to the Internet, it's time to start that connection and see what it can do!

Connecting to the Internet on a Linux PC used to be a combination of voodoo and science, much like picking the number one–ranked college football team is today. No longer. All you need to connect to the Internet is the RH PPP Dialer application, called "RP3" for short.

In this task, you will see the steps needed to access the Internet on your PC, as well as how to configure RP3 to suit your needs.

TASK

Connecting to the Internet with RH PPP Dialer (RP3)

This task demonstrates the ease with which you can connect to the Internet.

1. Click the Main Menu icon to open the Main menu.
2. Choose System, RH PPP Dialer. The Choose dialog box will open (see Figure 5.13).

TIP

If you frequently connect to the Internet, you might consider adding an icon for RP3 to the GNOME panel using the technique described in Chapter 4, "Configuring Your Environment."

3. Click the connection you want to use and then click OK to continue. The Change Connection Status dialog will appear (see Figure 5.14).
4. Click Yes. RP3 will begin the dial-up and login process, all the while displaying the Waiting dialog (see Figure 5.15). Click Cancel at any time if you want to stop the connection.

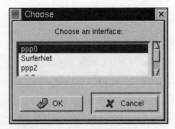

Figure 5.13   *Select the PPP connection you want to start.*

Figure 5.14   *Confirm that you want to start the connection to your PPP account.*

Figure 5.15 *One ringy-dingy...*

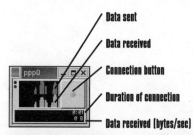

Data sent

Data received

Connection button

Duration of connection

Data received (bytes/sec)

Figure 5.16 *The RP3 application window.*

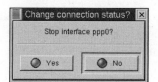

Figure 5.17 *Confirm that you want to stop your Internet connection.*

5. Once the connection is made, the main RP3 window will appear. Although not much to look at, this window displays quite a bit of information, as shown in Figure 5.16.

6. When you want to disconnect from the Internet, simply click the Connection button in the RP3 window. The Change Connection Status dialog box will appear once more, this time asking if you want to stop the connection (see Figure 5.17).

7. Click Yes to confirm this action. All of the RP3 windows and dialog boxes will close.

I find RP3's default method of asking for confirmation every time you want to start or stop an Internet connection to be a bit annoying. While useful in preventing the accidental logoff of an Internet connection, it certainly is bothersome when you're trying to connect.

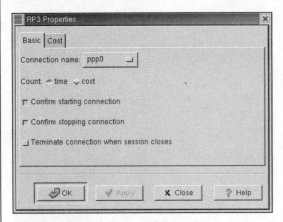

Figure 5.18 — *Configuring your RP3 settings.*

Despite the apparent lack of interface within the RP3 application, there is a way to adjust some of the program's settings. To do so, right-click in the application window used to start the RP3 menu. Select Properties to open the RP3 Properties dialog box (see Figure 5.18).

Here, you can disable the confirmation messages that appear at the start and end of RP3 sessions, as well as determine whether you want the application to monitor the time or cost of the connection, based on a per-hour, minute, or second rate. The latter option is especially useful when you have an ISP that bills you for connection time or if you must pay a toll for local telephone calls.

Using Netscape Communicator

As indicated earlier in this chapter, several Internet tools for users are included with Red Hat Linux 7. Of these, the most encompassing application is surely Netscape Communicator 4.7.4.

Netscape Communicator is actually a suite of three applications: Navigator, Messenger, and Composer. Navigator is the Web browser component of the suite, Messenger the e-mail and newsgroup reader component, and Composer the HTML file builder used to create your own Web pages.

With all these capabilities, you might think you would have a bit to set up—and you'd be right. The Navigator component alone has several settings that can make surfing the Web even faster.

Configuring Netscape Navigator

In the olden days of the Internet (all of seven years ago), life was uncomplicated. There was the simple concept of hyperlinks on a text page. Some links went to other pages, others to files to be downloaded—perhaps a picture or two. Browsers such as Lynx only had to contend with text. Life was good.

In 1993, this all changed forever. The National Center for Supercomputing Applications (NCSA) at the University of Illinois created Mosaic—a browser capable of displaying text and pictures. Suddenly, users could see illustrated Web pages, which facilitated the flow of information. A year later, one of the Mosaic developers left NCSA and launched his own browser: Netscape Navigator 1.1.

Since then, the capability of browsers has grown even more in response to more complex content. Need to hear a sound file? No need to download the file, save it, and then play it using another application. Browsers can now either play the sound themselves or automatically start that third-party application for you. Need to view a Shockwave file? Not only will a browser display it for you, the browser can automatically go get the required viewer if you don't already have it.

This is a long way from the early Internet days, that's for sure.

To make all of this work for you, there are a few settings you can adjust within Navigator, such as the rudimentary home page and personalized start page settings. You can also alter the size of the cache and choose which helper applications Netscape will use when it encounters a file it can't display itself.

Home Page and Other Easy Stuff

Most of you have used browsers before and know that a user's home page is the first HTML file loaded when the browser starts. That home page can be a local file or one on the Internet. You can easily specify what's displayed, as shown in the following task.

Configuring the Navigator Home Page

This task shows how to configure the Netscape Navigator home page.

1. Click the Netscape icon in the panel to open Netscape.
2. Click Edit, Preferences. The Netscape Preferences dialog box opens (see Figure 5.19).

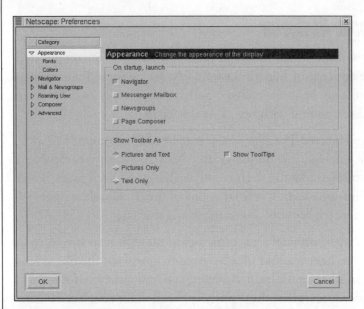

Figure 5.19 *All the Netscape configuration changes are made in this dialog box.*

3. Click Navigator in the Category pane to open the Navigator settings window.

4. Type the URL of the Internet page you want to use as your home page (see Figure 5.20).

If you want your home page to be a local file, click the Choose button to open the Netscape File Browser dialog box. There, navigate to the desired file and click OK. The full path to the file will appear in the Location field.

5. Click OK. Navigator will now display the selected home page each time the browser starts or you click the Home button on the Navigator toolbar.

When the Netscape Communicator icon is clicked on the GNOME or KDE panel, by default the Navigator component starts first. If, for example, you want to check your e-mail before doing anything else, you may prefer to have Messenger start before Navigator.

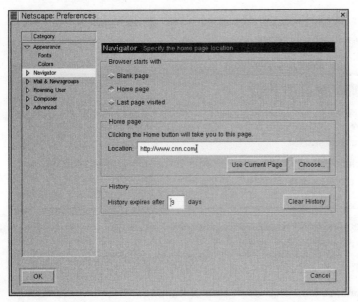

Figure 5.20 *Any page on the Internet can be your home page.*

Configuring the Communicator Starting Component

This task shows how to specify which Netscape Communicator component will be the first to start.

1. In Netscape, choose Edit, Preferences. The Netscape Preferences dialog box opens.
2. Click any of the four options in the On Startup, Launch group.

> If you want more screen real estate in Netscape, change the Toolbar setting in this dialog to Picture Only or Text Only.

3. Click OK. Communicator will now open the selected component each time the application starts.

Netscape also enables its registered users to create their own personalized start page. This start page, which can also serve as a home page, is a custom Web page provided by Netscape that can contain information from a variety of categories that you pick. What's nice about these pages is that you can access them from anywhere, not just your Linux PC and not just with Navigator as your browser. All you need is a connection to the Internet.

Configuring the Personalized Start Page

This task shows how to choose personal settings to be displayed each time Netscape Communicator starts.

1. In Netscape, click the My Netscape icon in the toolbar. The NetCenter Web page will appear (see Figure 5.21).

If you are already a registered Netscape user, click the Find it! link on the default NetCenter page to enter your user name and password.

2. Click the Personalize icon on the left side of the page. The New Member Sign-Up page will open (see Figure 5.22).

If you are a returning NetCenter member, click the Sign In icon to customize your page.

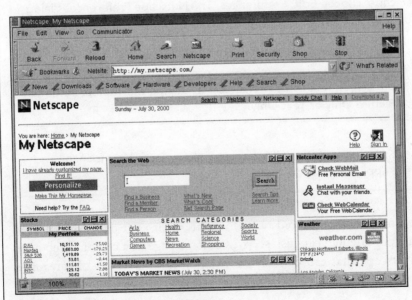

Figure 5.21   *The default NetCenter Web page.*

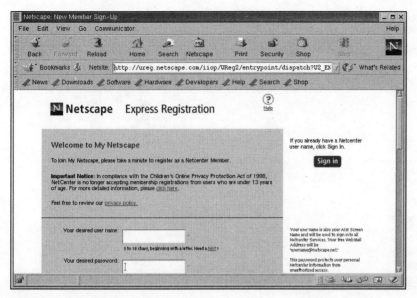

Figure 5.22 *Express Registration enables you to register with NetCenter before personalizing your start page.*

3. Enter the appropriate information in the Sign-Up page. When finished, click the Next button at the bottom of the page to continue.

4. The Email Confirmation Sent screen will appear. Read the screen to confirm the information, and then click Next to continue.

5. Figure 5.23 displays the Welcome page that appears. On this page, click an option's check box to include it on your start page, clicking the check box again to clear any that you want to remove.

To see a preview of the information each option will display, click the option's link to get a peek. Click the toolbar's Back button to return to the Welcome page.

---

6. Next, select your time zone using the drop-down list near the bottom of the Welcome page.

7. When finished, click one of the Build My Page buttons on the top or bottom of the page.

8. The new start page will appear, as shown in Figure 5.24.

9. Besides selecting the channels that will appear, you can also customize each channel. This is especially handy if you chose a local channel and your city is not the default. To begin, click the Customize channel button for the channel you want to modify.

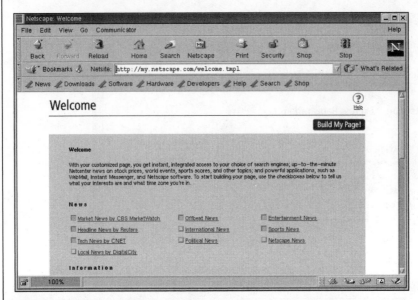

Figure 5.23   *Choose the options you want to appear on your start page.*

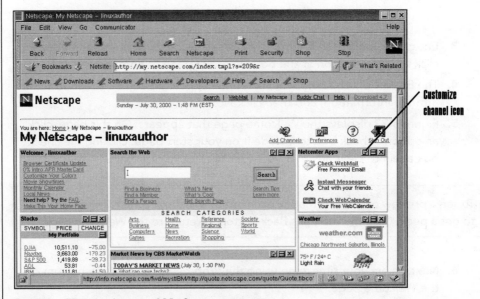

Figure 5.24   *The new improved NetCenter page: yours.*

10. In this example, I chose to customize the local news channel. Find and select your desired city in the Select a News Category field. (See Figure 5.25.)

11. Click the Add icon to move the selected city to the Selected News Categories field. Repeat if you want to add more cities.

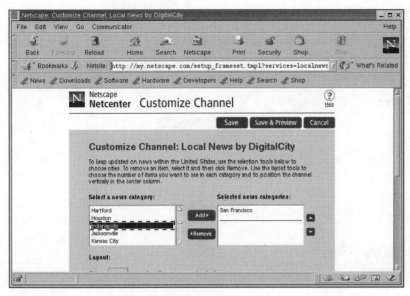

Figure 5.25 *Local news at 11? Get it anytime!*

12. To remove any cities you no longer want displayed, click their names in the Selected field and then click the Remove button.

13. Click the Save button to apply your changes. The updated channel will appear in your start page (see Figure 5.26).

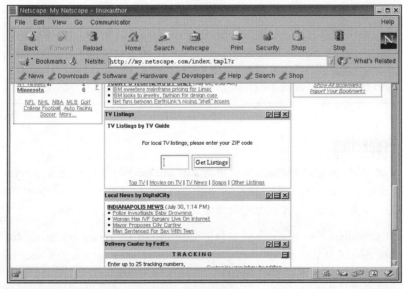

Figure 5.26 *My city's news. Maybe I should move…*

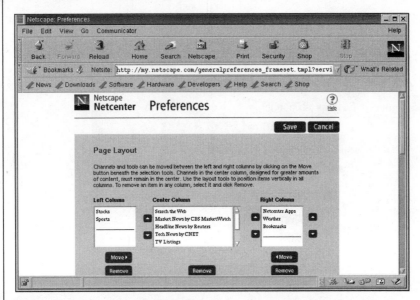

Figure 5.27 *Page layout, color, and other personal preferences are handled from this page.*

14. If you want to change the layout of the page itself, select the Preferences link that appears near the top of the page. The Preferences page will open (see Figure 5.27).

15. Make the changes you desire and click the Save button. Your updated page will be displayed with all of your changes, as shown in Figure 5.28.

If you decide to customize both color and general preferences in a single trip to the Preferences page, be aware that only your color changes will be applied to the start page when you click Save. Therefore, you should set your general preferences first and then set your color choices later.

Setting Cache Properties

A vast majority of Web pages to which you may surf are heavily laden with graphics and other little gimcracks that take up bandwidth and therefore lengthen download times. Caching is a way to accelerate the downloading process.

When it is first installed, Netscape has a fair amount of memory set aside for caching: a total of 8MB. If you often visit graphic-intense sites (or a lot of sites in general), you may want to change this figure.

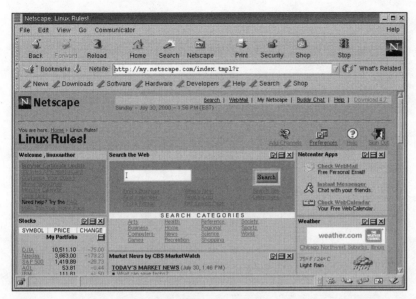

Figure 5.28 *You may want to practice some restraint in designing your page.*

Configuring the Navigator Cache

This task steps you through changing cache settings within the Navigator.

1. In Netscape, choose Edit, Preferences. The Netscape Preferences dialog box will open.
2. Click the expansion icon next to Advanced.
3. Click Cache. The Cache window will open (see Figure 5.29).

> Unless your system has a lot of RAM, it is a good idea to leave the memory cache settings where they are. You do not want to devote a lot of system resources to caching.

4. Increase the disk cache value to a level you feel is appropriate for your system. I recommend at least 10MB, unless you are using a smaller or older PC.
5. Click OK.

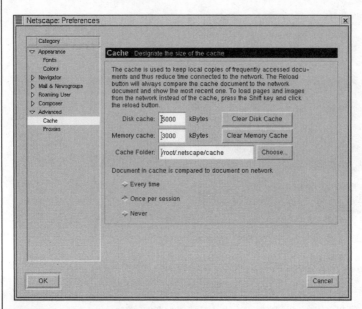

Figure 5.29   *The cache preferences.*

Defining Helper Applications

Helper applications are those used by Netscape to display or otherwise use certain file types you may find on the Internet. There are basically two types of helper applications: plug-ins, which are essentially mini-applications that work seamlessly with Netscape to open or display a file, and true third-party applications started by Netscape when a particular file type is encountered.

The next task demonstrates how to add third-party helper applications to Netscape Navigator.

Specifying a Third-Party Application as a Helper Application

This task shows how to set an existing application as a helper application—in this case the StarOffice application for reading WordPerfect files.

1. In Netscape, choose Edit, Preferences to open the Preferences dialog box.

2. Click the expansion icon next to the Navigator listing.

3. Click the Applications listing. The Applications window will appear.

4. Scroll to the WordPerfect description and select it.

5. Click Edit. The Application dialog box will open.

6. Click the Application option and then click the Choose button. The File Browser dialog box will appear.
7. Navigate to the StarOffice application file and click OK.
8. Click OK to close the Preferences dialog box.

You can also configure StarOffice to open any Microsoft Office file.

TIP

Configuring Netscape Messenger

One of the more useful features of Communicator is the all-in-one capability to receive e-mail and read newsgroups. Before you can begin, however, you will need to tell the Messenger component where your Internet mailbox is, as well as where your newsgroup server is.

The next two sections of this chapter examine exactly how to provide Messenger with the information it needs.

Setting Up E-Mail

E-mail messaging has changed the course of the business world considerably. It's gotten to the point where using the phone is considered a last resort for many companies.

So that you can receive e-mail on your PC, you first need to tell Messenger where to pick up your mail. E-mail rarely arrives directly at your computer. Instead, it resides on a mail server (usually at your ISP's location) until you query that server and download your messages to your computer.

The following task demonstrates how to enter this information.

BUZZWORD

Cache: A specific amount of memory set aside to keep compressed versions of visited Web pages and their graphics. On a return visit to the Web site, any unchanged elements from the page are loaded from the cache first, thus rendering their download unnecessary.

Configuring E-Mail

TASK

This task demonstrates how to set up e-mail services in Messenger.

1. In Netscape, select Edit, Preferences to open the Preferences dialog box.
2. Click the expansion icon for the Mail & Newsgroups listing.
3. Click the Identity listing. The Identity window appears (see Figure 5.30).
4. Enter all the necessary information.
5. Click Mail Servers in the Category pane to open the Mail Servers window (see Figure 5.31).

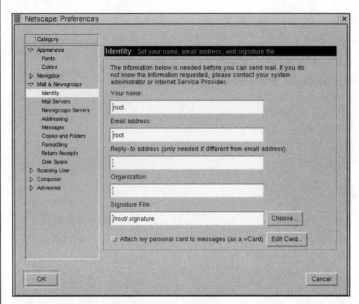

Figure 5.30   *Telling Messenger who you are.*

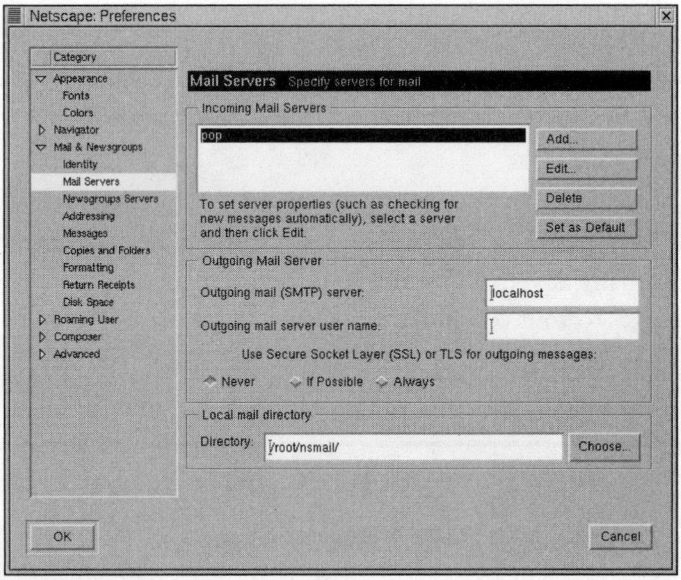

Figure 5.31   *Finding your Internet mailbox.*

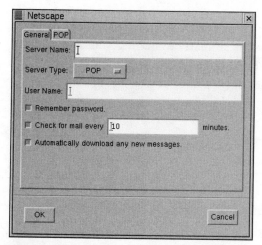

Figure 5.32   *Configuring the incoming mail server.*

6. Select the default Incoming Mail Server and then click Edit. The POP dialog box will open (see Figure 5.32).

Click on the Remember Password option to facilitate mail pickup.

7. Set any options you require in the General panel.
8. Click the POP tab to view the POP panel.

If you use more than one computer to check your e-mail, I recommend choosing one computer to be the central client repository and setting all other computers to leave messages on the mail server. In this way, all incoming mail is seen in at least one place.

9. When finished, click OK.
10. Enter the pertinent information in the Outgoing Mail Server fields.
11. Click OK to complete the task.

Messenger can now pick up your messages.

Setting Up Newsgroups

Reading newsgroups on the Internet works similarly to getting your e-mail. The only differences here are that you are looking at servers to which everyone has access, and you can view a lot more messages! Think of newsgroups like the old bulletin boards: Just post a message for all to see, and wait for the replies.

Configuring Newsgroups

This task demonstrates how to set up newsgroup services in Messenger.

1. In Netscape, select Edit, Preferences to open the Preferences dialog box.
2. Click the expansion icon next to the Mail & Newsgroups listing.
3. Click the Newsgroups Servers listing. The Newsgroups Servers window appears (see Figure 5.33).
4. Click Add. The news server dialog box opens (see Figure 5.34).
5. Type the descriptive name of your news server and click OK to close the dialog box.

> The port setting should be left alone, unless you know for sure that your news server uses a different port.

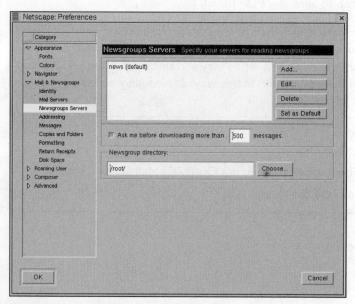

Figure 5.33 *Identifying from where newsgroups will be read.*

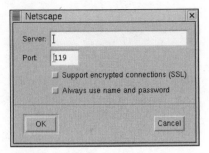

Figure 5.34   *Configuring the news server.*

6. Select the new newsgroup and then click the Set as Default button.
7. Select the original newsgroup (which is a dummy setting) and click Delete.
8. Click OK to close the Preferences dialog.

To begin using the news server, start the newsgroup reader, right-click the server listing, and then select Subscribe to Newsgroups.

Conclusion

This chapter led you through a lengthy exploration of how to configure your Linux system to connect to the Internet and how to use one of the more versatile tools within Red Hat Linux 7: Netscape Communicator.

But Netscape is certainly not the end-all-be-all of Linux's Internet tool set. Nor is the Internet the full extent of Linux's networking capabilities. Chapter 6, "Configuring a Network Connection," continues exploring connectivity issues with your Linux system and demonstrates how to configure your PC to work with a network.

Chapter 6: Configuring a Network Connection

Networking Settings During Installation

Stars, Cards, Cables, and Hubs——A Few of My Favorite Things

Open the History Books

Networking and IP Addresses

Network Configuration

Command-Line Tools

Problem Cards and Plug and Play

R ed Hat Linux 7 is a very capable operating system on its own, but like the old saying goes, there's strength in numbers. Hooking your computer to the Internet is one way to improve your productivity, but to really share the resources of your co-workers or even family members, you need to use the networking capabilities of Red Hat.

There are many tools and help systems to connect you to your local area network (LAN), if you are part of one, and to the outside world via the Internet. Important networking settings appear during the initial Red Hat installation, so it's best to be ready to address these settings then.

Networking Settings During Installation

During installation, you will be prompted to enter information that identifies your computer and network. You will also be asked for information concerning your connection to the Internet. Gathering this information ahead of time will make your network configuration faster and easier.

Configuring Your Network Settings

If a network card is detected during the initial installation of Red Hat Linux 7, the Network Configuration screen will appear, as shown in Figure 6.1. This task demonstrates what information you should supply.

```
┌─ Online Help ──────────┬─ Network Configuration ──────────────────┐
│                     ▲  │  ┌─ eth0 ─┐                                │
│                     │  │  │                                        │
│  Network            │  │  ▢ Configure using DHCP                   │
│  Configuration      │  │  ▣ Activate on boot                       │
│                     │  │                                           │
│  If you have a      │  │   IP Address: [          ]                │
│  network card, you  │  │   Netmask:    [          ]                │
│  can set up your    │  │   Network:    [          ]                │
│  networking         │  │   Broadcast:  [          ]                │
│  information.       │  │                                           │
│  Otherwise, click   │  │                                           │
│  Next to proceed.   │  │                                           │
│                     │  │   Hostname:      [                  ]     │
│  Choose your device │  │   Gateway:       [          ]             │
│  type and whether   │  │   Primary DNS:   [          ]             │
│  you would like to  │  │   Secondary DNS: [          ]             │
│  configure using    │  │   Ternary DNS:   [          ]             │
│  DHCP. If you have  │  │                                           │
│  multiple ethernet  │  │                                           │
│  devices, each      │  │                                           │
│  device screen will │  │                                           │
│  keep the           │  │                                           │
│  information you    │  │                                           │
│  have given to it.  │  │                                           │
│  You can switch     │  │                                           │
│  between device     │  │                                           │
│  screens, for       │  │                                           │
│  example eth0 and   │  │                                           │
│  eth1; the       ▼  │  │                                           │
│                        │                                           │
│  ? Hide Help           │          ◁ Back      ▷ Next               │
└────────────────────────┴───────────────────────────────────────────┘
```

Figure 6.1 *Your networking options can be entered during installation.*

1. Click the Configure using DHCP option if you have a dynamic IP address or know that your Internet service provider (ISP) uses dynamic addressing.

2. Click the Activate on Boot option if you want the network to start automatically when you start Red Hat Linux.

3. If you're not using DHCP on your network, enter your IP address in the next field. This is your own IP address, assigned by your ISP or possibly your system administrator.

If you want to use only a private LAN and have no direct Internet connection, you can use the group of IP addresses that has been set aside for this purpose. Probably the most common group used is 192.168.1.1 through 192.168.1.254. There are others that are reviewed in the "Networking and IP Addresses" section later in this chapter.

NOTE

4. Linux will attempt to automatically assign a netmask setting according to your IP address. Check to see that it matches the one you are assigned.

5. Linux will automatically attempt to fill in an address in the Network field, based on information it gleans from your network. This will be part of the information assigned to your PC by the network administrator if you are part of a large system.

6. The Broadcast field will need to be filled in with a broadcast IP address if your PC is a broadcasting component of your network.

7. If you are connecting directly to the Internet from your computer, you will be assigned a host name by your ISP or system administrator. Enter that information in the Hostname field.

8. Enter your gateway or router IP address in the Gateway field.

9. The primary DNS address may or may not be your gateway IP address; enter whatever is given to you.

10. If you have an alternate domain name server IP address, enter it in the Secondary DNS field.

11. Some networks provide access to more than two name servers. Enter the address of any additional DNS, if you have it, in the Ternary DNS field.

12. Click the Next button to continue with the installation process, which is detailed in Chapter 2, "Installing Red Hat Linux 7."

Your initial networking configuration is now complete.

BUZZWORD

Dynamic IP address: Every computer on the Internet must have its own Internet Protocol (IP) address. To share an increasingly finite number of available addresses, many private networks and ISPs distribute temporary or dynamic IP addresses from a pool of IP addresses.

Stars, Cards, Cables, and Hubs— A Few of My Favorite Things

It is most likely that you are entering the Red Hat Linux world with a computer that is set up and functioning with another operating system (OS)—one that is already connected to a network and/or the Internet. If you computer is not connected to a network and you'd like it to be, this section will discuss some of the popular networking choices you will have to choose from.

NOTE

> For a more thorough examination of networks, see the *Red Hat Linux Administrator's Guide* (Prima, 2000).

BUZZWORD

Netmask: Also known as a *subnet mask*, a netmask is used to determine the subnet to which an IP address belongs. For example, the IP address 150.216.19.31 with a netmask of 255.255.0.0 is part of the Class B subnetwork on the Internet.

The first step in building or configuring a network is deciding what form the network will take. The most common *topology*, or *form*, for a small-to-medium network is known as the *star topology*. Star networks are formed by machines that use twisted pair cable. One end of the cable is connected to the computer's network interface card (NIC) and the other end is connected to a hub. Although twisted pair cable resembles ordinary phone cable, it is not the same thing, and phone cable will not work. The connectors on the ends of twisted pair cable have RJ45 connectors, which resemble the RJ11 connectors on your telephone but are larger.

Each computer in your star-shaped LAN will have its own cable and a connection to your hub. A *hub* is a simple device that allows several devices to connect to a series of receptacles built into the central hub via twisted pair cables.

Another networking form is the *bus topology*. The bus network cabling is connected from computer to computer. Each computer, except the first and the last, has two cables connected to an Ethernet card. The cable used in the bus network is different from the cable used in the star network. Bus networks use coaxial or thin Ethernet cable. Coaxial cable, often referred to as "coax," resembles the cable running to your cable TV, but it is not the same. The last computer in a bus network is *terminated* on the empty side of the coaxial connector with a special resistor known as a terminator. The first computer in the chain is usually connected on one side to the network and to either a modem or another LAN on the other side.

BUZZWORD

Topology: The shape of a local area network (LAN).

Bus networks can only function at a speed of 10Mbps; there are no 100Mbps bus networks. This limits the future potential for the bus network. A bus network is fine, however, for a small LAN—whether it's in an office or you use it at home.

> It is possible and common in larger networks to combine a star and a bus topology. You can hang stars from a central bus network. This combination is beyond the scope of this book.

There is also a *ring topology* that is based on IBM's token ring protocol. It is seldom used in a small LAN, so I don't discuss it here.

Network Interface Cards or Ethernet Cards

These cards come in two different bus types and three separate speeds (10Mbps, 100Mbps, 1Gbps). The older types fit into one of your computer's ISA bus slots. The ISA-type NIC is perfectly acceptable from a performance standpoint, especially in a smaller LAN. Its 10Mbps transfer rates exceed that of all modems and will scarcely slow information transfer within your LAN. This type of NIC will work fine on a Linux network. However, there can be a few configuration problems with ISA NICs. For more information on dealing with ISA devices, see Chapter 7, "Configuring Printers, Sound, and Other Devices."

Ethernet: A local area network (LAN) protocol developed in 1976. Ethernet uses bus or star topologies.

If you must purchase new Ethernet cards for your Linux network, buy PCI bus cards whenever possible. The PCI bus is a more modern bus architecture that allows for better speed and easier configuration. PCI NICs generally can be found in the 100Mbps speeds, which should be plenty fast for a long while. The use of PCI cards also makes the computer more flexible to use and configure. The cost difference between PCI and ISA card is negligible.

There are dozens of different makes and brands of network cards offered for sale, so which do you buy? Although I can't give you an absolute recommendation (there are just too many choices), I have always used and had excellent luck and performance with both ISA and PCI cards that are NE 2000 compatible. NE200 cards are older and only run at 10Mbps, but they are among the longest lasting network cards around. Perhaps the best advice is to look at Red Hat's compatible hardware lists and then look for the best deal on one of the listed cards.

Hubs

Hubs are very simple devices that are almost fail-safe. The only problem with hubs is that you tend to outgrow them. It is simply amazing how quickly a hub (that had so many empty sockets when new) fills up. New networking equipment just seems to appear. If possible, buy hubs in the extra large size so that you have plenty of growth room—you won't be sorry.

Hubs also come in two speeds, 10Mbps and 100Mbps. The difference in price is not huge, but you will notice the difference in speed. Buy hubs for future growth and only pay for them once. One economical option is to get a dual-speed hub, which can use either speed. This is a great buy if you don't have the time or funds to swap your 10Mbps cards out right now but want to keep your future expansion plans open.

Switches

In networks, a device that filters and forwards packets between LAN segments is called a *switch*. Switches are much faster network devices than hubs because they do not accept packets whose destinations are not on the local LAN segment. Therefore, switches reduce unnecessary traffic and speed up your LAN. Another cool feature is that, like hubs, they can pass along data from any protocol. You have to pay for this kind of power, though, which is why switches are not a great option for a home or small network.

Cables

You can buy cable in bulk length and easily make your own custom cable lengths, or you can buy pre-made cables in every length and color under the sun. Color-coding is very handy when you have a dozen or so cables coming and going everywhere. The real choice is which type to buy: coaxial or twisted pair. Your choice of network topologies will make that decision easier.

Open The History Books

A brief review is in order for those of you not keen on the finer details of the Internet.

TCP/IP is the main protocol of the Internet. A protocol is the "language" that two computers connected to each other use to pass information back and forth. There are other protocols, such as IPX/SPX and NetBIOS via SMB, but TCP/IP is the most commonly used and is nearly universal. Other protocols usually function with TCP/IP. It follows, then, that a nearly universal system such as Linux will use TCP/IP. Red Hat Linux 7 excels at communications and the use of TCP/IP.

Applications such as File Transfer Protocol (FTP), Simple Mail Transfer Protocol (SMTP), and Hypertext Transfer Protocol (HTTP)—as well as Telnet and SNMP— exclusively use TCP/IP.

TCP/IP is as old as the Internet; indeed, it is almost synonymous with the Internet. TCP/IP had its beginning when the U.S. Government's Advanced Research Project Agency was looking into methods of keeping communications between computers alive should normal communications systems be disrupted in the advent of a nuclear war. The Internet, and hence TCP/IP, have since grown, or more nearly exploded, beyond that capacity. I like to think of this as a perfect example of the "beating swords to plowshares" concept.

There are five classes of IP address: A through E. Classes A, B, and C are used for networking and hosts. The three classes available (A, B, and C) can be identified by their dotted-decimal address, which is called the IP address.

- Class A: 1.*nnn.nnn.nnn* through 126.*nnn.nnn.nnn*
- Class B: 128.*nnn.nnn.nnn* through 191.*nnn.nnn.nnn*
- Class C: 192.*nnn.nnn.nnn* through 223.*nnn.nnn.nnn*
- Class D: 224.*nnn.nnn.nnn* through 239.*nnn.nnn.nnn* (for multicast)
- Class E: 240.*nnn.nnn.nnn* through 248.*nnn.nnn.nnn* (reserved for future use)

An IP address that is connected to the Internet must be unique; there can be no duplicate addresses anywhere on the Internet. This is why unique IP addresses are rapidly disappearing. The solution is a new 128-bit addressing concept for the IP protocol called *IPv6*. Ipv6 will be implemented over the course of time and will work with the current IPv4 system. For now, Internet users are concerned with using IPv4, the current version of IP. There are changes coming in the near future.

Networking and IP Addresses

As mentioned in the previous section, no two computers can share the same IP address. The system used to assign an address to a computer is known as the dotted-decimal address, usually referred to as an *IP address*, or just an IP. The Class A, B, and C addresses are assigned to certain functions.

Class A addresses are normally used for loopback communications and for very large organizations. Usually, 127.*nnn.nnn.nnn* IP addresses are used for applications and processes that communicate with other applications and processes on the same computer.

Class C addresses are the most commonly used, especially for networks that are not part of a widespread organization. Class C addresses are discussed here. Most Class C addresses are part of a LAN, which can consist of any number of computers (from 2 to 254 computers, or *hosts* as they are known in networking jargon). Two sets of IP addresses are assigned for use by LANs that are not part of the Internet:

- 172.16.0.0 to 172.16.255.255
- 192.168.0.0 to 192.168.255.255

These blocks of addresses are used for LANs and will not be assigned to Internet addresses. Any of these blocks are private network IP addresses. Probably the most commonly used block is the 192.168.*nnn.nnn* group. More discussion of these blocks of reserved addresses for LANs can be found in a bit.

Network Configuration

While Red Hat Linux 7 was being installed, the installation program asked for information concerning your network (refer to Figure 6.1). Specifically it asked for the following:

- **Configure using DHCP.** A DHCP server on a network assigns a different unused IP address each time your PC connects to your network. If your network uses DHCP, use this option.
- **IP address.** This is the static IP address of your computer or host, if DHCP is not used.
- **Netmask.** The installation script attempted to enter this; be sure it is correct.
- **Network.** The installation script attempted to enter this also.
- **Broadcast.** The installation script attempted to enter this also.
- **Hostname.** This is the name your ISP assigned your computer or host.
- **Gateway.** This is the IP address assigned by your ISP for a gateway/router.
- **Primary DNS.** A name server that may or may not be your gateway IP address.
- **Secondary DNS.** A name server; at least one will be assigned.
- **Ternary DNS.** A name server.

If all the above was entered correctly during installation, you should be able to connect to the Internet with a Web browser such as Netscape Navigator or Lynx. If you cannot connect, check to make sure the information was entered correctly.

Changing Your Network Configuration

The most common reason for networking to fail is that the network configuration information is incorrect. To see what information was entered in the initial configuration, you can use one of three tools:

- Netconfig
- Network Configurator (netcfg)
- Linuxconf

Using Netconfig

To use Netconfig to verify or change your network configuration, log in as root, then go to a terminal window, and type **Netconfig**. You can then re-enter the entirety of your network information just as though you were configuring your network at the initial installation.

Using Network Configurator

Network Configurator is another tool that you can use to re-enter your configuration information. Network Configurator is very easy to use and understand. It can be started using one of three methods:

- By selecting Programs, System, Network Configuration in the Main menu.
- From the Control Panel (select Programs, System, Control Panel). The icon for the application is shown in Figure 6.2.
- By typing **netcfg** in a terminal window.

In the Network Configurator, clicking on the Names, Hosts, Interfaces, and Routing tabs will allow you to check and change your network configuration (see Figure 6.3).

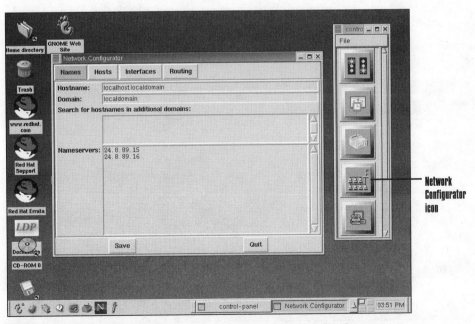

Figure 6.2   *The Control Panel is a fast way to start the Network Configurator.*

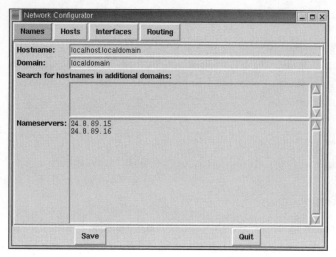

Figure 6.3   *The Names tab of the Network Configurator.*

If you want to modify information in the Hosts tab (shown in Figure 6.4), first click the line to be changed, then click Edit. The Add button works similarly, allowing you to add information for a newly added network interface card, for example.

The Interfaces tab, displayed in Figure 6.5, enables you to check on settings for your NIC. If you believe your card is not being activated, check the Active area. If the card is active, it will say so under this heading. If not, you can set a card to Active by selecting it in the list and clicking the Activate button.

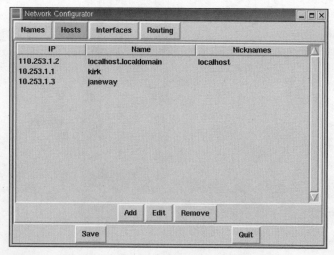

Figure 6.4   *The Hosts tab of the Network Configurator.*

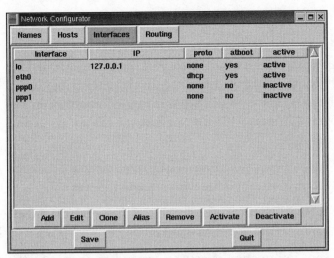

Figure 6.5 *The Interfaces tab of the Network Configurator.*

The Routing tab enables you to set your gateway IP address and your gateway device (your NIC), as shown in Figure 6.6. This is important only if you want to use your Linux PC as a gateway to the network. Red Hat will usually enter eth0 as your gateway device. You can, however, change or add a gateway device here. Additionally, you can verify that the Network Packet Forwarding option is selected, which is essential for a gateway server.

When you are finished with Network Configurator, click Save.

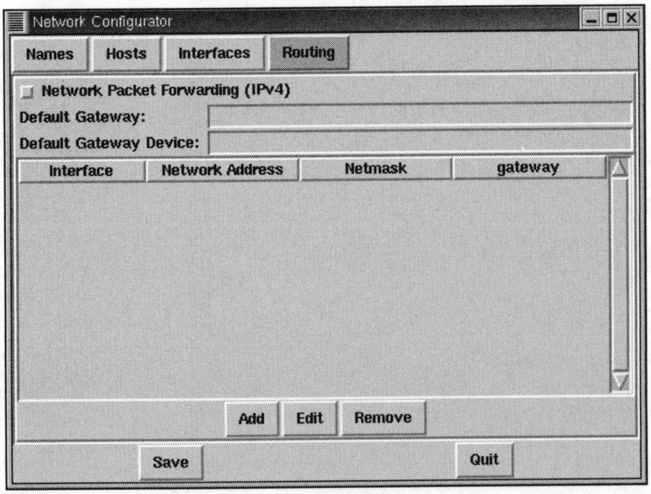

Figure 6.6 *The Routing tab of the Network Configurator.*

Using Linuxconf

Linuxconf has become the most popular configuration tool in Red Hat Linux and is used for making and changing settings for the entire Linux installation. This chapter is concerned with how to use Linuxconf to configure networking. If you are using Linuxconf for the first time, you will see some initial information describing how to use the program. After the initial dialog box, you can use Linuxconf to configure your network settings.

After you open Linuxconf (usually by typing **linuxconf** in the terminal), click the Client Tasks, Basic Host Information tab to show the screen in Figure 6.7.

Check to see that the host name is correct on this screen and then click the Adaptor 1 tab to open a screen similar to the one shown in Figure 6.8.

Notice that the basic network information is easy to see and to change in the Adaptor 1 tab. Click any box and modify or enter the desired information.

You can tell, from the presence of the eth0 device in Figure 6.8, that I am using a PCI NIC card. Red Hat quite capably handles the PCI bus, so if you use PCI cards, you do not usually need to enter a lot of parameters into your configuration. Also note that the pcnet32 kernel module for your NIC is usually already chosen by Linux, though this depends on what kind of card you have. This kernel module is the "driver" that Linux uses to interface with the device. If necessary, however, you can select a module for your NIC from the drop-down list.

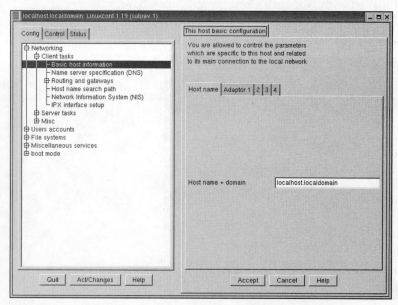

Figure 6.7   *You can verify and edit the host name on this screen.*

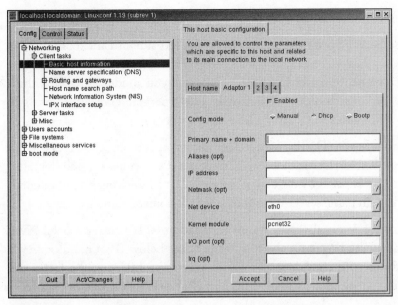

Figure 6.8   *Your network card's information can be found here.*

Be sure that the Enabled check box is selected, along with your method of IP address selection. If you have a static IP address, click Manual. If you have dynamic IP addressing, as I do on my network, click DHCP.

If you're not sure about one of the fields on the screen, select the field in question and then click Help. A Help window will open, offering insights on that particular area (see Figure 6.9). To exit the Help screen, simply click the Kill button.

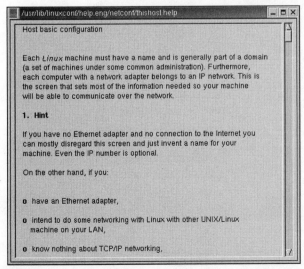

Figure 6.9   *You can get help on any of the fields in Linuxconf.*

When you are satisfied with the selections you have made, click Accept.

Click the Name Server Specification option on the left side of Linuxconf to open a screen that will allow you to enter your DNS IP addresses, as shown in Figure 6.10. The screen name, Resolver Configuration, gives you an idea as to what these lines do in the configuration of your network. These parameters enable your system to resolve host names to IP addresses via your network.

Click the check box next to DNS is required for normal operation. An interesting fact about the Default domain line is that it will blank out if you enter a search domain a few lines down. This is perfectly normal; if it happens, it means your configuration is using a search domain name server instead of a default domain name server.

IP of name server 1 is usually your gateway IP address. If you have been given additional name server IPs, enter them into the boxes below IP of name server 1. The more methods your computer can use to access the Internet, the faster and more reliable your connections will be. This helps balance the loading of your ISP's servers and system.

When you are satisfied with your entries, click Accept and then close Linuxconf. You will be asked to activate the changes you have made as the application shuts down.

If you have entered the correct information in Linuxconf, you should be able to connect to the Internet. If you are still unable to do so, it may be time to call up the big guns: the command-line tools.

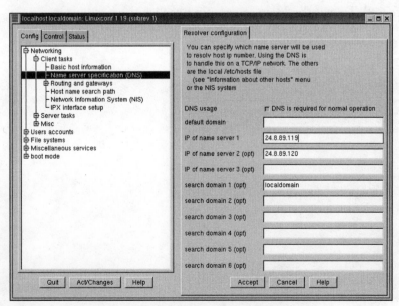

Figure 6.10   *Domain name server information is entered here.*

Command-Line Tools

Many people who are new to Linux avoid using a command-line interface (CLI) because they are accustomed to the graphical interface of other operating systems. The Linux CLI, also known as the *console*, is a powerful, lightweight method for controlling your computer. It is not difficult to use the control line in a terminal—it is only different. A bit of familiarization will have you working in a text screen before you know it. Many people come to prefer the command line for its speed and direct approach to computer input.

Getting Help with Control-Line Commands

Almost all control-line commands have a help function that can be accessed by adding -h after the command. (Note the space between the command and -h.) Almost all control-line commands are lowercase, but there are exceptions. If a command does not work as expected, check both spelling and case, as all Linux commands are case-sensitive.

> In some tools, you can use the command –help in addition to -h.

Using iconfig to Check Your NIC Configuration

The command ifconfig (located in /sbin) can be used to check your current NIC configuration. In any terminal window, type **ifconfig**. A screen similar to the one shown in Figure 6.11 will appear.

```
root@localhost.localdomain: /root                              _ □ ×
 File   Edit   Settings   Help
[root@localhost /root]# ifconfig
eth0      Link encap:Ethernet  HWaddr 00:60:B0:A4:FC:F6
          inet addr:10.253.1.2  Bcast:10.253.1.255  Mask:255.255.255.0
          UP BROADCAST RUNNING  MTU:1500  Metric:1
          RX packets:23710 errors:0 dropped:0 overruns:0 frame:0
          TX packets:23868 errors:0 dropped:0 overruns:0 carrier:0
          collisions:0 txqueuelen:100
          Interrupt:9 Base address:0xd600

lo        Link encap:Local Loopback
          inet addr:127.0.0.1  Mask:255.0.0.0
          UP LOOPBACK RUNNING  MTU:3924  Metric:1
          RX packets:16 errors:0 dropped:0 overruns:0 frame:0
          TX packets:16 errors:0 dropped:0 overruns:0 carrier:0
          collisions:0 txqueuelen:0

[root@localhost /root]# ▊
```

Figure 6.11 *Configuration information can be easily obtained.*

The eth0 lines show your type of configuration, the hardware codes, IP address (inet addr), broadcast IP, and the configured netmask. Immediately following the eth0 lines is a line that displays UP, meaning that your card is activated. The broadcast IP runs using multicasting, which allows sending and receiving TCP/IP packets to a subset of hosts—other computers with which your computer is communicating. MTU is a measurement of the maximum size, in bytes, of a packet. Below that are several lines that give the status of TCP/IP packet transfer. Do not be too concerned if you have numbers other than 0 on some of these; TCP/IP will resend or request new packets until your information is complete. The last line tells you the IRQ and I/O addresses of your NIC.

The lo category displays information about the loopback configuration for your computer. Typically, this configuration is automatically set; it allows your computer to communicate with computer processes. Since this is a self-contained communication system, it is much less susceptible to erroneous settings. Notice how much larger the MTU number is. Your computer and its hardware are not subject to the vagaries of the Internet and can transfer much larger packets without losing information to lost or corrupted packets.

Using netstat –i to Research the Network

Another useful command is netstat -i. (Note that using netstat without the -i argument will return a huge amount of information about your network, which is interesting, but not too useful for configuration.) As you can see in Figure 6.12, the information presented in netstat -i is similar to the information in the Ifconfig

Figure 6.12   *Configuration information is also revealed with* netstat.

screen. `netstat` is easier to use if you understand the initials on the header, but the Ifconfig screen is more self-explanatory.

Using route to Trace the Path of Your Connection

Using the `route` command will give you information about the path your Internet connection is using or attempting to use (see Figure 6.13). The route screen displays the destination IP address, the gateway used, and the genmask or netmask used by `route`. The `Flags` column lists abbreviations for your configuration, which are listed in Table 6.1. These abbreviations will help you determine whether your network and NIC are actually working.

Table 6.1   Route Flag Parameters

Flag	Definition
U	Up
H	Host
G	Gateway
R	Reinstate
D	Dynamic
M	Modified
!	Reject

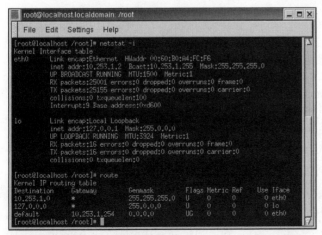

Figure 6.13   *Network routing revealed.*

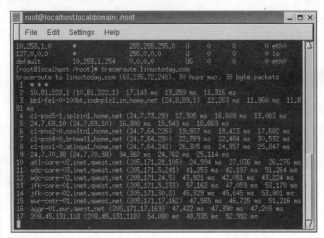

```
root@localhost.localdomain: /root                          _ □ ×
 File   Edit   Settings   Help
10.253.1.0      *          255.255.255.0  U   0   0      0 eth0
127.0.0.0       *          255.0.0.0      U   0   0      0 lo
default         10.253.1.254  0.0.0.0      UG  0   0      0 eth0
[root@localhost /root]# traceroute linuxtoday.com
traceroute to linuxtoday.com (63.236.72.248), 30 hops max, 38 byte packets
 1  * * *
 2  10.81.222.1 (10.81.222.1)  17.143 ms  13.259 ms  11.316 ms
 3  bb1-fe1-0-100bt.indnpls1.in.home.net (24.8.89.1)  12.263 ms  11.960 ms  11.8
81 ms
 4  c1-pos5-1.iplsin1.home.net (24.7.73.29)  17.305 ms  16.609 ms  13.083 ms
 5  24.7.69.10 (24.7.69.10)  16.308 ms  15.549 ms  15.869 ms
 6  c1-pos2-0.nsvltn1.home.net (24.7.64.226)  19.937 ms  18.423 ms  17.602 ms
 7  c1-pos4-0.brhwal1.home.net (24.7.64.230)  22.783 ms  22.484 ms  30.532 ms
 8  c1-pos1-0.atlnga1.home.net (24.7.64.242)  26.305 ms  24.957 ms  25.847 ms
 9  24.7.70.38 (24.7.70.38)  34.387 ms  24.762 ms  25.114 ms
10  atl-core-02.inet.qwest.net (205.171.21.105)  24.994 ms  27.036 ms  26.276 ms
11  wdc-core-03.inet.qwest.net (205.171.5.241)  41.253 ms  42.197 ms  51.264 ms
12  wdc-core-02.inet.qwest.net (205.171.24.5)  43.921 ms  42.051 ms  43.224 ms
13  jfk-core-01.inet.qwest.net (205.171.5.233)  57.162 ms  47.059 ms  53.178 ms
14  jfk-core-02.inet.qwest.net (205.171.30.2)  45.329 ms  45.645 ms  53.801 ms
15  ewr-cntr-01.inet.qwest.net (205.171.17.162)  47.565 ms  46.725 ms  51.216 ms
16  aggr-01.ewr.qwest.net (205.171.17.169)  47.422 ms  47.390 ms  47.203 ms
17  208.45.131.118 (208.45.131.118)  54.080 ms  48.535 ms  52.992 ms
```

Figure 6.14   *Getting from Point A to Point B on the Internet.*

Using traceroute to Trace Your Connection

traceroute is a handy command to use when you are trying to find where along the line of communications a problem exists. The Internet is far from a sure thing and sometimes overloading, equipment failure, backhoe operators, or snowstorms conspire to cut the convoluted routing that takes place. If you enter the command traceroute [your ISP's name] or traceroute [your ISP's IP address], you will get a printout of the various connections that were made to connect to your ISP, as shown in Figure 6.14. Terminate traceroute by pressing Ctrl+C.

Using ping to Test Your Connection

The ping command (for example, ping 192.nnn.nnn.nnn using your gateway IP) is employed by most savvy Internet users. It actually tells your computer to send a batch of packets to another computer. The receiving computer will answer your "ping", and your computer will then count how many packets were sent and how many were returned. ping can be used within your LAN or out to the Internet and is very useful for determining whether you are actually transmitting and receiving information from your computer. You can also use a known functioning computer to ping a questionable machine. ping will also help to establish whether your communications lines are causing problems with excessive packet loss.

The ping command is not self-terminating, which means that your machine will continue to ping the designated computer forever if you let it. (It is considered very bad form to ping a gateway or someone else's computer continuously.) In their Acceptable Use Agreements, many ISPs forbid the pinging of their routers or DNS servers for periods of time. Also, some firewalls do not allow pinging in one direction, or altogether. To stop a ping, press Ctrl+C. The ping will terminate and the program will return a count of the number of packets sent and the number received.

Problem Cards and Plug and Play

If you must purchase a new NIC to use with Red Hat Linux 7, be sure to first go to the Red Hat site (**www.redhat.com/support/hardware**) and check for hardware compatibility. Red Hat maintains an extensive list of hardware known to work and not work, which makes selecting hardware easier and installation smoother.

Problems with Plug and Play

If you already have a card that is listed and does not seem to work (but functions fine under Microsoft Windows), it may be an ISA PNP card. Linux support for Plug and Play (PnP) is limited, as Plug and Play was created for a proprietary operating system, Windows, which is not open source.

I/O address: A specific memory address used exclusively by a device connected to the PC.

The easiest way to get an unwilling ISA PnP card to work under Linux is to disable its Plug and Play function. Older PnP cards had small DIP switches or jumpers that could be moved to disable Plug and Play. You will need to consult the card's documentation or the manufacturer's Web site for the settings. PnP settings for newer (meaning *most*) cards are set in the BIOS on the card. To disable a software Plug and Play card, you need to go to MS-DOS, insert the driver disk for the card, and then follow the instructions for the card.

Once the PnP function is disabled, you can use Linuxconf to set the card to the kernel module for the card and assign an I/O address and an IRQ for the card in the Adaptor tab of the Basic Host Information category. The card will then usually function fine under Linux. For example, the computer used to write this chapter includes two NICs, one of which is an ISA PNP card that was installed in this way.

IRQ: Abbreviation of interrupt request line. IRQs are hardware lines over which devices can send interrupt signals to the CPU chip.

You can also assign a module, I/O, and IRQ addresses in the /etc/conf.modules file. To do so, add the following lines

```
alias eth0 ne
options ne I/O=0xnnnn Irq=nn
```

where ne is a module. To see if an Ethernet card is properly configured and working as expected, try the following:

```
ifconfig eth0 up
```

Then, check to see if the card is now working by using the `ifconfig` command. The Ethernet card known as eth0 should show up. You may need to set it to start automatically at reboot in Linuxconf or netcfg.

The Linux Plug-And-Play-HOWTO text can be found in the HOWTO documentation on your computer if you installed the Extra Documentation option. Look in /usr/doc/HOWTO. HOWTOs are also available online at **howto.tucows.com/ LDP/HOWTO/** and **www.redhat.com/mirrors/LDP/HOWTO**. Many answers to other questions can be found in the HOWTOs, as well as instructions on getting ISA PnP cards to operate under Linux.

Other Problem Cards

A few Ethernet cards simply will not work with any Linux distribution. The necessary drivers cannot be created because the card manufacturers refuse to release the information needed. These cards are listed in the Unsupported Card list in the Hardware Compatibility List. Try checking this list if nothing seems to enable your card under Linux. As the open-source movement gains strength, look for fewer and fewer hardware manufacturers to refuse to release technical information.

Multiple Networking Cards

If you want to use Red Hat Linux 7 on your LAN as a gateway or router between the rest of your computer(s) and the Internet or another LAN, you will need to have two networking cards installed and configured on your machine. One card will communicate with your LAN, and the other will take care of communications via the Internet or other LAN.

Linux can easily use multiple networking cards, but with one small complication: The kernel will detect only *one* networking card at startup. The answer is to add both cards' module, I/O, and IRQ addresses to the boot commands of LILO. You can do this by editing file /etc/lilo.conf with the vi text editor. Using your own module, IRQ, and I/O addresses, add the following line at the end of the file:

```
append="ether=10.0x300.eth0 ether=9.0x320.eth1"
```

Sometimes two Ethernet cards that use the same kernel module will confuse the system and will not be enabled properly. If everything appears to be working properly and one of the cards still does not seem to be functioning, run the command `ifconfig -v`. You may see only one networking card listed, usually eth0. If so, try the command `ifconfig eth1 up`. Then run `ifconfig` again to see whether the card eth1 is now listed.

If the card is still not working, you probably need to modify your files to start both cards. This can be done by making an entry into the /etc/conf.modules file.

Add the following lines, substituting your module, I/O, and IRQ addresses:

```
alias eth0 ne
alias eth1 ne
options ne i/o=0x300,0x320 irq=10,9
```

These command lines will instruct the kernel to look for both networking card modules and to assign the proper IRQ and I/O addresses to both Ethernet cards.

Assuming you have entered the correct IP address into each card's configuration, you should be set to go. Both cards should be fully configured and the kernel modules in place with the proper I/Os and IRQs assigned to both cards. You should be able to communicate with your own LAN and with the Internet or another LAN, which, in reality, is all the Internet is—one huge LAN. In other words, you should be connected. Congratulations!

Configuring the Computers on Your LAN to Use a Single IP Address

Linux has many more networking capabilities for you to use. Now that you have your computer set up as a router, wouldn't it be nice if you could use *any* of your computers on your LAN to talk to the outside world, rather than just the one computer that has an outside IP address? Remember that because no two computers can share the same IP address, two computers cannot use the Internet with one IP address even through a Linux router. Of course, you can always pay your Internet provider for more IP addresses, if they will even sell you the privilege. Your company may have more than one IP address, but those addresses will be guarded zealously. So how can all of your computers use one IP address? Can it even be done?

The answer is of course it can, and in the Linux world it's free!

NAT or IP Masquerading

IP masquerading, or network address translation (NAT), is a method of changing packets from machines that do not have a legal IP address to appear as though they are coming from the one machine on the LAN that does have a legal IP address. This enables all the machines on your LAN to use the Internet or to reach other LANs using the IP address of the Linux router. Please note that the word *legal* does not mean to imply that the use of IP Masquerading or NAT is a shady thing.

Legal is used here to mean an IP address that is recognized as a valid address. Indeed, many ISPs encourage the use of IP masquerading as a means of extending the use of a limited number of IP addresses.

IP masquerading may already be set up on your machine. To check this, type **ls /proc/net** in a terminal window. Verify that there is a file named /proc/net/ip_masquerade. If there is no entry by this name, you will need to recompile your kernel to support IP masquerading. While you're checking, look also for a file named /proc/net/ip_fwchains by typing **ls -la /sbin/ipchains** at a terminal prompt. If the file /proc/net/ip_fwchains exists, you are ready to set up IP masquerading on your computer.

To learn more about recompiling your Linux kernel, see Chapter 12, "Compiling a Kernel."

You may want to check out the IP-Masquerade mini-HOWTO at /usr/doc/HOWTO/mini for more information, along with the IPCHAINS-HOWTO in the HOWTOs. You can also find manual pages in the Red Hat Linux regarding IP masquerading.

If you plan to use IP masquerading to access the Internet or external LANs, it would probably be a good idea to also provide some form of firewall protection for your system. There are some unsavory characters in cyberspace who would like nothing more than to crack your system and delete, corrupt, or even steal your information. A firewall can be created easily, costing nothing more than the time it takes to write a rule set. Many sites provide rule sets and information to create extremely secure firewalls. Take the time to make sure you have a good rule set and that your resulting firewall works the way you want it to; a poorly done firewall is worse than no firewall at all.

Some good information on IP masquerading and firewalls can be found at the Linux IP Masquerade home page, **ipmasq.cjb.net**.

Creating an IP Masquerade Firewall Rule Set

You can easily create a very basic and minimal IP Masquerade firewall rule set by following these steps:

1. First, figure out the interdependencies of the IP Masquerade kernel modules using the following command:

   ```
   /sbin/depmod -a
   ```

2. Support the masquerading of FTP file transfers with the following command:

   ```
   /sbin/modprobe ip_masq-ftp
   ```

3. Allow use of Dynamic IP Addressing (DHCP) if your ISP uses it by typing the following command (place a comment [#] at the beginning of the next line if your ISP doesn't use DHCP):

   ```
   echo "1" > /proc/sys/net/ipv4/ip_dynaddr
   ```

4. Allow the kernel to perform IP forwarding to enable IP masquerading by typing the following command:

   ```
   echo "1" > /proc/sys/net/ipv4/ip_forward
   ```

5. Set timeouts for IP Masquerade with this command:

   ```
   ipchains -M -S 7200 10 160
   ```

6. Allow IP masquerading for your LAN 192.168.0.*nnn* (use your LANs IP address range) using these lines:

   ```
   ipchains -P forward DENY
   ipchains -A forward -s 192.168.0.0/24 -j MASQ
   echo "/etc/rc.d/rc.firewall done."
   ```

7. Save your IP Masquerade and firewall rule set into a file named /etc/rc.d.rc.firewall.

8. Protect your /etc/rc.d/rc.firewall rule set so that only the user logged in as root can use it, using the command:

   ```
   chmod 700 /etc/rd.d/rc.firewall
   ```

9. If you want IP Masquerade to automatically start after a reboot, it must be added to your startup scripts. Do so by appending the line `/etc/rc.d/rc.firewall` to the end of the /etc/rc.d/rc.local file.

You may be thinking that it must require quite a powerful computer to run all these communication protocols and to take care of all your LAN firewall needs. Well, Linux will save you even more money. You know that old 486 with the s-l-o-w 50MHz processor and a puny 16MB of RAM—the one you can't run any of your programs on? That 486 will quite easily and happily work as your Red Hat Linux router. It will have no trouble keeping two dozen computers connected and protected. A 486 computer can easily saturate a T1 line or keep up with your cable and DSL modem.

IP Masquerade will work almost any way you want it to. It can use your PPP POTS modem, cable and DSL modems, or FDDI corporate communications. IP Masquerading will allow the use of the most popular services found on the Internet, including POP, SMTP, HTTP, FTP, NNTP, Telnet, and VRML. The TCP/IP tools traceroute and ping are also available when you use IP Masquerading.

A Proxy Server Named Squid

Red Hat Linux will allow your Linux computer to provide a connection between your LAN and the Internet without using routing—that is, through the use of a proxy server. The biggest advantage of using a proxy server is that no one needs to know anything about all the arcane numbers demanded from ISPs—no one, that is, except the person who configures and maintains the proxy server. The only information a person on your LAN needs to know is the name or IP address of the Red Hat Linux proxy server. There may be a few people who would like to use services other than just HTTP, however; if they know a few port numbers, they will have access to those services.

One such server, Squid, is installed in all but the smallest Red Hat Linux installations. The basic package is easy to configure, and Squid can grow in capability as your networking needs and knowledge grow. The basic configuration of Squid will allow the most popular services found on the Internet, namely HTTP and FTP. Another advantage to Squid is that it allows the use of disparate operating systems. Everyone can use the operating system of his or her choice and painlessly use the Internet or access external LANs.

First, you need to check to see if Squid is properly installed. You can do this easily by issuing the following command:

```
rpm -q squid
```

Linux will reply with either the package version number or a statement saying that the package is not installed. To install the package from the Red Hat 7 CD, type the following command (after placing the CD in the drive of course):

```
rpm -iv /mnt/cdrom/RedHat/RPMS/squid*
```

To see if the Squid process (known as a daemon) is installed, type the following:

```
ps x | grep squid
```

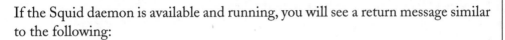

The symbol | is referred to as a *pipe*.

If the Squid daemon is available and running, you will see a return message similar to the following:

```
860 pts/0   S  0:00 grep squid -D
```

Once you have determined that Squid is available on your computer, go to the Squid home page at **squid.nlanr.net**. There, you can find a better configuration file to use to get Squid up and running. This new configuration is still a very basic one; Squid can be expanded to include a staggering number of services and restrictions. The default installation from the Red Hat 7 CD puts a basic configuration file in the proper place, and there is really only one change you will need to make. The line

```
http_access deny all
```

must be changed to

```
http_access allow all
```

From within Linuxconf you can start the service and enable it so that it starts upon boot.

You can use one of your LAN computers to set up the Squid server as a proxy server. You probably have Netscape as a Web browser on your system. To set Netscape to use the Squid proxy, open Netscape and then choose Preferences, Advanced, Proxy. Set the proxy setting to Manual, add the Squid server's name (which you defined earlier in the Squid installation process), and set the proxy port to 3128. You should then be able to connect to the Internet from the LAN computer on which you just configured Netscape. Repeat the browser configuration on each of your LAN computers.

Should Squid not work as you expected, make sure all the configuration entries are correct and that both your Squid server and your Red Hat Linux computer are connected to the Internet. If you still cannot connect from your LAN, look at your debugging files at /var/log/squid. The Squid home page at **squid.nlanr.net** also has debugging suggestions you may want to review.

Conclusion

In this chapter, you learned a lot of the tricks of the networking trade. This is by far not all of the information you can learn about this huge and ever-growing subject, but it's a healthy start.

In Chapter 7, you will examine how to configure the most basic types of hardware for your PC: printers, sound cards, and other devices.

Chapter 7: Configuring Printers, Sound, and Other Devices

Printers

Sound

Plug and Play Using the isapnptools Utility

Working with Non-Linux Partitions

E arly computers did not communicate well. The first digital calculating device that could safely be called a computer was the Harvard Mark I, a five-ton, 750,000-component device that read its programming code from paper tape and its data from punch cards. Data was output on a similar medium. Multimedia was a bit of a wash as well; the only sound the Mark I generated was the internal clicking of its components, which sounded a bit like a "roomful of ladies knitting."

For those of you old enough to remember the Apple I and II microcomputers released in 1976 and 1977, respectively, you'll recall that they weren't big on multimedia, either. Little beeps and clicks were about all the sound they emitted. Printing was coming along, though, as dot-matrix printers wound out reams of perforated paper.

Today, however, the number of communication devices that can be connected to PCs is phenomenal: printers, speakers, television tuners, cameras, alarm systems— you name it. This chapter focuses on connecting such peripheral communication devices to your Linux machine.

Printers

Think about this: You can make a book on your PC. Right now. All you need are some good typing skills and about three cases of soda and you're set. Believe me, I know.

This may not seem like such a big deal to you because you are likely accustomed to the PC/printer combination. But a mere two decades ago, you would have had little chance of finding software and printers capable of performing such a feat. Thirty years ago, you would have had no chance.

Again, what's the big deal? It's just technological advancement, right? True, but it is also a huge shift in social dynamics as well. No longer is the ability to distribute and publish information in the hands of a select few. Now almost anyone with the will can generate published works. This decentralization is aided by the nature of the Internet, which provides even more avenues of communication. Now a writer can generate work and send it electronically, letting the reader print it out as needed.

Linux, like any other operating system worth its salt, can use printers seamlessly from any application with a print function. First, though, you need be sure that communication occurs between Linux and your printer, whether connected directly or through a network.

Adding a Local Printer

Printers either can be local to your own PC or can exist on a network. Either way, accessing them in Linux is not difficult, especially when you work with a local printer.

Local printers are almost always connected to your PC's parallel port—the device known as lp in Linux. In DOS and Windows, the ports are named lpt1, lpt2, and so on; in Linux they are given the nomenclature lp0, lp1, etc.

It's important to remember that Linux handles devices as extensions of its file system. Any files (that are not plain-text to begin with) that need to be printed are first converted to something the printer can use through Ghostscript, a utility that uses an additional printer filter to perform the conversion. After the conversion is finished, the data is loaded into the device's file system directory—for example, the printer's file system directory, which is typically /var/spool. Finally, the data is automatically read by the device (in this case, the printer).

In the next task, you will learn the steps necessary to connect a printer to your Linux system.

BUZZWORD

Bus: A device used to transmit data from one part of a computer to another.

TASK

Connecting a Local Printer

This task demonstrates connecting a local printer to your system.

1. Click the Main Menu icon to open the Main menu.
2. Choose Programs, System, Control Panel. The Control Panel opens (see Figure 7.1).
3. Click the printer icon to start the Red Hat Linux Print System Manager.
4. Before the Print System Manager starts the first time, an Error dialog box may appear warning you that ncpfs is not installed. If you do not intend to ever connect to printers through NetWare, click Ignore (see Figure 7.2).
5. The Red Hat Linux Print System Manager will be displayed, as shown in Figure 7.3. Click Add to begin the printer-connection process.
6. The Add a Printer Entry dialog box appears, as shown in Figure 7.4. Select the Local Printer option, and then click OK to continue.
7. A message indicates what ports, if any, Linux was able to detect. Although not critical, it is important that Linux detects the port to ensure the right port address is obtained. Click OK to continue.

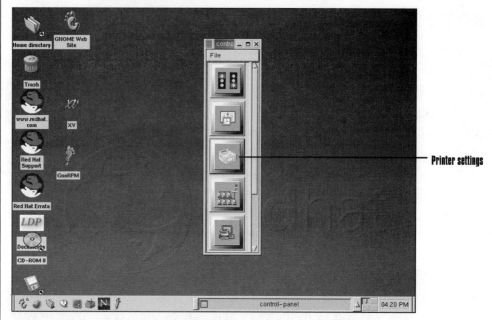

Printer settings

Figure 7.1 *You can create and edit printer settings from the Control Panel.*

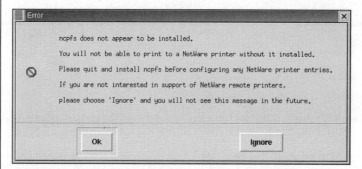

Figure 7.2 *Print System Manager's cautious message about NetWare.*

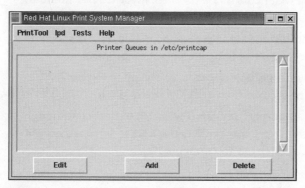

Figure 7.3 *The Print System Manager coordinates all of your PC's printers.*

Figure 7.4 *You can specify the type of printer you want to add.*

8. The Edit Local Printer Entry dialog box appears (see Figure 7.5). Linux typically auto-detects the active printer port, completing the Printer Device and remaining fields for you. If needed, however, type **/dev/lpX** in the Printer Device field, where *X* is the number of the device, starting with 0.

9. To select your printer device, click the Select button that appears adjacent to the Input Filter field. This opens the Configure Filter dialog box (see Figure 7.6).

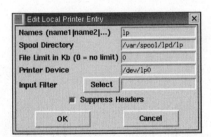

Figure 7.5 *Many device parameters are entered in this dialog box.*

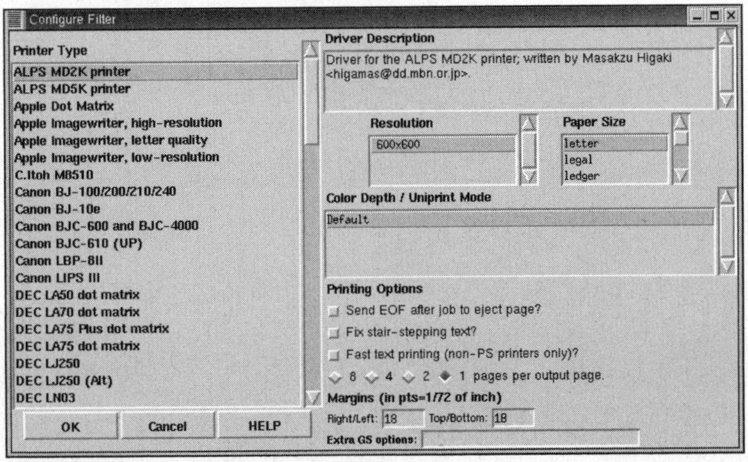

Figure 7.6 *Choose your printer filter here.*

10. Select your printer from the Printer Type list.

> If your printer does not appear on the list, try getting the latest version of Ghostscript from the Red Hat FTP site (**ftp.redhat.com**), which lists additional filters.

11. Select the default resolution and paper-size settings you want to use, as well as any available color-depth settings.

> If you plan to buy a printer in the future and are worried about compatibility, I recommend choosing a PostScript printer. No matter what the model, the printer language for PostScript printers is consistent.

12. Click OK to finish the filter settings. The Input Filter field in the Edit Local Printer Entry dialog now displays the selected filter (see Figure 7.7).

13. Click OK to continue. The Print System Manager now lists the new printer (see Figure 7.8).

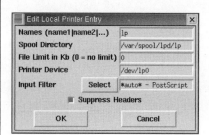

Figure 7.7   *A completed set of printer parameters.*

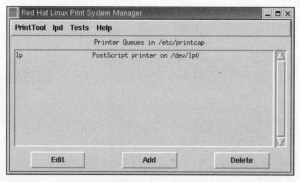

Figure 7.8   *A connected printer.*

Adding a Network Printer

Getting to a printer on a network is no big deal, either. There are three types of network printers that Linux can be configured to use:

- UNIX/Linux printers
- Windows printers
- NetWare printers

Configuring these printer types is similar to configuring a local printer. However, rather than pointing the data to a device's spool directory in the local file system, the data is directed to a remote printer's queue—the storage area where print jobs are held until printed.

Table 7.1 illustrates the information you will need to connect to a remote printer for each network type.

Table 7.1 Remote Printer Settings

Network	Protocol	Other Values
UNIX/Linux	TCP/IP	Remote host, Remote queue
Windows	TCP/IP, SMB	Host name of printer server, IP number of server, Printer name, User, Password, Workgroup
NetWare	NCP	Printer, server name, Print, queue name, User, Password

When printing to a network printer, it is important that the network recognize the user name and password of the Linux user. In a UNIX or Linux scenario, this is a given; but you must make sure the incoming Linux user has access rights to the network print queue.

In NetWare, the user must have rights to access a network printer. In Windows, the printer itself must be set to be "shared" first.

> For security reasons, the user names and passwords used to access a remote NetWare or Windows printer must be different from any user names and passwords that access your Linux PC. This is because the printer passwords are stored unencrypted before being used by NetWare nprint or the Samba smbclient programs. Be creative!

BUZZWORD

PCI (Peripheral Component Interconnect) bus: a local bus standard developed by Intel Corporation. PCI comes in 32- and 64-bit flavors, although it is usually implemented as a 32-bit bus in all but the most expensive of computers.

CAUTION

Connecting to a Windows printer, a common scenario, will entail the use of the Samba, the tool needed to use the SMB protocol to converse with Windows machines. While the configuration of Samba is a bit beyond the scope of this book, an excellent tutorial on Samba configuration can be found at **http://www.linuxnewbie.org/nhf/intel/network/samba/samba1.html**.

Presuming your Samba settings are configured correctly, you should have little trouble connecting to a Windows printer.

Configuring a Windows Network Printer

This task demonstrates connecting to a Windows printer on a TCP/IP network.

1. Click the Main Menu icon to open the Main menu.
2. Choose Programs, System, Control Panel. The Control Panel will open.
3. Click the printer icon to start the Red Hat Linux Print System Manager.
4. Click Add. The Add a Printer Entry dialog box appears.
5. Select the SMB/Windows 95/NT Printer option, and then click OK to continue. A warning box will appear, emphasizing the point about password caution (see Figure 7.9).

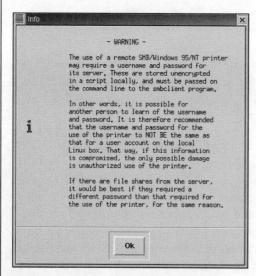

Figure 7.9 *It can't be said enough: Don't use passwords that can compromise your Linux PC.*

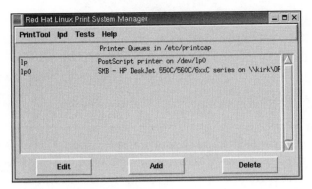

Figure 7.10   *The new network printer.*

6. Click OK. The warning box will close and the Edit dialog box will open.

7. Complete the Edit dialog box. Be sure to use the exact spellings of the names for your network devices. You can get this information from your network administrator.

8. Click the Select button (adjacent to the Input Filter field) to open the Configure Filter dialog box.

Be sure that your Windows printer is set to "shared."

9. Select the filter that matches the remote printer configuration.

10. Select the default resolution and paper-size settings, as well as any available color-depth settings.

11. Click OK to finish the filter settings. The Input Filter field in the Edit SMB/Windows 95/NT Printer Entry dialog will display the selected filter.

12. Click OK to continue. The Print System Manager will now display the new network printer (see Figure 7.10).

Sound

One of the most popular peripherals today is a sound device. No computer should be without one. Applications use sounds in increasingly creative ways to generate signals about what's going on. Games rely heavily on sound to put you into the action. And don't get me started on the Internet: Entire radio and television broadcasts are now available.

All this sound content is worthless to you, though, if you don't have a decent sound device. Sound devices are typically composed of two sets of components: a sound card and a set of speakers. As you learned in Chapter 1, "Before You Install Red Hat Linux 7," Red Hat Linux is able to support quite a few types of sound cards, which are the heart of a PC sound system.

Speakers will work with any sound card—the interface is pretty standard. This is not to say you should not give the purchase of speakers any thought. If you're going to get speakers, get mid- to high-quality speakers. This is one area where I think more investment is worthwhile.

When Red Hat is first installed, your sound card will likely be configured automatically. On the off chance that it is not configured, don't worry. Setting up a sound card is not hard to do.

Configuring Sound with the sndconfig Utility

The sndconfig application is used by Linux to configure sound. sndconfig is a command-line, text-based program and needs to run independently of X in the console. You cannot reliably run it from a terminal emulation window.

For illustration and demonstration purposes, the sndconfig screens in Figures 7.11 through 7.15 appear in a terminal window. This is only for demonstration. Kids, don't try this at home.

To access the Linux console from any X mode, press Ctrl+Alt+F1. To return to X from Linux, press Alt+F7.

That said, it's a straightforward process to get your sound card configured, as you will see in the next task.

Setting Up Sound

This task will show you how to configure a sound card on your Linux PC. Before starting sndconfig, however, you must make sure that the sound server component of X is running.

1. Click the GNOME Configuration Tool icon in the GNOME Panel.

> In the KDE Control Center, click the enable system sounds checkbox in the Sound, Systems Sound pane.

2. Click the Sound category to open the Sound pane in the Control Center.
3. Make sure both Enable options are checked, especially the Enable Sound Server Startup option.
4. Click OK to close the Control Center.
5. Press Ctrl+Alt+F1 to go to the Linux command line.
6. Log in as the root user.
7. Type **sndconfig** to begin the application. The Introduction screen will appear (see Figure 7.11).
8. Press Enter to accept the selected OK button. The next screen should display the results of a probe of all of your computer's PCI devices. If any sound cards are displayed, the probe was successful (see Figure 7.12).
9. Press Enter to continue. A message appears advising that the conf.modules file will be overwritten.
10. Press Enter to continue. sndconfig will inform you that it will now test the sound card by playing a sound sample (see Figure 7.13).

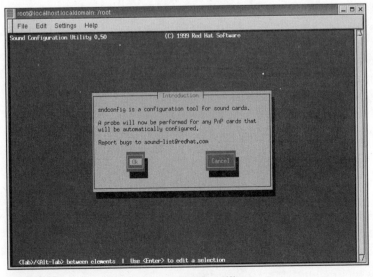

Figure 7.11 *The first screen of the sndconfig utility.*

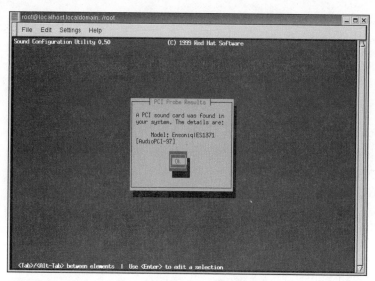

Figure 7.12 *Finding your sound card.*

Figure 7.13 *Testing your sound card and getting an answer to one of the great Linux mysteries.*

11. Press Enter to continue. A sample sound will play. (If you heard the sample, you will know the right way to pronounce "Linux," from the man himself, Linus Torvalds.)

12. If you heard the sound sample, press Enter to accept the selected Yes button. You can then proceed to Step 19.

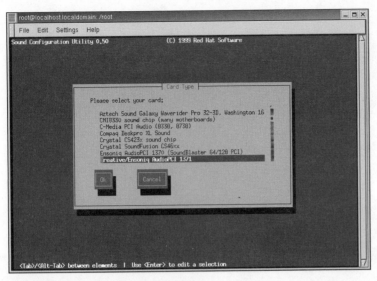

Figure 7.14   *Manually selecting a card type.*

13. If you did not hear the sample, press the Tab key to select the No button. Then press Enter. A message appears stating that auto-configuration has failed.

14. Press Enter to continue to the manual configuration process. The Card Type window will be displayed (see Figure 7.14).

15. Scroll though the list to select your card. When selected, press Tab to select OK and then press Enter to continue. The next screen enables you to select the port and IRQ settings for the card (see Figure 7.15).

> If you are not sure of the settings, check your card's documentation. If your PC has Windows installed, you might want to stop this process for now, boot to the Windows partition, and then check the settings used by Windows for the card.

16. Once again, press Tab until OK is selected, and then press Enter to continue.

17. The Sound Sample screen reappears. Select OK and press Enter to continue.

18. If the sample was heard, highlight Yes and press Enter to end the sndconfig program.

19. Log out of this X session and log back in to activate the changes you made in the GNOME or KDE control centers.

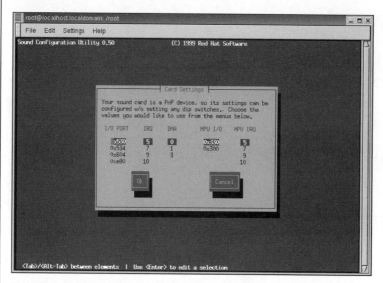

Figure 7.15   *Selecting the sound card's port and IRQ settings.*

Applying Sounds to Events

Once your sound card is configured, you can have sounds play at key events such as at an application's opening or closing. This capability will allow you to further personalize your PC.

TASK

Assigning Sound Events

This task will demonstrate how to assign sounds to certain system events on your Linux PC.

1. Click the GNOME Configuration Tool icon in the GNOME panel.
2. Click the Sound category to open the Sound pane in the Control Center.
3. Click the Sound Events tab to view the screen shown in Figure 7.16.
4. Scroll through the list of events, selecting the one you want to change.
5. Click Browse to open the Select Sound File dialog box (see Figure 7.17).
6. Select the file name for the sound you want to use, and then click OK. You will be returned to the Control Center.
7. Click Play to hear the sound sample. If you like the sample, click OK to save the configuration and close the Control Center.

TIP

Don't go too crazy applying sounds to your events. You'd be amazed at how tiresome it becomes hearing Homer Simpson saying "Doh!" with every menu selection.

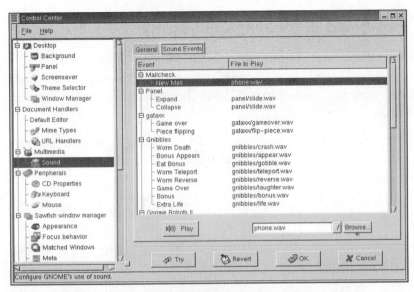

Figure 7.16 *You can browse sounds before applying them to system events.*

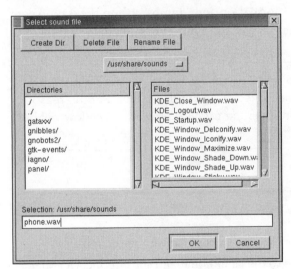

Figure 7.17 *You can use sounds from any WAV file source.*

For more information about applying entire sound schemes as part of a desktop theme, see Chapter 8, "Customizing Your Desktop's Appearance."

Plug and Play Using the isapnptools Utility

If you have a newer PC, it is very likely that you have a PCI bus on your motherboard. PCI buses are nice for Linux users because Plug and Play technology is built into the bus itself. Any device connected to a PCI bus, therefore, is likely to be detected by Red Hat Linux.

Older PCs, however, have ISA busses, with which Red Hat Linux needs a little help. Linux must probe an ISA device more directly to determine whether it is Plug and Play.

If your PC has an ISA device that is not recognized by Linux, you can use the isapnptools set of applications to help configure the device.

Performing a PnP Dump

The first thing you need to do is to perform a scan of all existing ISA PnP cards on your PC. This is done using the pnpdump application—an apt name for the program since it takes all of the PnP information and "dumps" it into the isapnp.conf file. From there, the isapnp application can configure the isapnp.conf file.

CAUTION

> Because pnpdump will try to use real-time scheduling to get the right I/O port settings, all other programs will be locked while pnpdump runs. For this reason, do not run pnpdump from within X, as the terminal emulation window will be locked as well.

TASK

Using pnpdump

This task will show how to create the isapnp.conf file with pnpdump.

1. Press Ctrl+Alt+F1 to switch to the Linux command line interface (if you're not there already).

2. Log in as root.

3. Type **/sbin/pnpdump > /etc/isapnp.conf**.

4. Check and record the settings for all other devices so that you will avoid conflicts when setting up your ISA devices. Type the following commands, each on a separate line, to obtain other device information:

- `cat /proc/dma`
- `cat /proc/interrupts`
- `cat /proc/ioports`
- `cat /proc/pci`

Editing the isapnp.conf File

Now that the isapnp.conf file is made, you can use the isapnp utility to configure your devices, as seen in the following task.

Using isapnp

This task will show how to edit the isapnp.conf file with isapnp.

1. At the Linux console, while logged in as root, type **/sbin/isapnp /etc/ isapnp.conf**.

2. isapnp will open and display the results of the pnpdump. If any ISA boards were found, remove the comment characters preceding the device listing. This will enable Linux to activate the board.

For more information on the format of the isapnp.conf file, see the isapnp Tools Home Page at **http://www.roestock.demon.co.uk/isapnptools/**.

3. Edit the values listed so that they match your card's exact specifications.

If isapnp is not installed, you can use a text editor such as vi to edit the file.

4. Once the isapnp.conf file is edited, save the file and reboot your system. Your device should be recognized by Linux now.

Working with Non-Linux Partitions

Although another file partition is not exactly a peripheral, it certainly is a device on your PC that can be exploited like any other. If you have another partition on your computer, such as a Windows partition, you can easily access its file system from Linux.

TASK

Connect to a New Partition

This task will show how to connect to a non-Linux file partition, such as a Windows drive on your PC.

1. While logged in as root, type **/sbin/fdisk –l** in the Terminal window. This will determine the device on which the partition exists.

    You will see a list of all logical and actual hard disks on your PC, including a line that includes Win95. At the beginning of that line will be a /dev/hdaX value. There should also be value such as FAT32 or FAT16. Keep these values in mind for later.

2. Type **mkdir /mnt/win** or **mkdir /mnt/windows,** naming the directory something that you can remember. This will create a mount point directory from which the Windows partition can be accessed.

3. Mount the partition by typing **mount –t vfat /dev/hdaX /mnt/win**. Remember to replace the **x** with the correct drive number. Your Windows file system can then be accessed like any other file directory.

TIP

To re-mount the partition after a halt or reboot, simply type the mount command once more. Or, add a line similar to this one in the /etc/fstab file:

```
/dev/hda1   /mnt/win   vfat   defaults   0  0.
```

This will mount the partition for you every time Linux starts.

Conclusion

In this chapter, you learned the finer points of connecting important peripheral devices to your computer. As Linux continues to grow, more devices will be included in the Linux world. This will cause the Linux configuration methods to become more simplified. Until then, use patience and care when dealing with peripheral set up.

In Chapter 8, "Customizing Your Desktop's Appearance," environments and window managers will be examined, as well as how to change fonts and mix audio.

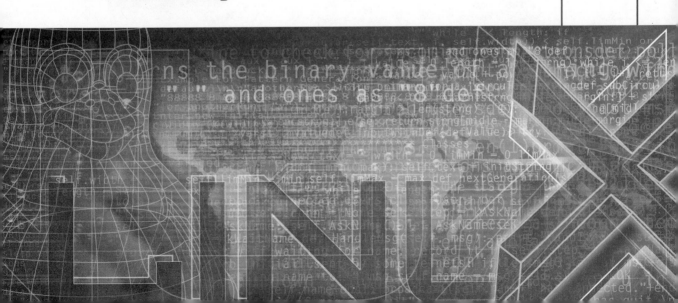

Chapter 8: Customizing Your Desktop's Appearance

T hey say that clothes make the man. If this is true, a lot of us are in big trouble. Looks are not, of course, everything, but the more pleasing to the eye something is, the easier it will be to work with.

In this chapter, you will learn how to customize many aspects of your desktop's appearance, making it more visually attractive and more personal than the default installation.

Selecting your preferred environment and window manager and then customizing them allows you to make your desktop look and act exactly as you want. You can also configure Linux to use a variety of fonts. For example, you may wish to use the same fonts under Linux as you do under Windows, so that Web pages look similar for both operating systems.

Linux can further be customized by attaching sounds to a number of events. This may not make you more productive, but it can be fun.

Desktop Environments and Window Managers

Linux, like most other UNIX-derived operating systems, uses the X Window system to provide basic graphics facilities. This system does not, however, dictate the look and feel of your desktop. The appearance is instead controlled by one or more separate programs. The most important of these is generically called a *window manager*. Window managers handle tasks such as drawing window borders, resizing windows, displaying icons representing minimized windows, and so forth. A window manager is not solely responsible for your desktop's appearance—other supporting programs can certainly be used to spice it up—but your selection of a window manager is one cornerstone in influencing how your desktop will look and respond.

A second major influence on the appearance of your desktop is your selection of desktop environment—GNOME, KDE, or perhaps none at all. A *desktop environment* is a collection of complementary software, including its window manager along with supporting utilities such as a menu system used to launch programs. Optionally, your desktop environment can include a selection of basic applications along with a GUI tool kit to provide these applications with a common look and feel.

Understanding X Client Startup Scripts

If you have several desktop environments and/or window managers installed, changing the one that starts first is simple. The next section will help you understand how to do so. If you want to customize your X startup, however, it is useful to understand the shell scripts Red Hat uses to load the X server and clients. If such background information (and the flexibility it offers) does not interest you, skip to the next section.

When a user starts X, either by logging in via the graphical xdm or by typing **startx** at a command prompt, the program xinit is launched. View the /usr/X11R6/bin/startx file to see how this is done. Near the top of the file are several lines of interest:

```
userclientrc=$HOME/.xinitrc
sysclientrc=/etc/X11/xinit/xinitrc
clientargs=""

if [ -f $userclientrc ]; then
    clientargs=$userclientrc
else if [ -f $sysclientrc ]; then
    clientargs=$sysclientrc
fi
```

The first two lines set variables referring to two possible scripts used to start X clients. The first is an optional custom script in the user's home directory; the second is the default system script (part of the xinitrc package). The `if` statement determines whether these scripts exist. If the user has developed a custom script, `clientargs` will contain its file name. Otherwise, the file name for a system script will be used, if it exists.

Other lines similar to these also exist. They differ, however, in that they are searching for a server startup script rather than a client script. The main purpose for server scripts is to find and run an X server appropriate for your video card.

Red Hat does not use server scripts, instead installing the correct X server during the Linux install. You may, however, find a use for custom server scripts. One user might install a nonstandard X server accelerated for games and use a custom ~/.xserverrc to start it.

Once a suitable client script is found (possibly even one passed from the command line), its file name is passed to xinit. The instruction line to do so can be found near the end of the startx script:

```
xinit $clientargs - $display $serverargs
```

xinit starts the X server on the specified display and then runs the client script to start the window manager and any other client programs.

If the system's default client script is selected to run, it first performs a bit of house-keeping—it loads X resources and a keyboard mapping. It then finds the clients to start. Here you might feel a bit of déjà vu: The script tries to run the clients listed in a user's ~/.Xclients; if that does not exist, it tries to run the system's /etc/X11/xinit/Xclients. These two files are the heart of the entire affair. They start GNOME, KDE, or something else entirely.

Changing the Desktop Environment

Red Hat 7 offers two major desktop environments: GNOME and KDE. GNOME and KDE are each complete environments with file managers, icons, and a number of useful programs. Each also has its own GUI tool kit—GNOME is built on a tool kit called gtk, and KDE is built on Qt.

Changing the Default Desktop Environment

One of the easiest ways to change the desktop environment is to use the Desktop Switching tool, outlined in Chapter 4, "Configuring Your Environment." Another fast way to start a different desktop environment is to create or edit the file /etc/sysconfig/desktop, first logging on as root. This file only needs to contain a single word: GNOME or KDE, according to your preference. When X starts, /etc/X11/xinit/Xclients examines this file and starts your preferred environment.

As an example, suppose you originally installed GNOME but now wish to try KDE. Here is a sample walk-though of how you might do this from the command line:

```
# mount /dev/cdrom
# rpm -iv /mnt/cdrom/RedHat/RPMS/qt1x*
# rpm -iv /mnt/cdrom/RedHat/RPMS/kde*
# echo kde > /etc/sysconfig/desktop

Press Ctrl+D when finished.
```

First you should mount the Red Hat Linux 7 CD-ROM. The next two commands install the Qt libraries and all KDE packages. Finally, you edit the file that will cause KDE to be started. The next user to start X will be greeted with KDE.

If your expected desktop environment does not start after you've put its name in /etc/sysconfig/desktop, there are several possible problems. First, you should ensure that the environment has truly been installed. Next, ensure that you don't have any old .xinitrc or .Xclients files in your home directory because these can override the global desktop selection.

TIP

Changing a Single User's Desktop Environment

Modifying /etc/sysconfig/desktop affects all users. If several people use your computer, they may not all agree to use one environment. Fortunately, personal preferences can be specified by each user, overriding the default desktop environment. One way to create a personal environment setting is to make a custom ~/.Xclients file that contains lines to start the desktop you want. For example, the code section here is a very simple file that causes the current user to use the KDE desktop, regardless of the settings in the /etc/sysconfig/desktop file.

```
$ cat > ~/.Xclients
#!/bin/bash
startkde
```

Press Ctrl+D when finished.

```
$ chmod +x ~/.Xclients
```

In the example, startkde is the shell script that starts the KDE environment. The equivalent program for GNOME is gnome-session.

After you have been using Linux for awhile, you will know that GNOME and KDE are not the only desktop environments on the block and may not even be the right ones for your system. For instance, on a computer with little RAM (less than 16MB), you will see better performance if you do not use GNOME or KDE, or even a complex window manager. This next sample code for the .Xclients file uses as little RAM as possible by starting only a clock, an xterm, and a simple window manager:

```
#!/bin/sh
xclock -geometry 100x100-5+5 &
xterm -geometry 80x35-50+100 &
exec twm
```

The `-geometry` option specifies the initial size and location of the window. If you plan to manually start older X applications (not KDE or GNOME applications) from a script such as this, you may want to read the X manual page for a full description of `-geometry` and other options. Type **man X** to view the X manual.

Changing the Window Manager

Dozens of window managers exist for Linux, varying in features, appearance, and speed. Red Hat Linux 7 includes three of them:

- Sawfish is a flexible window manager used in conjunction with GNOME. It can be configured to create attractive desktops.
- kwm is designed to be used with KDE. By default, KDE and kwm create an environment quite similar to Windows. For users most comfortable with Windows, this is a good starting point.
- twm is the most minimal window manager included with Red Hat. It is usually only used as a fallback should no other window manager be installed.

During the installation of Red Hat, you were given an option to install one of three desktop environments. If you selected GNOME, Sawfish was also installed and set as your default window manager. The kwm window manager was automatically installed for users of the KDE environment. If you elected to install neither GNOME nor KDE, your default window manager will be twm.

Even though GNOME and KDE each came with a window manager, it is possible to replace their default window manager with another. For example, if you like the GNOME environment but do not need all of Sawfish's features, you may want to save some of your computer's resources by using a simpler window manager such as twm.

Use Table 8.1 to guide you while configuring and starting window managers in the next few sections.

Table 8.1   Comparing Window Manager Startup, Configuration, and Features

Window Manager	Startup Command	Config Command	Default Config Files	User Config Files	Session Managed
Sawfish	sawfish	gnomecc	n/a	n/a	yes
kwm	kwm	kcontrol	n/a	n/a	yes
twm	twm	n/a	/etc/X11/twm/	~/.twmrc	no

These are not the only window managers you can use with Red Hat. If you purchased the Deluxe edition of Red Hat 7, you will have the PowerTools CD, from which you can install one of many window managers, including Blackbox, fvwm, icewm, and xvwm, just to name a few.

Changing GNOME's Window Manager

To try a different window manager with GNOME, open GNOME's Control Center, expand the Desktop category, and then select Window Manager. If the window manager you want to try is not already listed, you will have to add it.

To add xvwm as a possible GNOME window manager (assuming you installed it from your PowerTools CD), just click the Add button and fill in the information in the Add New Window Manager dialog box, shown in Figure 8.1.

> Be warned that the GNOME pager and drag-and-drop actions on the desktop will only work with a GNOME-compliant window manager. Sawfish is the only fully compliant window manager included in Red Hat.

CAUTION

Changing KDE's Window Manager

KDE's window manager can be changed by modifying the startkde script. If you do not want to modify the system's startkde script, remember that you can make a personal copy, modify it, and have ~/.Xclients start that instead.

Add New Window Manager	×
Name:	xvwm
Command:	xvwm
Configuration Command:	
⬜ Window manager is session managed	
	🔵 OK ✗ Cancel

Figure 8.1 *Changing GNOME's window manager.*

Changing KDE's Window Manager to Blackbox

To use Blackbox as a window manager with KDE, you must create a modified version of the startkde script. Follow these steps:

1. Make a copy of the startkde script so that you can modify it. You can use commands similar to the following:

```
$ mkdir ~/bin
$ cp /usr/bin/startkde ~/bin/mystartkde
```

2. Edit the last line in the file, changing it to start Blackbox, as it appears in this sample code:

```
sleep 2 ; exec blackbox
```

3. Now create or modify your X startup script to use ~/bin/mystartkde. The following commands create a new startup script:

```
$ cat > ~/.Xclients
#!/bin/sh
exec ~/bin/mystartkde
Press Ctrl+D when finished.
$ chmod +x ~/.Xclients
```

As with GNOME, using a different window manager causes some of KDE's features to be lost. Virtual desktops and the pop-up task list are two features that will not work in KDE without kwm.

Customizing Window Managers

Window managers often have settings that can be modified independently of the desktop environment's settings. You can customize each of Red Hat's six window managers.

Customizing Sawfish

Sawfish's settings can be changed using the graphical Sawfish configurator, part of the GNOME Configuration tool. Start the utility, shown in Figure 8.2, by choosing Run Configuration Tool Sawfish in the Window Manager section of the GNOME Control Center.

As part of the configuration, you can select from several themes. Essentially, a *theme* is a bundled set of customizations. The themes apply only to Sawfish. If you

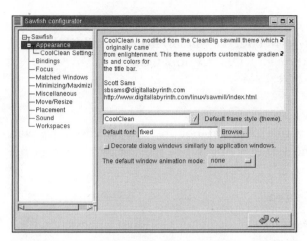

Figure 8.2 *Customizing the Sawfish window manager.*

also want to apply themes to GNOME applications, you will need to look at the theme option in GNOME's Control Center.

Customizing kwm

The behavior of kwm is modified through KDE's Control Center. KDE's Control Center can be launched from the menu if you are running KDE; otherwise use the command `kcontrol`. Figure 8.3 shows some of the settings available in the Control Center.

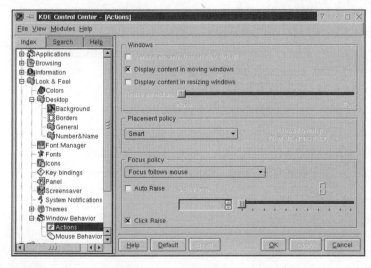

Figure 8.3 *Customizing the kwm window manager with the kcontrol utility.*

Like Sawfish, kwm supports themes. kwm's themes are more complete, however, since one setting changes the styles of both the window manager and KDE applications. You can select themes through KDE's Control Center.

Customizing twm

twm configuration is not done with a graphical tool. Instead, you customize twm by making a personal copy of the default configuration file. For twm, only one file is involved:

```
$ cp /etc/X11/twm/system.twmrc ~/.twmrc
```

The twm manual page describes at length the options for this configuration file.

TIP

If you are unable to modify your copy of the file, you may need to make it writable with the command `chmod +w .twmrc &`.

Fonts

Whether you're a command-line junkie or a GUI guru, it's essential to use a font that is easy to read. Fortunately, fonts can be changed almost everywhere in Linux.

Changing the Console Font

Even if you do not use X, you can still change the font used on your display, also known as the *console font*. The fonts from which you can choose are located in /usr/lib/kbd/consolefonts/. (If the directory does not exist, be sure that the console-tools package is installed.) Modifying the console font requires an EGA, VGA, or newer graphics card. Almost every computer has a suitable card.

The next code sample is a simple script that you can use to browse the existing fonts. Save it where it will be referenced by your path, perhaps as ~/bin/viewfonts. Also, remember that these are console fonts, so they cannot be viewed while in X.

```
#!/bin/sh
DIR=/usr/lib/kbd/consolefonts
for font in $DIR/*.psf*
  do
    clear
    consolechars -f $DIR/default8x16.psf*
```

```
    consolechars -f $font
    echo This is the font:
    echo $font
    /sbin/getkey
done
```

When you run this script, each font's file name will be displayed using the attributes of that font. Press any key to advance to the next font. When all fonts have been displayed, the routine will end.

> If a small font (such as an 8×8-pixel font) is loaded followed by a larger font (an 8×12, for example), it is possible that the number of lines on the screen will not reset correctly. This will cause the bottom half of the larger font to be cut off, making it hard to read. If this happens while you are viewing fonts, continue running the script; loading other fonts should fix it. If you run the script while logged in as root, you may avoid this problem.

CAUTION

If you find a font you like, it can be loaded automatically every time you turn on your computer. The place for customizations such as this (that is, simple commands that only need to run at boot) is in /etc/rc.d/rc.local. Add the `consolechars` command with your desired font to the end of this file. For example, if you decide you like the font t.psf.gz, add this line to the end of the file:

```
consolechars -f /usr/lib/kbd/consolefonts/t
```

The extension .psf.gz can be omitted; `consolechars` is smart enough to figure out which font you mean.

Changing Fonts in X

The method required to change fonts in X depends on which desktop environment you are using.

Changing KDE Fonts

The KDE Control Center includes an option to change the display fonts. These settings apply to all KDE applications and the desktop. They usually will not, however, affect GNOME or legacy X applications.

Unless a KDE application explicitly uses a particular font, all text in KDE applications falls into five groups: general, fixed, window title, panel button, and panel clock. You can select a font for each of these groups.

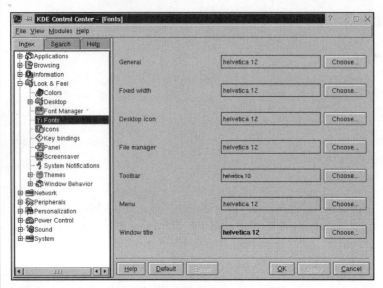

Figure 8.4   *Changing fonts in KDE.*

To change fonts, start the KDE Control Center, select Look & Feel, and then Fonts (see Figure 8.4).

Increasing the font size is not always handled gracefully in KDE. To see this, try increasing the General font from 12-point Helvetica to 16-point Helvetica, and then click Apply. Some of the labels beneath your icons will be clipped short.

A solution to this problem is to close the Control Center to save your changes and then restart KDE. Your larger font should now be displayed correctly.

Changing Fonts in GNOME

GNOME's Control Center does not have a configuration option to change the fonts of the desktop and applications. Loading a GNOME theme may change the font, but it also brings with it lots of other visual changes. There is, however, another way to change fonts in GNOME.

Before you learn how to change GNOME's fonts, you should understand how GNOME applications decide what visual settings to use. A gtk-based application first reads the settings in /etc/gtk/gtkrc. Next, it tries to open ~/.gtkrc, and finally, it reads the theme's settings from a file such as /usr/share/themes/Default/gtk/gtkrc. (The Default directory will be replaced by the name of the current theme.)

To set your own fonts, create a ~/.gtkrc file that sets the fonts you want to use. This will override the fonts set by any theme you may be using. You might want to follow the examples of some of the simpler themes in /usr/share/themes/. If you are adventurous, you might prefer to create your own entire theme. An excellent resource for more information on themes is **http://www.themes.org**.

Adding Fonts to X

Fonts used by your X server are installed in the directory /usr/X11R6/lib/X11/fonts/. They are further separated by type: Speedo, Type1, 75 dpi bitmap, and so on.

Adding Fonts to X

You can add your own fonts to X by following these steps:

1. Copy your own fonts to the correct directory (the file extension will usually tell you which directory). For example, suppose you have a font file named font0123.spd. A little investigation reveals that the spd fonts are in the Speedo directory, so that is a reasonable place to locate your font. Use this command to copy the font to the Speedo directory:

   ```
   # cp font0123.spd /usr/X11R6/lib/X11/fonts/Speedo
   ```

2. You must rebuild that font directory with the `mkfontdir` command. Use this command:

   ```
   # mkfontdir /usr/X11R6/lib/X11/fonts/Speedo
   ```

3. Although the font is now correctly installed, the X server has not yet updated its own list of fonts. To make the changes take effect, you can either restart X or use this command:

   ```
   # xset fp rehash
   ```

4. Now verify that your new font is available by running a font selection tool, such as xfontsel.

Adding True Type Fonts

True Type fonts require slightly more effort to set up. X does not natively understand True Type fonts, so you must install a True Type font server that X can use, as demonstrated in the next task.

Adding True Type Fonts to X

Installing True Type fonts is done a little differently from installing other types of fonts. Follow these steps:

1. Verify that the font server is installed by typing **locate xfs**. This command will find the font server if it is on your PC.

2. Verify that the font server is set to start automatically when you turn on your computer. To do so, first be sure that you are logged on as root, type **setup,** and then run the System services tool. Scroll down and verify that xfs is checked; then exit the setup utility.

3. You can now install True Type fonts. Here is an example of installing True Type fonts from the current directory, after downloading them from the Web:

```
# mkdir /usr/X11R6/lib/X11/fonts/TrueType
# cp *.ttf /usr/X11R6/lib/X11/fonts/TrueType
```

4. Tell the fonts server where to find the new fonts. Edit /etc/X11/fs/config and add the True Type font path to the list of existing font paths. The relevant section of this file initially reads:

```
catalogue = /usr/X11R6/lib/X11/fonts/misc:unscaled,
    /usr/X11R6/lib/X11/fonts/75dpi:unscaled,
    /usr/X11R6/lib/X11/fonts/100dpi:unscaled,
    /usr/X11R6/lib/X11/fonts/misc,
    /usr/X11R6/lib/X11/fonts/Type1,
    /usr/X11R6/lib/X11/fonts/Speedo,
    /usr/share/fonts/default/Type1
```

5. After you add the reference to the True Type directory in the first line, it should read:

```
catalogue = /usr/X11R6/lib/X11/fonts/TrueType,
    /usr/X11R6/lib/X11/fonts/misc:unscaled,
    /usr/X11R6/lib/X11/fonts/75dpi:unscaled,
    /usr/X11R6/lib/X11/fonts/100dpi:unscaled,
    /usr/X11R6/lib/X11/fonts/misc,
    /usr/X11R6/lib/X11/fonts/Type1,
    /usr/X11R6/lib/X11/fonts/Speedo,
    /usr/share/fonts/default/Type1
```

6. To make the new fonts usable, you must now either restart your machine or restart the font server using the following command:

```
# /etc/rc.d/init.d/xfs restart
```

7. Now start X and run a font-selection tool such as xfontsel to see if your new fonts are available.

Improving the Appearance of Legacy X Applications

You have certainly noticed by now that not all X programs look and act the same. These differences are very obvious among the three text editors shown in Figure 8.5. The current crop of X applications are usually built using either the gtk or Qt GUI tool kits, which gives them a particular look and feel. Older X applications predate these tool kits and therefore do not share these newer user interfaces. For example, such an application may have scrollbars that behave differently from those in gtk or Qt-based applications. Not only is it unsightly, it's also annoying to launch an older X application and have it ignore KDE color scheme and font settings.

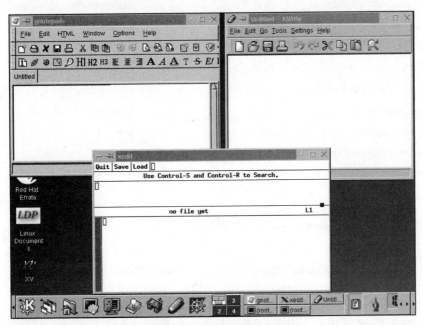

Figure 8.5 *Inconsistent look and feel due to multiple tool kits.*

There are two basic approaches to fixing this: You can either replace the older application or attempt to manually customize it.

Replacing Older Applications

Replacing the older application tends to be the easiest (and usually the best) solution. Remember, a newer application using gtk or Qt not only gains a more standard look compared to the older application, but it also may support desirable features such as drag-and-drop capability and Internet awareness.

Red Hat Linux 7 includes mostly modern versions of utilities and applications, but you may still encounter older incarnations. Table 8.2 suggests modern equivalents you might like to try. All software—both old and new—listed in this table is included in Red Hat Linux 7.

Table 8.2   Possible Upgrades of Legacy X Applications

Old	Description	New (gtk-based)	New (Qt-based)
gv	PostScript viewer	n/a	kghostview
xcalc	Calculator	gcalc	kcalc
xbiff	Checks for new mail	n/a	kbiff
xmh	Simple mail reader	balsa	kmail
ical	Calendar and organizer	gnomecal	korganizer
xfm	File manager	gmc	kfm
xrn	News reader	n/a	krn
xanim	Animation player	n/a	kaction

Manually Customizing Older Applications

Sometimes no modern equivalent exists for an older application. For example, many users have a long history with the editor emacs, and despite its less than aesthetically pleasing interface, they don't want to part with it. A version of emacs based on gtk or Qt would be ideal, visually speaking, but it does not exist. In a case such as this, manual tweaking of the older application is the only option.

These older X applications (specifically, those built with Motif or directly on top of Xlib) often have their colors and fonts controlled through a file in your home directory named .Xdefaults. If you view this file now, it probably contains settings for emacs and xterm. The possible settings vary for each program. Reading the manual pages for these programs will give you more information about setting these defaults.

Conclusion

In this chapter, you learned how to select and begin configuring your desktop environments and your window managers. You also learned how to configure fonts and to customize the look of older applications. Also, you learned how to associate sounds with events.

Chapter 9, "Customizing Your Desktop's Usability," teaches more practical concepts: It will help you make your desktop environment and window manager more usable by simplifying and automating a number of tasks.

Chapter 9: Customizing Your Desktop's Usability

Configuring Virtual Desktops

Making Drives Easy to Mount

Making Programs Start Automatically

Defining File Associations

Streamlining the Printing Process

n this chapter, you will learn how to make your desktop fit the way you work. One way to do this is to create virtual desktops, which gives you more space to work. Another is to make your removable drives easily mountable; making your removable drives mount with a simple command or a single mouse click will save you time. The same goes for learning how to make programs start automatically—both when you start X and when you click on a data file. Finally, you will learn how to streamline the printing process with drag-and-drop printing.

Configuring Virtual Desktops

Virtual desktops allow your screen to act as part of a larger, multi-screen desktop. I find this to be a useful way of organizing my running programs, which in turn helps me organize my thoughts. For example, at work I use virtual desktops one and two to develop and debug software. Useful programs not directly related to work (such as a Web browser, e-mail, and instant messaging software) are active on desktop three. Such programs are still available with just a keystroke when I want them, but they are not always present on my current desktop to distract me. (Not to mention, I can make the Web-browsing desktop disappear with just one more keystroke—especially useful when the boss pays an unexpected visit!)

Both KDE and GNOME come with virtual desktops. The KDE and GNOME panels display a grid of four buttons (referred to as the *desk guide* in GNOME), representing the four possible screens. With KDE, you can use handy keyboard shortcuts to switch among desktops: Ctrl+F1 to switch to the first virtual desktop, Ctrl+F2 for the second, and so forth. Similarly, GNOME uses the Alt key in combination with the function keys (such as Alt+F1).

Configuring KDE's Virtual Desktops

To change KDE's virtual desktop setup, start the KDE Control Center, expand Applications and then Panel, and then select the Desktops tab. The Desktops page will allow you to create between two and eight virtual desktops. You can also re-name each desktop to something descriptive, as is being done in Figure 9.1, if that will help you organize your windows.

Configuring GNOME's Virtual Desktops

You can configure GNOME's virtual desktops by right-clicking the desk guide. Choose Properties from the shortcut menu, and in the Desk Guide Settings dialog, click the Geometry tab (see Figure 9.2).

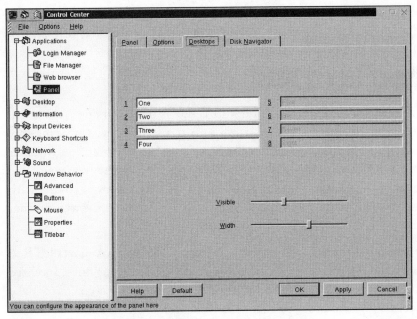

Figure 9.1   *Configuring KDE's virtual desktops.*

In this dialog box, you can change the size of the pager control itself with ease. It is important to remember to clear the Override desktop height/width with panel size options if you want to affect any size changes to the desk guide.

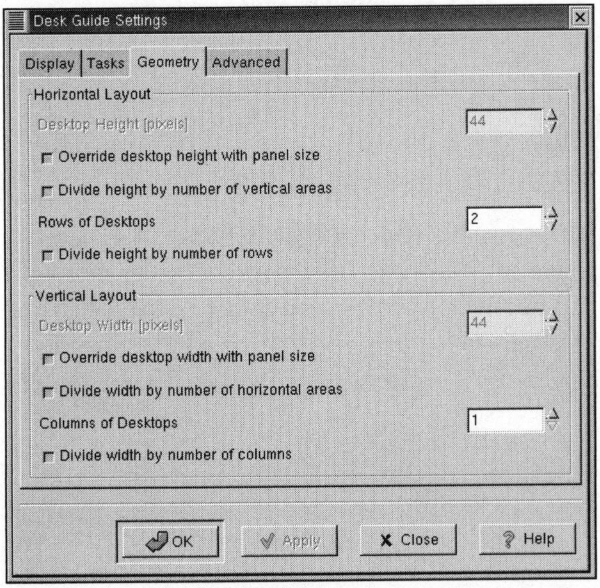

Figure 9.2   *Configuring GNOME's virtual desktops.*

You can also specify the number of desktops that will be shown on the pager by manipulating the number of rows and columns the pager control will display.

Making Drives Easy to Mount

One of the difficulties beginners encounter in Linux is how to mount removable drives—especially a drive that is added after Linux is installed. Even after mastering the commands to format and mount the new drive, incorrect settings (in /etc/fstab) might make mounting impossible for all but the user logged in as root. The Red Hat Linux installation sets up the KDE and GNOME desktops so that with a single click you can mount and access the floppy, but how do you add other removable drives?

To set the background for the following examples, suppose you have installed Red Hat Linux on a computer that already has a floppy drive, CD-ROM drive, and hard drive. Later, you decide to add an IDE Jaz drive to the system. Your goal is to make this new device mountable and accessible to normal users with minimal fuss, ideally even from X. The next sections outline the procedure for accomplishing this.

> Very little in this example is specific to a Jaz drive; this example could as easily refer to the addition of a second floppy or a second hard drive. For a floppy drive, you would skip the partitioning step. In the case of the hard drive, of course, a normal user probably wouldn't care about being able to mount and unmount it.

Determining the Device Name

After you've physically installed the Jaz drive, the first step is to figure out what device name it uses so that you can tell Linux which device to mount. Perhaps the simplest way to find the device name of your new drive is to watch the messages Linux displays as it first begins to boot. Don't fret if you didn't notice what was displayed; all messages from the kernel are logged to disk. To read them, log in as any user and view the file /var/log/dmesg. Scroll down until you see lines similar to the following:

```
hda: WDC AC36400L, ATA DISK drive
hdc: ATAPI CDROM, ATAPI CDROM drive
hdd: Iomega Jaz drive, ATA DISK drive
```

From this information you can learn that the hard drive is /dev/hda, the CD-ROM drive is /dev/hdc, and most importantly, the new Jaz drive is referenced as device /dev/hdd.

> Devices /dev/hda, /dev/hdb, /dev/hdc, and so forth are IDE devices. If you had installed a SCSI drive, you would look for /dev/sda, /dev/sdb, /dev/sdc, and so on. Your first floppy drive is /dev/fd0; your second, if any, is /dev/fd1.

Partitioning a Disk

Once you've determined the device's name, you must know how the disk is partitioned so that you can decide which partition to mount. (Floppy disks are usually not partitioned.) New Jaz disks come already partitioned; partition 4 fills the entire disk. Most other disks, whether removable or not, do not come partitioned. In these cases, you must partition them yourself. This can be done using the fdisk, cfdisk, or linuxconf command.

To help you understand how to partition your own drive, the sections that follow first delete the Jaz drive's fourth partition and then re-create it in the first partition slot as a native Linux partition. This example, which is performed from the command line while the user is logged in as root, uses the fdisk utility; you can apply the concepts to the friendlier cfdisk, if you'd prefer.

Repartitioning a Disk

Partitioning a disk must be done as the user root. The following steps use the fdisk utility:

1. First, load the disk-partitioning program and print the list of existing partitions using the p command:

```
$ fdisk /dev/hdd


Command (m for help): p


Disk /dev/hdd: 255 heads, 63 sectors, 522 cylinders
Units = cylinders of 16065 * 512 bytes


   Device Boot    Start      End    Blocks   Id  System
/dev/hdd4    *        1      121    931770    5  FAT16
```

2. For a hard drive or for most removable drives besides the Jaz drive, no partitions will be listed. Since my Jaz drive does display a partition, you'll see how to delete the existing partition and then create another. Use the d command to delete, as shown in this example.

```
Command (m for help): d
Partition number (1-4): 4
```

3. The next example demonstrates how to create a new partition using the n command. The new partition is created as *primary*; the *extended* option is only useful if you want more than four partitions on a disk. For removable disks, make the partition as large as possible.

```
Command (m for help): n
Command action
   e   extended
   p   primary partition (1-4)
p
Partition number (1-4): 1
First cylinder (1-522, default 1): 1
Last cylinder or +size or +sizeM or +sizeK (1-522, default 522): 522
Command (m for help): p


Disk /dev/hdd: 255 heads, 63 sectors, 522 cylinders
Units = cylinders of 16065 * 512 bytes


    Device Boot    Start      End    Blocks   Id  System
/dev/hdd1                1      522   4192933+   83  Linux
```

Setting the Partition Type

You will often need to set the partition type for partitions you create. Table 9.1 lists some common partition and file-system types supported by Linux.

Since this sample disk will be used only with Linux, set the partition type to ext2, the standard Linux file system. Here are the relevant lines from fdisk:

```
Command (m for help): t
Partition number (1-4): 1
Hex code (type L to list codes): 83
Changed system type of partition 1 to 83 (Linux)
```

If this Jaz disk is to be shared between Windows and Linux, the type should be set to FAT16. Windows and Linux can both read and write the FAT and VFAT file

Table 9.1 Common Partition Types

Hexadecimal Partition Type	Partition Type	File-System Type for mount -t
01	FAT12	msdos
02	XENIX root	sysv
03	XENIX usr	sysv
04	FAT16 <32M	msdos, vfat
05	Extended	n/a
06	FAT16	msdos, vfat
07	HPFS, NTFS	hpfs, ntfs
0b	Win95 FAT32	msdos, vfat
0c	Win95 FAT32 (LBA)	msdos, vfat
0e	Win95 FAT16 (LBA)	msdos, vfat
0f	Win95 Extended (LBA)	msdos, vfat
4d	QNX 4.x	qnx4
4e	QNX 4.x 2nd partition	qnx4
4f	QNX 4.x 3rd partition	qnx4
63	GNU HURD or SysV	ufs
81	Minix, old Linux	ext (obsolete)
82	Linux swap	n/a
83	Linux	ext2

systems, but setting the type to FAT16 would result in the loss of ext2 features such as links. Your expected use of the disk should guide which partition type you select.

These final example lines from fdisk write the changes to disk and then exit fdisk:

```
Command (m for help): w
The partition table has been altered!

Calling ioctl() to re-read partition table.
Syncing disks.

WARNING: If you have created or modified any DOS 6.x
partitions, please see the fdisk manual page for
additional information.
```

Unless fdisk warns you otherwise, you do not have to reboot after partitioning. Before the partition can be used, however, it must be formatted. Since the device is /dev/hdd, the partition created was number 1, and the partition type is ext2, use the following command to format:

```
$ mkfs -t ext2 /dev/hdd1
```

Had the partition type been set to FAT16, the format command would have looked like this:

```
$ mkfs -t msdos /dev/hdd1
```

All FAT partitions (FAT12, FAT16, and FAT32) are formatted as type msdos.

Mounting the New Partition

You have now collected the information you need (the device name and partition number), and the partition is formatted. (If you are installing an unpartitioned disk, you would not have a partition number. For example, you would use /dev/hdd instead of /dev/hdd1. Everything else is the same. Also, recall that floppies are not partitioned even though they are named with numbers, such as /dev/fd0.) It is now possible to issue a mount command, specifying the partition, mount point, and any mount options you want. First create the mount point, and then mount the new disk:

```
$ mkdir /mnt/jaz
$ mount -t ext2 /dev/hdd1 /mnt/jaz
```

Improving the Mount Command

Typing a long mount command each time it was necessary to mount a Jaz disk would certainly be annoying—thankfully it's not necessary. By placing these values as defaults in /etc/fstab, the mount command can be shortened. To do so, edit /etc/fstab and add the following line anywhere in the file:

```
/dev/hdd1        /mnt/jaz        ext2    defaults    0 0
```

You can edit the file with a text editor while logged in as root, but if you prefer, you can use the more extravagant linuxconf to enter the values.

In the last example, the first column specifies the partition to mount. The second column is the mount point and the third column lists the file system with which the disk is formatted. The last three columns are optional settings describing how to mount the partition. The disk does not need to be mounted in any special way, so specify default for the options. For removable devices, the last two columns can usually be set to zero.

After saving this change to the file, the disk can be mounted with a much simpler command. You only need to specify the device to mount; all other options are filled in from the file system table. First unmount the disk so that you can start fresh, and then remount it using a more terse command:

```
$ umount /dev/hdd1
$ mount /dev/hdd1
```

A difficulty occurs if you also share disks with users of Microsoft Windows. Your own disks might be formatted as ext2, but those you share will be formatted as FAT or even NTFS file systems. If you are logged in as root, you can cope with other file systems by overriding the settings in /etc/fstab as needed. (This is not allowed when you are logged in as a normal user.) Use this command as root to mount a disk formatted as FAT:

```
$ mount -t vfat /dev/hdd1 /mnt/jaz
```

> The file-system type msdos truncates the base file name to eight characters and the extension to three, just as DOS does. The vfat file system behaves just like Windows, allowing long file names. Normally you will want to use vfat.

An easier method to use when mounting various file-system types is to have Linux pick the correct file system automatically. To accomplish this, specify the file-system type as auto in /etc/fstab.

Another difficulty with the current settings occurs when you attempt to mount the Jaz disk while not logged in as root. Typically, you don't do most of your work while logged in as root, so why should you have to be root to mount a removable disk? The user option enables any user to mount the disk; only the user who mounted it can then unmount it. This setting would be particularly useful on a computer with multiple simultaneous users. Once one user mounts a disk, no other user can interfere and unmount it. A more relaxed setting is users, which is more suitable for a shared home computer. All users may mount and unmount the disk, without restriction. For example, if one user mounted a Jaz disk, used it, and then left without remembering to unmount it, the next person who used the computer would be allowed to unmount it.

All drives listed in /etc/fstab will be mounted when Red Hat boots unless the noauto option is specified. Automatic mounting usually doesn't make sense for removable media, so include this option for your Jaz drive.

Finally, you might want to consider whether you will always remember that /dev/hdd1 is your Jaz drive. If not, you can give it a better name. Perhaps /dev/jaz is more memorable. Use this command to create a link from jaz to the real device:

```
$ ln -s /dev/hdd1 /dev/jaz
```

Taking all of these customizations into account, the line in /etc/fstab should now read:

```
/dev/jaz    /mnt/jaz    auto    noauto,user    0 0
```

Now your Jaz drive can be mounted and unmounted by any user with the simple command mount /dev/jaz. This is a good start, but wouldn't it be even better if it were mountable via your mouse in X?

Mounting Drives in KDE

Initially, your KDE desktop should have included several icons to mount, unmount, and browse drives. These are convenient, especially for beginning Linux users or users who prefer the GUI over the command line. Icons for the CD-ROM and floppy drives are on your desktop by default, but if you add a new removable drive, it would also be nice to have an icon for that drive.

TASK

Creating Drive Icons in KDE

You can create icons to mount, unmount, and browse drives in KDE by following these steps:

1. If you have the Jaz drive mounted, unmount it and then start KDE as a normal user. To create an icon for your Jaz drive (or any other drive or partition), right-click your desktop and select New, File System Device. The krootwm dialog box will appear.

2. Type in a name for the new device's link, such as jaz.kdelnk.

3. Click OK. The krootwm dialog box will close, and the kfm dialog box will open. You now have a generic device icon on your desktop, but it is useless until configured in kfm.

4. The kfm dialog box has three tabs: General, Permissions, and Device, as shown in Figure 9.3. On the General page, the name you entered in the krootwm dialog box will appear.

5. The settings on the Permissions page affect the Jaz.kdelnk icon itself, not /dev/jaz. You can leave these as they are.

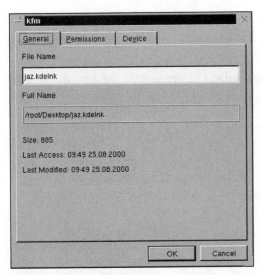

Figure 9.3 *Configuring a drive icon in KDE.*

6. On the Device page, type the name of the device to mount. You might also want to pick icons to represent the mounted and unmounted drive.

Only users logged in as root can set the drive as read-only, define a different mount point, or define a different type of file system. These settings are already defined in /etc/fstab. For security reasons, the settings cannot be overridden unless one is logged in as root.

7. After you click OK, you should be able to mount and display the files on the drive with a single click of the Jaz icon. To unmount, right-click the icon and choose Unmount.

If the drive fails to mount, KDE will give you the error message from the mount command. This is usually enough to diagnose any problems, but if not, here are some things to try.

First, see if you can mount the drive from a terminal (still as the same user) with the command mount /dev/jaz. If this works, there is a problem with the icon. Double-check the icon's properties. If it fails, verify that jaz is linked to /dev/hdd1 as you expect, that the correct line is in /etc/fstab, that the disk is partitioned correctly, and that the partition is formatted.

For completeness, you might want to set the text for the tip that appears when a mouse pointer rests on the icon for a few seconds. For example, the trash can's tip reads "Contains removed files." In similar fashion, you might want the Jaz icon's tip to read "IDE Jaz drive" or something similar. Unfortunately, the kfm dialog box does not provide a way to edit these tips, but it's easy to do by hand.

The drive icons exist in ~/Desktop/ as files ending with the extension .kdelnk. Open ~/Desktop/Jaz.kdelnk in your favorite editor. To create a tip, you need to define a Comment line. Notice that you can specify multiple translations, as is done with the Name keyword, by appending the language abbreviation in square brackets. KDE decides which translation to use based on the current language as set in the KDE Control Center.

Unless you know how to translate "IDE Jaz drive" into other languages (more than a dozen languages are possible), you can simply omit the translations. The final Jaz.kdelnk file is shown here:

```
$ KDE Config File
[KDE Desktop Entry]
UnmountIcon=3floppy_unmount.xpm
Name=Jaz
Comment=IDE Jaz drive
MountPoint=
Icon=3floppy_mount.xpm
Dev=/dev/jaz
ReadOnly=0
FSType=Default
Type=FSDevice
```

Because this file appears within your home directory, the new icon will only appear for you. If you want all user accounts that are created in the future to also have this icon, copy it into the directory /etc/skel/Desktop/.

Mounting Drives in GNOME

The GNOME desktop also provides for mounting and unmounting drives using buttons on GNOME's panel. GNOME's method is simpler than KDE's, although the same troubleshooting tips apply to GNOME.

Creating a Drive Mounting Button in GNOME

It is quite easy to add a button to GNOME's panel that will allow you to mount, unmount, and browse your removable drives. Use these steps:

1. Click on the Main Menu button. The Main menu will appear.
2. Select Applets, Utility, and Drive Mount. The Drive Mount launcher appears on the panel (see Figure 9.4).
3. Right-click on the Drive Mount launcher. The context menu appears.
4. Click on Properties. The Drive Mount Applet Properties dialog box appears (see Figure 9.5).

    Initially the applet is set to control the floppy drive, but you can change its options. The Mount point refers to the directory defined in /etc/fstab; the Update in seconds box refers to how often the applet checks to determine whether the drive has been mounted or unmounted from the command line.

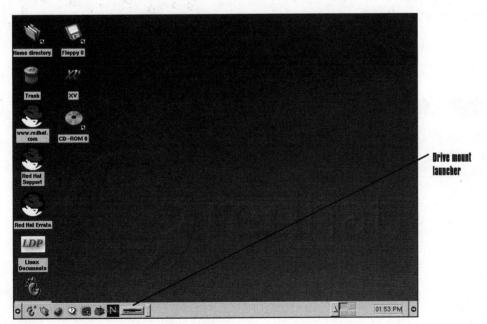

Figure 9.4 *Setting up a drive mount launcher.*

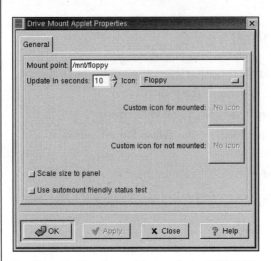

Figure 9.5   *Configuring a drive applet in GNOME.*

> **5.** Make the appropriate changes and click on OK. The Drive Mount Applet Properties dialog box closes.

You can start multiple drive mounting applets. Each has independent settings, and all will be restarted automatically each time you start GNOME.

Improving Red Hat's /etc/fstab

Before you decide that you are finished with drive mountings, you should consider modifying several other lines in /etc/fstab. A typical /etc/fstab for Red Hat Linux looks like this (after including the /dev/jaz entry created by a previous example):

```
/dev/hda1   /            ext2     defaults        1 1
/dev/cdrom  /mnt/cdrom   iso9660  noauto,owner,ro 0 0
/dev/hda5   swap         swap     defaults        0 0
/dev/fd0    /mnt/floppy  ext2     noauto,user     0 0
none        /proc        proc     defaults        0 0
none        /dev/pts     devpts   gid=5,mode=620  0 0
/dev/jaz    /mnt/jaz     auto     noauto,user     0 0
```

In this sample code, look at the default file-system type for the floppy drive. I like the ext2 file system as much as Red Hat does, but explicitly listing it in the /etc/fstab file is not a good idea. This setting prevents normal users from mounting floppies formatted with anything but ext2. I recommend that you change the ext2 entry to auto.

If you are security conscious, you might want to specify the `nodev` and `nosuid` options for all removable devices. The `nodev` option instructs Linux to ignore device files on the disk; `nosuid` causes Linux to ignore all set-user-identifier or set-group-identifier bits on the disk. These options will prevent anyone from mounting a specially prepared disk and using it to snoop on your hard drive (bypassing any file permissions in the process) or to cause damage.

> The `owner` option is specific to Red Hat Linux. It is not yet documented in the `mount` manual page, but its purpose is to allow only the owner of the device file to mount the device. This option currently will not work on other distributions.

Making Programs Start Automatically

You may want certain programs to start automatically when you start X. This can be done in most desktop environments, although KDE and GNOME go one step further by supporting session management.

Session management is the ability to remember which applications were running when the desktop was exited so that they will be restarted automatically next time. The applications must support the type of session management offered by the environment. This means that GNOME's session management supports only gtk-based programs, and KDE's only supports those that are Qt-based.

Automatically Starting Programs in KDE

On the KDE desktop is a folder titled Autostart (see Figure 9.6). All files in this folder are started when KDE starts. You can place anything in the Autostart folder: programs, data files, links to other files, drive icons, or even URLs.

KDE will load each file as if you had clicked on its icon, which leads to a number of interesting possible uses of the Autostart folder:

- Text files will be loaded into an editor, so placing a link in this folder to a to-do list will create a simple reminder system.

- Putting a URL in this folder will cause KDE's Web browser to load the page. This can be useful, for example, if you want to start your mornings by checking a stock quote.

- You can also place links to programs in this folder. Starting a large clock is a common thing to do.

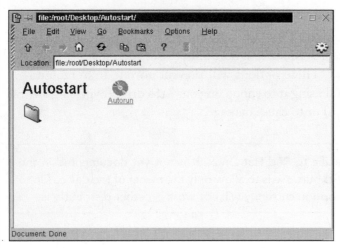

Figure 9.6   *Autostarting objects in KDE.*

You could depend on KDE's session management to restart KDE applications, provided you do not close them before exiting KDE. However, the Autostart folder tends to be a better solution for two reasons. First, it allows programs that are not session managed (that is, non-KDE programs) to be started when you log in. Second, the Autostart folder can guarantee that an application starts with a particular file or URL.

Automatically Starting Programs in GNOME

GNOME is less flexible than KDE in this respect because it only allows actual programs to be started; you cannot add data files of any sort to the startup list. To define programs that should start automatically, open GNOME's Control Center and then select Startup Programs (see Figure 9.7). You should specify only non-qtk-based applications in the startup list, leaving the session manager to handle all the rest. If you would like to use GNOME's session management, select Automatically Save Changes to Session. Select Add to incorporate an application into the startup list.

Defining File Associations

File associations bind particular types of files (based on MIME types and/or file-name extensions) to an application. A MIME type is a property of every file that

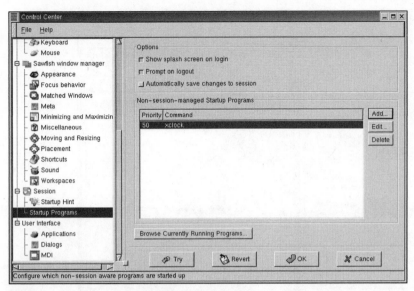

Figure 9.7 *Autostarting programs in GNOME.*

tells any application looking at the file what kind of file it is. So, if you try to open a file in StarOffice, StarOffice will look at the file's MIME type first to see whether it is compatible with StarOffice. It's that simple. KDE and GNOME both support file associations, but sometimes you have to help the environments out by manually defining file associations.

The following sections show how to create an association between MP3 files and xmms, the X Multimedia System. You will want to have the xmms package installed to follow along.

Defining File Associations in KDE

File associations in KDE are done using MIME objects. KDE's MIME objects associate three things: file-name extensions, a MIME type, and a program. If you click an icon on your desktop, KDE will decide what program to launch based on its extension. If you download a file from the Web, KDE will decide what program to launch based on the MIME type.

KDE supports a global set of MIME types as well as a user's custom set. This example shows you how to modify a global MIME object so that all users will benefit. Referring to Figure 9.8 may be helpful.

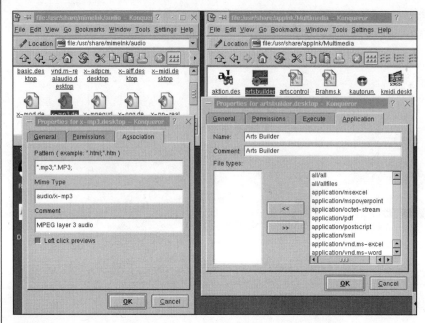

Figure 9.8 *Associating an application with a MIME type in KDE.*

Defining a File Association in KDE

File associations are a powerful feature of KDE. In this task, the mp3 file type (a music file type you may have heard of) will be associated with the xmms application. These are the steps you should follow to create your any kind of file association.

1. To associate MP3 files with xmms, you must first create a MIME object for MP3 files. Start KDE while logged in as root and then open the file manager window (such as your home directory).

2. From the Edit menu, choose Global Mime Types.

3. Because MP3 is an audio format, open the Audio folder. In this example, an x-mp3 object already exists. (If it doesn't exist, you can create your own by right-clicking while the mouse pointer exists somewhere in the window and then choosing New, Mime Type.)

4. Right-click the x-mp3 object and choose Properties to open its Properties dialog box.

5. Click the Binding tab, and then list all file-name extensions that should be tagged as this MIME type. For MP3, not only should you list *.mp3, but

also the MP3 play list extension *.m3u because the xmms program can handle both.

Because Linux is case-sensitive, you may want to enter both upper- and lower-case extensions.

6. Type the MIME type; in this case, it is **audio/x-mp3**. You cannot yet select a default application for this MIME object since no application object exists for xmms. Click OK to close the Properties dialog box.

If you are creating a new MIME object and do not know the correct MIME type, it's okay to guess. At worst, such files will not be handled correctly when downloaded from the Internet, but clicking local files will work.

7. Create the application object by returning to the file browser. From the Edit menu, choose Global Applications. A number of categories appear; open the Multimedia folder.

8. In this folder, create a new program object for xmms by right-clicking and choosing New, Application.

9. Name the object **xmms.kdelnk**.

10. The Properties dialog box for xmms.kdelnk should open. Click the Execute tab of the Properties dialog box, and then type **xmms**.

11. Change to the Application page, select the new audio/x-mp3 MIME type, and click the left arrow to add it to the list. This is a list of all MIME types the application can handle. You can list several; try adding audio/x-wav also. (Now, whenever you open a shortcut menu by right-clicking MP3 or WAV files, xmms will be offered as a choice.)

12. Give the application a name. For this example, use **X Multimedia System**.

13. Click OK to close the Properties dialog box.

14. Associate the application object with the MIME object. To do so, open the Properties dialog box of the x-mp3 MIME object once again, click the Binding tab, and then select X Multimedia System as the default application.

15. Click OK to close the Properties dialog box. Now, clicking on MP3 files will cause them to load into xmms.

NOTE

If a MIME type or an application does not appear in a list when you believe it should, try closing the Properties dialog box and opening it again. This will force KDE to re-scan all MIME types and applications. Alternatively, from the View menu, choose Rescan Bindings to force a re-scan at any time.

Defining File Associations in GNOME

GNOME's method of creating file associations differs from KDE's in several ways. First, only one application can be associated with a given MIME type. Second, GNOME allows different applications to be defined for each of the open, view, and edit tasks. KDE's method only defines an application to be used when opening an object.

GNOME has no global set of mappings between MIME types, file-name extensions, and applications. Every user must create his or her own mappings. Modifying these while logged in as root is not specially handled; only those associations for the root login are affected.

TASK

Defining a File Association in GNOME

Use these steps to associate an application with a MIME type in GNOME. Again, while this example specifically deals with mp3 being associated with xmms, these steps will work for any association.

1. Open the GNOME Control Center and select Document Handlers, Default Editor, Mime Types. A long list of existing MIME types is displayed (see Figure 9.9).

2. If your MIME type does not exist, click Add. The type audio/x-mp3 does exist, so for this example, click Edit. The Set Actions dialog will open (see Figure 9.10).

3. Add the file-name extensions that you want to be handled by this association. These are case sensitive, so you may want to add all four: mp3, MP3, m3u, and M3U.

4. GNOME allows separate applications to be associated with the MIME type for the actions open, view, and edit. For MP3 files, open should be defined but it doesn't make sense to define the other actions. Type **xmms %f** into the open field (%f is a placeholder for the file name).

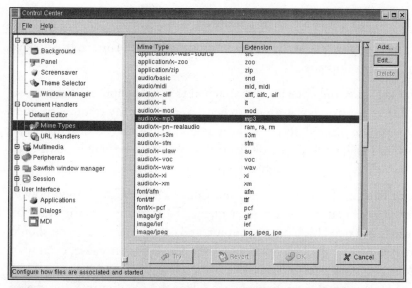

Figure 9.9 *Associating an application with a MIME type in GNOME.*

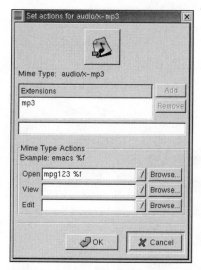

Figure 9.10 *Editing MIME types.*

Streamlining the Printing Process

Although by now you've already set up your printer and hopefully have it working fine, here are two additional customizations that may make it easier to use.

Creating New Print Queues with Common Settings

This customization applies primarily to dot matrix and inkjet printers. If you have a laser printer, you can skip ahead.

Although you likely have only one printer attached to your computer, at times you may use it in different ways. For example, when I'm printing my resume, speed is not an issue. I want the printed output to be as good as possible. At other times—for example, when I am printing a to-do list for the weekend—there is no need to waste extra time or ink creating a high-quality copy.

Chapter 7, "Configuring Printers, Sound, and Other Devices," explained how to configure your printer and create a printer queue. To best support the way you work—sometimes you need high quality output, and other times not—you should actually create two printer queues. Such a setup is convenient because, even if an application does not allow you to define the print quality, you can still control its quality by sending the job to a particular queue. Use the Configure Filter dialog box (shown in Figure 9.11) to configure individual queues.

Creating a Low-Quality Print Queue

Start X while logged in as root and run printtool as you did in the "Printers" section of Chapter 7. Create a new print queue, duplicating the settings of the existing one. Give it a different name, such as "draft." Click Select. Select your printer as before, but choose a lower resolution.

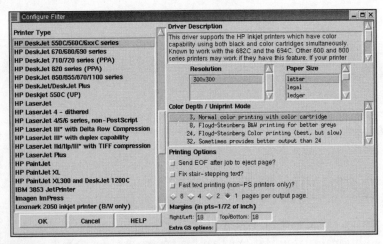

Figure 9.11   *Creating a new print queue.*

Creating a High-Quality Print Queue

Some inkjet printers are capable of slightly overlapping the print passes, so that horizontal banding is lessened. This is often referred to as *weaving* or *interleaving*. If your printer does not do this by default, you might want to add this option to your high-quality print queue. To do so, start printtool and then edit your high-quality print queue. Click the Select button, and locate the Extra GS options field in the lower-right corner of the window. Add either the `-dMicroweave` or `-dSoftweave` option to force interleaving. Not all inkjet printers support these, so you may have to experiment.

Enabling Drag-and-Drop Printing

A printer icon on the desktop to which you can drop files makes printing a snap. This is easy to set up in KDE and GNOME.

KDE

KDE's desktop does not come with a printer icon, but you can set one up very quickly by creating a desktop icon that points to the application klpq (shown in Figure 9.12).

To make the new desktop icon, follow the steps in the next task.

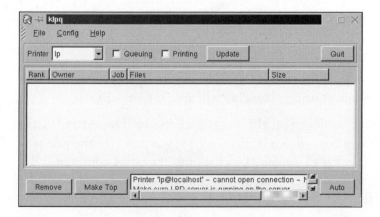

Figure 9.12 *klpq will let you drag-and-drop files to the printer queue.*

TASK

Creating Desktop Icons in KDE

You can create icons to start applications in KDE by following these steps:

1. Right-click your desktop and select New, Application. The krootwm dialog box will appear.

2. Type in a name for the new application's link, such as **klpq.kdelnk**.

3. Click OK. The krootwm dialog box will close and the kfm dialog box will open.

4. Click on the Execute tab. The Execute page will open.

5. Type the command to start the application in the Execute field.

6. Click OK. The kfm dialog box will close and the new icon will appear on the desktop.

After the icon is made, all you need to do is click it and verify that it refers to the correct print queue. It defaults to the BSD style `lpr daemon`, which is correct for Red Hat.

You might want to make a copy of the printer object and modify it for your draft print queue. It's a little difficult with KDE to make a copy of an object on the desktop. You may want to simply make a copy of it from the command line:

```
$ cp ~/Desktop/klpq.kdelnk ~/Desktop/draft.kdelnk
```

If the copy does not appear on the desktop, you may need to right-click on the desktop's background and choose Refresh Desktop. Edit the properties of the copied printer so that it prints to your draft queue rather than to the high-quality queue. For example, on the Execute page, change `klpq %u` to `klpq -Pdraft %u`.

GNOME

To create a drag-and-drop printer icon in GNOME, select Applets, Utility, Printer Applet in the Main Menu. A printer launcher will appear on the panel.

Right-click the printer launcher on the panel and choose Properties. In the Printer Properties dialog box, shown in Figure 9.13, you can give the printer a different name and direct it to a queue by changing the print command. Because of GNOME's session management, these icons will reappear whenever you restart GNOME.

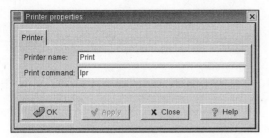

Figure 9.13   *Creating a drag-and-drop printer applet for a queue in GNOME.*

Conclusion

In this chapter, you learned a number of ways to make your desktop more usable, including how to configure virtual desktops, how to make drives mountable from the desktop, and how to start programs automatically when you start X. You also learned how to assign file types to particular programs and how to customize your printer icons. In the Chapter 10, "Installing Software," you will learn how to make Linux even more useful by learning how to install new software.

Chapter 10: Installing Software

Installing Software Packages

Installing Software with Setup

O ne of the biggest complaints about Red Hat Linux, and Linux in general, is its apparent lack of software applications. What good is an operating system that doesn't run anything useful?

First off, this is simply not the case. As any experienced Linux user will tell you, there are thousands of applications that run on Linux. The misperception lies in the fact that many of these applications are either very, very specific in their performed tasks or they are designed to run completely in the background from the command line. In either case, it becomes a case of "out of sight, out of mind." A Linux application is not perceived as "real" by an inexperienced observer unless that observer can see and manipulate the application. This infuriates long-time Linux users, and for good reason.

But if Linux is ever to make an impact on the personal desktop market, Linux distributors must continue to accede to the perceptions of the general public a bit and incorporate more flashy and robust applications within their releases. Red Hat has made significant strides in this direction with the development of GNOME and many of the GNOME-based tool sets.

Still, Linux purists decry this as the "Microsoftization" of their beloved operating system, failing to realize that there is room in Linux for both pure command-line users and pure GNOME users. Even today, Linux is having incredible success in embedded systems, where a graphic user interface is not needed.

To take this a step further, any student of the martial arts will tell you that the best way to stop an opponent's attack is to use the opponent's energy against him—so why not embrace a popular interface? Using this philosophy, Linux will then be in a better position to surpass Microsoft Windows.

When you install applications on Red Hat Linux, there are three ways of accomplishing the task: using packages, using the original source code, or using a third-party setup program. Each of these methods is examined within this chapter.

Installing Software Packages

Nothing is more exciting than opening a new package. Okay, well, a few things are more exciting. But, you must admit, it's kind of cool to crack open that cardboard box and rifle through the Styrofoam peanuts to find that special item you've always wanted.

Packages are great ways of moving objects around. They keep items together and they keep the items protected from both the elements and postal workers. The idea of a package can be used electronically as well. Many of you have already used compressed files, such as Zip, gzip, or tar. These compressed files are essentially packages of separate files that are all mashed together into one compact file.

Red Hat has developed a way to group the open-source code of Linux and its applications into packages as well. This method has proven so popular that many of the other Linux distributions have incorporated it into their tool sets. The method uses the Red Hat Package Manager (RPM) to track packages and their contents for the purpose of installing applications.

RPM comes in many forms. Within Linux, it is known simply as RPM; in GNOME it is GnoRPM; and in KDE it is referred to as Kpackage. Regardless of its form, the application always follows the same procedure: A package is examined, and RPM determines whether all the files necessary for the application to function are contained within the package or anywhere else on your Linux system. This is called a *dependency check*, and it's one of RPM's great features.

The average application requires a lot of code to run, especially in a graphic environment. If all the necessary code were included within every application, the executable files would be huge. To circumvent this, programmers often make use of code libraries, which are essentially redundant pieces of code necessary or useful to all applications. Why make a section of code to create a dialog box when a library of code already has the appropriate information? As a programmer, now all you must do is create a command in your program that references the necessary code in the correct library. Thus, your application is smaller, faster, and easier to install. The catch in all of this is that the user's PC must have the correct type and version of the code library present for use by the application. This is where RPM comes in handy. RPM looks at the packaged application and determines what code libraries (or any other helper application) are required for the packaged application to work. The neat thing is that RPM will look at all packages on your PC. If something is missing, it tells you what is needed to perform a successful installation.

Finally, once the dependencies have been cleared, RPM will enable you to install new applications or upgrade existing ones. The next two sections examine both ways to use RPM.

Installing a New Desktop Environment

In Chapter 4, "Configuring Your Environment," you saw how simple it was to switch between desktop environments. When installing Red Hat, however, you could choose whether to include both environments on your system. For the sake of this example, let's say you only installed GNOME, and now you want to try KDE. The next task shows you what to do.

Installing an environment is something that usually requires more than one package. If you learn how to do this, the installation of a single-package application will be a breeze.

Installing a Desktop Environment

This task guides you through the methods of installing a separate desktop environment on your Linux PC.

1. Click the Main Menu icon to open the Main menu.

2. Choose Programs, System, GnoRPM. The GNOME RPM window opens (see Figure 10.1).

3. Click on the Install button. The Install dialog box opens and begins to scan the Red Hat Linux CD-ROM for available RPM packages (see Figure 10.2).

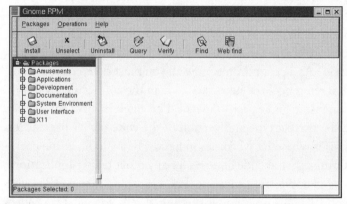

Figure 10.1 *Installation typically begins with the GNOME RPM.*

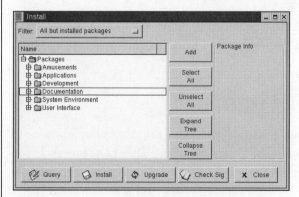

Figure 10.2 *Pick and choose the applications you want to install.*

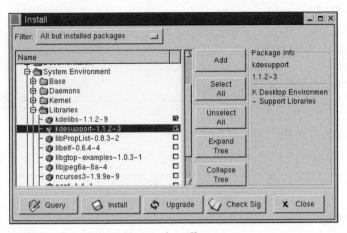

Figure 10.3 *Selecting packages to install.*

4. To install KDE on your GNOME workstation, first expand the System Environment category, and then expand the Libraries subcategory.

5. Select the kdelibs and kdesupport packages. Selected packages are indicated with check marks, as shown in Figure 10.3.

6. Expand the User Interface category and then the Desktops subcategory.

7. Select the kdebase and switchdesk-kde packages.

> If your monitor does not display colors, be sure to select the kdebase-lowcolor-icons package as well.

8. Expand the Amusements category and then the Games subcategory.

9. Select the kdegames package.

10. Click Install to begin the installation process. A dialog box appears that displays the progress of the installation (see Figure 10.4).

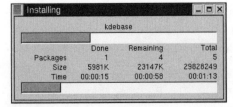

Figure 10.4 *Monitor the process of installing your packages.*

> Don't worry if you miss a package when installing a multi-package set like the KDE desktop environment. If something is missing, a message box will appear informing you of dependencies that need to be added. Just select the necessary packages and click Install again.

11. When complete, click Close.

12. Click the Close application icon to close GNOME RPM.

Using the Update Agent

Everything in the universe moves. Do you think you're sitting still reading this book? Not a chance. You, the chair, the room, and everything else around you are careening through the universe at tremendous speeds. On the other end from the macroscopic, your body is composed of ever-moving atoms.

Nothing is static; all is in motion.

It stands to reason that software constantly evolves. The need to fix what is broken and improve what works is a big driving force in human history, and software engineering is no different. Because we live in a universe of entropy and chaos, it should come as no surprise that the software in the nice white and red box has some flaws. It is, quite literally, a law of nature.

To combat these flaws and improve existing features, Red Hat has provided a great tool in this release of Linux: the Update Agent. The Update Agent is an application that will monitor your installed applications and check the Red Hat FTP site for any newer versions of your programs that may exist. If any are found, it will create a Web-based checklist where you can select the applications you want to upgrade. Update Agent will then coordinate downloading of the packages.

The steps to accomplish this procedure are outlined in the following task.

Using the Update Agent

This task guides you through configuring and using the Red Hat Update Agent.

1. Click the Main Menu icon to open the Main menu.

2. Choose Programs, System, Update Agent. The Red Hat Update Agent window opens (see Figure 10.5).

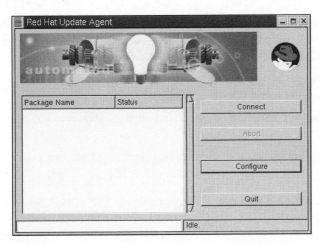

Figure 10.5 *The Red Hat Update Agent, ready for action.*

When using Update Agent, be sure you are already connected to the Internet and have already registered your product with Red Hat at **http://www.redhat.com/now**.

3. To begin using the Update Agent for the first time, click Configure. The Configuration—Up2Date dialog box appears (see Figure 10.6).

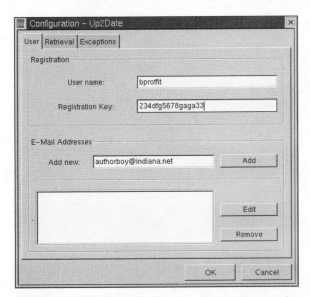

Figure 10.6 *User information is entered in the first panel of the Configuration dialog box.*

4. Enter the name you used when you originally registered your Linux software with Red Hat. You'll need to also provide the registration key from the Personal Product ID card, found in the Red Hat Linux documentation.

5. Enter at least one e-mail address in the Add New field and click Add. You may enter additional e-mail addresses, if applicable.

6. When finished, click the Retrieval tab to open its panel, as shown in Figure 10.7.

7. Verify that the Package Server settings are set to priority.redhat.com.

> To retain control over the upgrading process, be sure to select the option Retrieve Packages, But Do Not Install.

8. Select Red Hat Linux 7 as the override version. The default package storage directory can be left as is, but make a note of the path for later use.

9. Click the Exceptions tab to open its panel, shown in Figure 10.8.

10. The Exceptions panel allows you to skip announced packages and files. To skip additional packages or files, click Add.

> It is not recommended you allow Update Agent to download and install kernel upgrades, so you should make sure that the kernel* exception is present in the Skip Packages section.

Figure 10.7 *You must indicate from where the Update Agent will locate package information.*

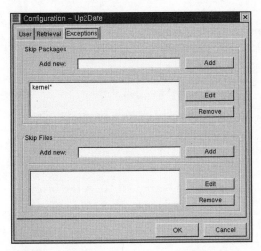

Figure 10.8 *You can choose to skip downloading certain package types.*

11. When finished, click OK. Update Agent is now configured for future use.

12. Click Connect. Update Agent will poll the priority FTP site to determine whether needed updates are available.

13. If any packages are found for those included in the Exceptions panel, a list of those packages will appear in a Warning dialog box (see Figure 10.9). Click OK to continue.

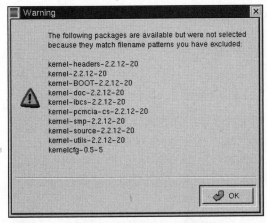

Figure 10.9 *Package exceptions will be listed.*

If you begin to see exceptions listed in the Kernel category, it's a good sign that a new kernel version exists. You should think about compiling it to your system as explained in Chapter 12, "Compiling a Kernel."

14. The Update Agent will process and then display a Web page detailing what packages are available. You can select specific packages and then click Request Selected Packages. Alternatively, you can simply click Request ALL Packages.

15. The download process will begin, as shown in Figure 10.10. A red arrow indicates those packages that were successfully downloaded. When downloading is complete, click Quit.

Now that the updated packages reside on your local PC, you can install them using GnoRPM, as detailed in the previous section. The only difference in the procedure is that you will now need to locate the packages on your PC by clicking Add while in the Install dialog box. Once the packages are selected, you will then need to select the Upgrade option rather than Install.

Installing Software with Setup

As more applications are built for Linux, the size and complexity of the applications will increase. As this happens, developers will start using entire setup applications to install programs. Windows users are very familiar with these types

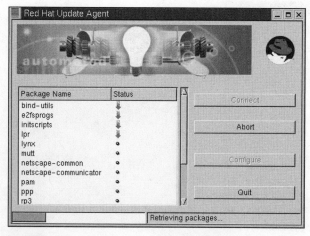

Figure 10.10 *Downloading the selected packages.*

of setup applications—virtually every Windows application makes use of an installation program of some type.

Using similar applications in Linux is just as simple. The following task demonstrates how StarOffice, a robust and free office suite, is installed on Red Hat Linux.

> You can download the StarOffice installation file from **www.sun.com/staroffice**. Follow the instructions on the Web site to get the file.

Installing StarOffice 5.2 Using Setup

Complete this task to install StarOffice 5.2 for Linux.

1. Open a terminal window on your GNOME or KDE desktop and navigate to the directory where you saved the installation file.

> You may need to type **chmod 777 *.bin** before starting the setup in order to give yourself permission to run the downloaded file.

2. Type **./so-5_2-ga-bin-linux-en.bin**. This starts the installation program, as shown in Figure 10.11.

3. The first dialog box welcomes you and tells you how to quit the program. Click Next to continue.

Figure 10.11   *The StarOffice Installation program.*

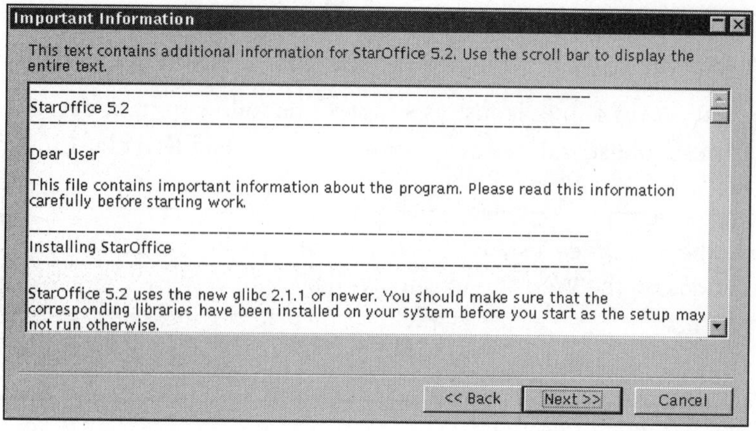

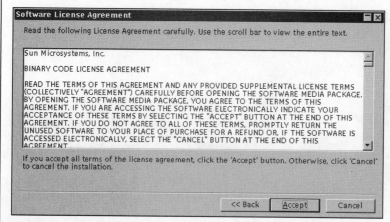

Figure 10.12 *A good chance to read the README file.*

4. In the second dialog box (see Figure 10.12), you see the Important Information dialog box, which essentially displays the README file. Read the contents, and click Next to continue.

5. The next dialog box presents the Sun license agreement to you (see Figure 10.13). Read it carefully and click Accept if you agree to its stipulations.

6. In the fourth screen, enter your personal data and click Next.

7. Choose which installation type you want, as shown in Figure 10.14. For now, select the Standard Installation choice and click Next to continue. Don't worry, you can always come back later to customize your settings.

8. Choose the directory to which you want to install StarOffice (see Figure 10.15). The suggested default directory is usually a safe bet. Click Next to continue.

Figure 10.13 *Good reading? No, but important nonetheless.*

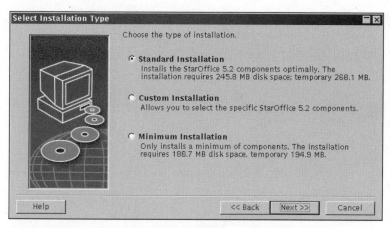

Figure 10.14 *Choose between Standard, Custom, or Minimum Installations.*

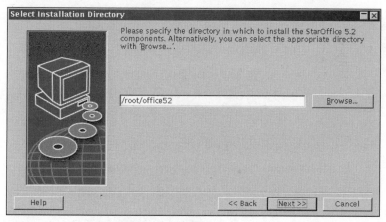

Figure 10.15 *Select the installation directory.*

9. When asked whether the directory name you entered or accepted should be created, click Yes.

10. You have reached the end of this section of the installation journey (see Figure 10.16). Click Complete, and then sit back and relax while installation is completed.

11. If the setup application cannot find a Java environment on your PC, it asks you what, if any, Java environment you want StarOffice to use. If you do not plan to use the StarOffice browser as your main Web browser—which I don't recommend—then there's no problem. Just click No Support for Java or JavaScript and then click OK to continue. StarOffice continues its installation, as shown in Figure 10.17.

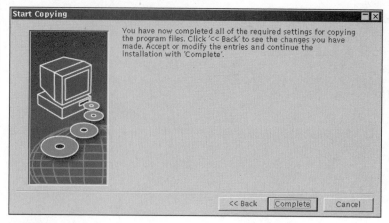

Figure 10.16 *You have given StarOffice all the information it needs. Click Complete and let it do the work.*

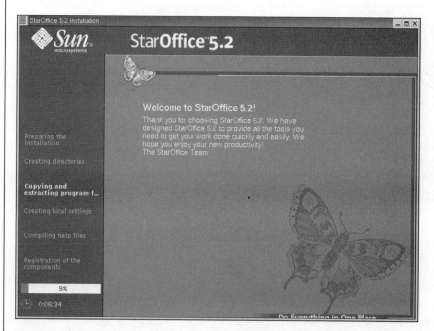

Figure 10.17 *The automated installation process, complete with advertisements.*

12. Near the end of the installation process, a message box appears, indicating that StarOffice was added to the KDE panel (even if KDE is not your default desktop environment). It also advises that you should restart KDE to complete the installation for that environment. Click OK to continue.

13. At the very end of the process, the Installation Complete dialog box appears. Click Complete to end the setup program.

When you want to start StarOffice in KDE, you will find it within the Application Starter menu. In GNOME, the fastest way to start StarOffice is to create a new launcher in the GNOME window or panel. See Chapter 9, "Customizing Your Desktop's Usability," for more information.

Conclusion

This chapter examined the three primary methods used to get new software on your program: RPMs, source code, and setup applications. As Linux grows in popularity, you can expect that these processes will become even more automated.

Chapter 11, "Adding New Hardware," journeys into another installation realm of Red Hat Linux: installing hardware. From /proc files to linking new kernel drivers, there's a lot to learn about configuring machines to talk to each other.

Adding new hardware to a system consists of two phases: the hardware phase and the software phase. You need to add the hardware device to the system, and you need to tell your operating system how it should be managed. The hardware phase is machine dependent, and the software phase is operating system dependent. Assuming you are working on a PC, regardless of its brand (AT, ATX, IBM, Compaq, and so on), installing new hardware is straightforward and is the same whether you are using Linux or some other operating system. The interface of the PC system is made in such a way that any device can be accessed in a standard and documented method, and any operating system can then handle it. (There are a few exceptions to this rule that are discussed later in this chapter.)

In this chapter, both phases are discussed, but more emphasis is placed on the second phase because it is perhaps the most confusing. You may have installed new devices such as printers or sound cards in the past, but you may not be familiar with the way Linux handles them. First, you will see the various types of devices, including internal and external ones, with a warning about those devices you can safely install and those you should not touch unless you are a computer expert. Then, you will learn how the Linux kernel detects and configures hardware devices. You'll learn about the various configuration files and how you can change parameters for your new devices. Finally, you will learn about Plug and Play (PnP) devices.

Similar to the steps you took before installing Red Hat Linux, before beginning any installation you should check the hardware compatibility list to see if your device is Linux compatible. In theory, any device conforming to the standards in PC technologies should work. However, in recent years many companies have started to make devices that were missing several important chips and then using proprietary drivers to do their work. Although making devices less expensive to the public, this strategy has resulted in two big side effects. The drivers are published for Windows 95/98 only, and, because the hardware device cannot work without the special Windows driver, it is incompatible with Linux or any operating system other than Windows. Secondly, the driver needs to do much more work, which means that your CPU will be busy doing what the chips were supposed to do. Hence, your system will feel much slower, even in Windows. The sad thing about this is that most of these components, commonly referred as *winmodems* and *winprinters*, are not identified as such on the packages. Contacting the manufacturer is often the only way you can be sure.

Adding New Devices

In this section, you will see the different types of devices that can be added to a personal computer and how they differ from each other. Table 11.1 lists a few common hardware devices and their specifications, which may help you to configure them.

Table 11.1   Common Hardware Devices

Device	Internal/ External	Type of Plug	Auto-Detected?
Modems	External	COM port (/dev/cua0)	No, easy to set up
Modems	Internal	ISA or PCI	No, configuration needed
Monitors	External	VGA port	Yes
Video cards mode: no	Internal	PCI or AGP	In text mode: yes; in GUI
RAM	Internal	Sockets	Yes
Sound cards	Internal	ISA or PCI	No, configuration needed
Mice	External	COM port (/dev/cua0)	Yes, for standard models

Adding External Devices

External devices are the easiest to add because you simply plug them in. Further, because no vital system part is outside the case, you don't risk corrupting your machine. You can install an external device even if you are still new to computers. For example, to add a printer, you simply connect the printer cable to both the printer and the back of the computer and then plug in the power supply.

There are many types of external devices. Specific devices exist for each of the ports on the back of your system, and, because they all have different socket sizes, you really can't connect the wrong device to the wrong port. For example, a standard parallel printer port is a female connection with 25 holes, and a mouse or modem serial port is a male connection containing either 9 or 25 pins. You already know how to connect a printer to your machine; connecting any other external device (keyboard, monitor, mouse, Zip drive, Ethernet-based cable modem) is just as easy.

For instance, if you want to add an Ethernet device to your system, it is generally recommended that you turn off the power before adding any new device. Most manuals also warn you of this fact. This will allow three things:

- The system BIOS will attempt to detect the new device when you reboot.
- The kernel auto-detect process will detect the device (this is discussed in the section "What is Auto-Detection?").
- The device will benefit from a fresh system start.

Some devices won't work right if they are plugged in while the power is on, especially external removable drives. Note that this does not apply to hot-swappable devices, such as special RAID arrays or rack-mounted servers, but most personal desktop systems do not use these device types.

Adding Internal Devices

Internal devices are more difficult to install only because they require you to work inside your computer case. Thankfully, very few devices need to be added in this way. With the advent of external removable devices such as the Iomega Zip drive and the universal serial bus (USB), it isn't necessary to crack open the computer case nearly as often.

The most common internal devices are sound cards, network cards, and hard drives. In most systems, you can also add memory, change the motherboard, or even upgrade the CPU, although I would advise you against doing so unless you know exactly what you are doing. There are factors to consider when changing a CPU and memory such as bus speed, clock multiplier, and memory timing. For a fee, local computer stores will gladly install any internal device you require. This section briefly shows you how to add the three most common internal hardware devices.

First, for your physical safety, you must turn off your computer's power. This is especially important when you are working with internal devices because you can literally blow up your motherboard or CPU if you try to install internal hardware with the power on.

After you have turned off the power and unscrewed the screws to remove the case, you can add the device in an empty slot. If you want to add a device that has a standard card, you simply have to insert it next to the other cards in your system. Any slot on the PCI bus (the white ones) will work for a PCI card; any slot on the ISA bus (the black ones) will work for ISA cards. Video cards may go in the recently introduced AGP slot (the gray one). It's easy to determine the three types of slots because each has a different size and color. You can't plug an ISA card into a PCI bus slot by accident.

A hard drive is typically added near the front of the case, grouped with the existing hard drives and CD-ROM drives. After positioning the drive, you must connect the power cable and its ribbon. Ribbons connect the drive to its controlling card. (If you are working with a SCSI hard drive, the SCSI controller is either on your main board or on a slotted card.) Be sure to refer to the manual for your device for proper installation procedures.

The Kernel Boot Process

Once the system is turned back on, some program code is executed to detect and configure new devices. The first code executed when a PC starts is the bootstrap code, which is a small program located in static memory (ROM) inside your computer. The code checks the internal system parts to see if any major failure can be detected, such as memory corruption.

Control is then passed to your BIOS, which is the heart of your input/output (I/O) subsystem. Its job is to detect the system components at start time and to work with the operating system to handle device calls. The code that appears on your monitor just after the video card name and before Linux starts is part of the BIOS. You may see a list of hard disks and then an information screen about your main system components. The BIOS is responsible for first detecting your hard disks, determining which one contains the kernel you want to boot, and optionally configuring any Plug and Play devices.

Once the BIOS completes its various functions, control is passed to the first sector of your bootable hard disk (known as the Master Boot Record, or MBR for short). The MBR was used to contain DOS-MBR if you used MS-DOS or Windows; it now contains LILO, the Linux boot loader, which simply tells the processor to load your Linux kernel.

> LILO can, in fact, do much more, such as set a password, load many operating systems, and set disk geometry information for Linux. For the purpose of this chapter, it is assumed that only the kernel is loaded. You can find more information on LILO by typing **man lilo** at the command line.

Once the BIOS and LILO have finished executing, the really complex part begins. The Linux kernel takes over and must detect, configure, and manage all the internal and external devices. It does that using complicated data structures, device drivers, and kernel processes. All the text that appears on the screen before you see the first Linux prompt explains what is being found by the kernel and various device drivers (see Figure 11.1). It is important for you to understand that text so that you can later troubleshoot any hardware problems:

- The first line displays the kernel version and the version of the compiler that built it. It isn't really important to know this unless you later want to recompile your kernel.

- Next, the speed of your CPU is displayed. That speed is detected at boot time by the kernel. It should be pretty close to the speed you know your CPU to be. For example, the CPU on the system shown in Figure 12.1 is a 333MHz Intel Pentium II; the kernel detected a speed of 334MHz, which is pretty close.

- The console line tells you the currently used display font. You can set your Linux console to display any other font, but the default is standard fixed VGA 80 columns by 25 lines.

- You should ignore the line about BogoMIPS. It is commonly not the same as your CPU speed, and that is quite normal.

- One very important line is the memory line. Here, the kernel is reporting how much RAM it detected in your system. This is a place where the kernel may be mistaken, especially if you have more than 128MB of memory or if you have an old system. The details as to why this happens are unimportant, but it is easy to fix. For example, if you see a number near 16000K and you really have 24MB of RAM, you will need to correct the kernel; you'll learn how in the "LILO" section later in this chapter.

- The next lines display information gathered about your CPU.

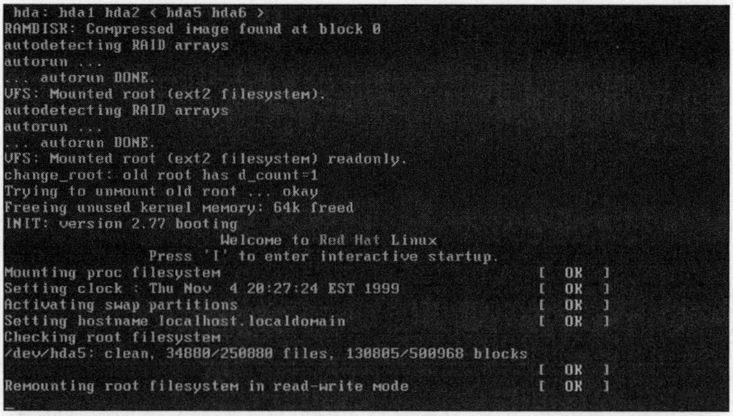

```
hda: hda1 hda2 < hda5 hda6 >
RAMDISK: Compressed image found at block 0
autodetecting RAID arrays
autorun ...
... autorun DONE.
VFS: Mounted root (ext2 filesystem).
autodetecting RAID arrays
autorun ...
... autorun DONE.
VFS: Mounted root (ext2 filesystem) readonly.
change_root: old root has d_count=1
Trying to unmount old root ... okay
Freeing unused kernel memory: 64k freed
INIT: version 2.77 booting
                    Welcome to Red Hat Linux
            Press 'I' to enter interactive startup.
Mounting proc filesystem                              [  OK  ]
Setting clock : Thu Nov  4 20:27:24 EST 1999          [  OK  ]
Activating swap partitions                            [  OK  ]
Setting hostname localhost.localdomain                [  OK  ]
Checking root filesystem
/dev/hda5: clean, 34800/250880 files, 130005/500968 blocks
                                                      [  OK  ]
Remounting root filesystem in read-write mode         [  OK  ]
```

Figure 11.1 *The boot process can inform you of any potential problems.*

> You should print the boot messages and read them all at least once. This will help you know your hardware a bit more and can help you diagnose problems. If you can't print messages while your system is booting, you can always review them by typing the `dmesg` command at your Linux console. If you have a printer attached, you can print the messages using the command `dmesg |lpr`.

When the kernel has finished setting up the main hardware, it passes control to device drivers, which are small portions of code that can set up and control a particular device. For example, to handle a SoundBlaster card, you need a SoundBlaster-compatible sound driver. There are also less specific drivers that deal with things such as networking and your serial devices. All of these drivers are loaded at start time.

What Is Auto-Detection?

The device drivers must configure your hardware to work with Linux. These drivers, however, must first find the hardware. Fortunately, Linux has a very good auto-detection process, in which drivers look in the likely places to see if a device can be found. For example, the NE2000 networking card driver knows that such a card will most likely be located at I/O address 0x300, 0x280, 0x320, 0x340, 0x360, or 0x380; it probes these addresses to see if a card can be found. If found, a message appears on the screen when your system starts.

If your card is at another address, however, the driver may not find it and you must tell the driver where to look. These settings can be found using various methods. If you have older hardware, settings can be altered using jumpers on the board itself. The default settings can usually be found in the board's manual, including the method used to change them.

Red Hat Linux 7 features a utility called Kudzu, which attempts to detect new hardware on startup. Kudzu is an advanced form of device auto-detection. It keeps a database of installed hardware and, when the system starts, compares the installed hardware with the database. If new hardware is detected, Kudzu should allow you to configure it. This utility does not make your job much easier if your device isn't detected by the Linux kernel, but I believe that Red Hat will be moving in that direction in the future. You can review the database by looking at the file /etc/sysconfig/hwconf.

Configuring Your Devices

The main devices in a system have device drivers already compiled in the kernel and will be detected on system startup. These include your CPU, memory, monitor, video card, floppy drive, IDE hard disks, and most CD-ROM drives—which means that most of the time you needn't worry about them. This section focuses on those devices that may not be so easily detected.

If a device is not detected at startup time, you first must determine whether the driver for that component was loaded. A driver can be loaded in two ways: by being compiled into the kernel itself or by being loaded as a module, which is a separate piece of code that works with the kernel to run your device. Although this may seem complex, Red Hat has made it very simple, providing several graphical utilities that enable you to easily configure most new devices. Because most drivers have been compiled into modules, you will seldom need to recompile your kernel.

To determine whether a device has been detected, you can use the command `cat /proc/devices`; this command lists all devices detected by your Linux system that access an IRQ.

Red Hat Utilities

Various Red Hat utilities can help you configure the most common hardware devices and protocols. Many of these utilities, including kernelcfg, timetool, printtool, and netcfg, must be run in the graphical mode. To see a complete list of utilities available on your Red Hat system, type **setup** for console-based utilities and **control-panel** for graphical ones.

> You must be logged in as root on your Red Hat Linux 7 machine to use Red Hat's various configuration utilities.

Configuring Your Sound Card with sndconfig

As you read in Chapter 7, "Configuring Printers, Sound, and Other Devices," you can configure a sound card by typing **sndconfig** at your Linux prompt. Doing so opens a sound configuration utility, called sndconfig, that can detect and configure many sound cards. It probes your system to find a Plug and Play card and reports what was detected. It then tests the sound card. If the test is successful, the utility saves the information and closes. If not, it tells you what went wrong and allows you to manually select a card. If this doesn't work, you may be

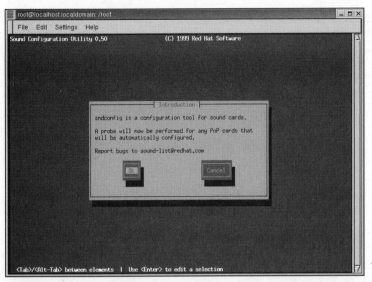

Figure 11.2 *sndconfig is the best way to add sound to your PC.*

forced to troubleshoot the device (see the section in this chapter titled "Trouble-shooting" for more information).

The sndconfig utility, shown in Figure 11.2, uses a probe that is part of the small but very useful package isapnptools. This package detects any ISA Plug and Play device and then allows you (or in this case, the sound utility) to set a small configuration file in the /etc directory. This file enables your Linux kernel to detect the sound card the next time it boots. The isapnptools package is also useful in trouble-shooting any type of ISA Plug and Play device; its documentation is available in the /usr/doc directory.

An interesting thing about sndconfig is the method it uses to handle modules. Selecting a card and parameters for that card results in the creation of a small configuration file called /etc/conf.modules, which lists all the modules loaded at startup, not just for sound cards.

Configuring Your Ethernet Card with netcfg

/etc/conf.modules is a very important configuration file because it contains all device parameters. For example, my NE2000 Ethernet card requires the following two lines in conf.modules:

```
alias eth0 ne
options ne io=0x220
```

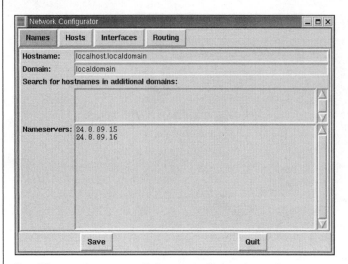

Figure 11.3   *netcfg gets your Ethernet card up and running.*

You will often find two lines in conf.modules, the first telling Linux which module to load and the second specifying which options to set. In this case, the module for the first Ethernet card (eth0) is ne; the card should be located at I/O address 0x220.

You can also test modules from the command line. For example, to load the NE2000 module with the parameters shown above, simply type **insmod ne io=0x200**.

Another card you may need to configure is an Ethernet card, whether it is used to link your computer to a local network or as a cable modem for Internet access. To do so, you use the utility called netcfg (see Figure 11.3); click Interfaces to add a new card. You should select Ethernet in the list of possible devices (note that PPP is also present, which means that you can configure a basic PPP interface with netcfg).

> netcfg will not add networking modules to /etc/conf.modules and will assume the module is already loaded at bootup time. You may need to add the module yourself, as discussed in the section "Using Modules."

Video Configuration

Video configuration can be unusual and requires a bit of discussion. Every device is handled by a driver, but the video card must also be recognized by the X server. Although every other device must be detected by a driver at the time you boot your system, you must tell X what video card you have so that everything looks right when you go into graphical mode. Therefore, if you install a new video card, you will need to run the Xconfigurator utility. Xconfigurator will ask you for the card's information so that your system won't fail the next time you use graphical mode as your Linux desktop. The same is true for your mouse.

External Devices

Similar to sound cards and other internal devices, external devices are also configured with drivers. For example, if you add a printer, you must run the printtool utility to tell Linux which printer you installed, to which port it is connected (usually lp0), and which filter to use. The *filter* is the type of printer you have, which you learned about in Chapter 7. In the same way, the current date and time can be changed using timetool (see Figure 11.4).

Configuring Modems

Configuring a modem can be a very complex process, especially when combined with the process of connecting to an Internet provider. Fortunately, graphical tools are available to help with configuration issues.

The first thing you must do is get your system to recognize the modem. Red Hat Linux systems recognize external modems; the process for internal modems, however, is complex.

Most modems are ISA Plug and Play modems and can be detected with the isapnptools package. Start by running the pnpdump utility to determine whether your system detects the modem. PCI modems should be detected automatically, but you may need to change the Plug and Play settings in your BIOS to enable them to work. Consult your BIOS manual to find out how to properly configure your PnP settings.

Figure 11.4 *timetool synchronizes your PC with the time and date.*

If your modem should be detected but is not or if the modem is detected but refuses to work, you may have what is called a "winmodem." Such a modem lacks several important chips and will never work outside of Windows 95/98. If you need to buy a new modem, I suggest that you purchase one that is external—sure not to be a winmodem.

After the modem has been detected, you can use one of the many graphical dial-out clients such as gnome-ppp or kppp to connect to your Internet provider.

Using Modules

Ordinarily, you must edit conf.modules manually, using a text editor such as vi. Thankfully, Red Hat Linux includes a neat utility to help you with this task: kernelcfg, which you start by typing **kernelcfg** on your console. In this utility, you can select a type of module to add, such as networking, and which module you want to load. Then you can specify parameters to pass to the module. You can also edit and remove modules from the same utility.

Modules are useful because you can add functionality to the kernel without recompiling. Hardware manufacturers use modules to provide hardware support without releasing the source code to the Linux community. For example, last year Creative Labs released a Linux driver for its SoundBlaster Live card and then posted both its module and installation instructions on its Web page.

USB

A few pages regarding universal serial bus (USB) devices have been included here for two reasons. First, the USB bus is unlike any other port on your system. Although you can't connect a monitor to a serial port, or a modem to your keyboard port, you can connect any type of supported device to a USB port. There are USB monitors, modems, network interfaces, mice, sound devices, scanners, printers, and so on. Because of this, USB is the wave of the future—which is the second reason USB is discussed.

USB is a bus. It may look like a simple port on your system, but its inner working is unlike the other ports. On a serial port, unless you use some special circuit workaround, only one device can be connected. On a USB port, you can connect hundreds of devices. Additionally, you can connect a USB hub to the USB port; hubs offer 6 or 12 ports to connect various other devices. Another interesting thing about USB is that it provides electrical power to the devices connected. Most serial devices must be plugged directly into an electrical outlet, but many USB devices don't have the same requirements. Devices that require a large amount of power include a power supply, but many won't.

When configuring USB in Linux, you must be aware that there are two parts of the USB bus to be supported: the USB controller and the device. USB controllers are made by various companies, but they follow a few standards. Linux currently supports those that comply with the UHCI and OHCI standards. Most USB controllers comply, so your controller should be supported.

Although there are many USB devices now on the market, not all are supported. Table 11.2 lists a few of the supported, popular USB devices. For a complete list and more information about the devices listed below, refer to the USB project Web site, **www.linux-usb.org**.

Table 11.2   Supported USB Devices

Type of Device	Supported Models
Mice and keyboards	Many Logitech USB mice are supported, including the N48, M-BA47 and Wingman Gaming Mouse. The Microsoft IntelliMouse Explorer is supported also. A few keyboards from Belkin, Cherry, Chicony and QTronix are supported.
Video and imaging products	The ZoomCam 1595, Kodak DC 240, 260, and Mustek MDC 800 are supported.
Hub devices	The USBH-600 hub from ADS Technologies is supported. Asante FriendlyNet also makes a supported hub. The Cherry MY3000 and Edimax hubs are also supported.
Mass storage	The Iomega USB 100MB Zip drive is supported.
Printers	The Lexmark Optra S 2450 is supported.
Audio devices	The Philips Electronics USB Digital Speaker System is partially supported.
Scanners	HP Scanjet 4100C and 6300C scanners are supported.
Misc. devices	The Anchorchips EZUSB and Cypress Thermometer are supported.

You should note that all the supported devices are not in your current kernel. You *may* need to download a recent development kernel and may also need third-party software. Kernel 2.2.7 and later contain the basic USB code and support for a few devices. Each new kernel supports new devices. You must also recompile the kernel to enable USB support in the configuration screen, where you also must enable support for a controller and device.

You can determine whether USB support was installed correctly and whether your USB device was loaded by looking at the logs in /var/log/messages. Once the controller is detected, you can start configuring your devices.

Configuring a USB Mouse

If you have a USB mouse, begin configuring it by creating the device node like so:

```
mknod /dev/usbmouse0 c 180 16
```

When complete, edit your XF86Config file and change the protocol to IMPS/2 and the port to /dev/usbmouse0.

Configuring a USB Keyboard

USB keyboards should require no configuration; they should work normally. Make sure that your BIOS supports the USB keyboard by contacting your manufacturer.

Configuring a USB Printer

To support a USB printer, create a special device node using this command line:

```
mknod /dev/usblp0 c 180 0
```

When complete, you can configure the printer like any other printer in your /etc/ printcap file or by using the printtool utility.

Troubleshooting

When everything fails, it's time to troubleshoot. This section introduces a few actions you can take to make Linux detect your hardware and where you can look for the scripts that control the bootup process and the detection of new hardware.

Before looking for scripts to modify, refer to any manuals and other documentation that came with your system and with the device you are trying to install.

Although they may not talk about Linux configuration, they will include useful information such as the IRQ and I/O ports supported by the device.

You should also determine the purpose for any jumpers that may exist on the device. Some newer devices don't have jumpers, but you should check any troublesome devices to see whether they exist.

LILO

The initial system configuration is done in /etc/lilo.conf. This file tells LILO what parameters to pass to the kernel, which file is the actual kernel, and which hard disk should be booted on startup. If you have problems with the initial startup, type **man lilo.conf** to refer to the complete syntax of commands.

One such parameter you may need to add is the amount of memory (RAM) you have. If Linux detects 16MB and you know you have 24MB, add the following line to the configuration file:

```
append = "mem=24M"
```

If you have a problem where a device is not detected by the kernel, you need to look elsewhere for a solution. For example, most drivers are loaded from the configuration and startup scripts, as we will examine in the next sections.

Configuration Scripts

The scripts used by the Red Hat utilities are stored in /etc/sysconfig, which contains files describing the mouse, network card, network configuration, and PCMCIA. Unless you are confident that you know exactly what you are doing, you should not attempt to modify any file in this subdirectory.

If you find that the Red Hat utilities are not able to complete the settings you require and you have tried everything else, you may need to edit the configuration files manually. They are text files, so you can edit them with your favorite text editor—but again, you must be very careful. You may want to check the Red Hat Linux Web site to search for a solution to your specific problem before delving into this procedure.

Startup Scripts

The scripts that display PASSED or FAILED on the screen when you boot your system are stored in /etc/rc.d. You may need to edit one of these scripts if you can see (by looking at the bootup messages) that a parameter needs to be changed for one driver.

The way startup files are installed on your Red Hat Linux system is called *System V init*. This means that each startup script is stored in /etc/rc.d/init.d and is linked to the other rc.d directories. Each file can also be called to perform three actions: start, stop, and restart. For example, if you want to stop the httpd device, you could type the following:

```
/etc/rc.d/init.d/httpd stop
```

The most pertinent file concerning device drivers is /etc/conf.modules, which specifies all the modules and options that will be loaded at boot time. You can use the kernelcfg utility to configure this file; you may need to edit the file by hand to add more modules or to change some settings. The modules are always loaded first, and then the Option line gives the parameters to these modules.

The only way to know those options accepted by a module is by looking at the kernel documentation. Sometimes the Documentation directory contains information about the driver you want to load. In other cases, however, you must look in the source files themselves. You may also want to ask for that information in Internet newsgroups.

A Note about Plug and Play

Plug and Play (PnP) is a Microsoft and Intel standard designed to make detection of hardware easier. It has both good and bad effects. Both ISA and PCI devices can be Plug and Play. The PCI bus has been constructed so that every device can be configured with Plug and Play. This is a good thing and makes configuration easier. However, a few ISA cards are also Plug and Play. This makes things more complicated because not all ISA Plug and Play devices behave in the same way. The isapnptools package has been made to handle these ISA Plug and Play devices.

If you know you have Plug and Play devices (and most computer users do…) and your BIOS is Plug and Play aware, a setting exists in your CMOS set up to turn on or off Plug and Play configuration in the BIOS. In most cases it is easier to set this to on so the BIOS can assign IRQ and I/O ports to all the Plug and Play cards. You then only provide the correct parameters to the drivers.

Conclusion

Adding new devices is always a mystery. You add a piece of hardware and hope that the system will see it. Sometimes it works, sometimes it doesn't. Then begins the perhaps long and complex task of troubleshooting. Thankfully, the Linux system becomes better every year, and with new kernel releases, more hardware is auto-detected. With more users, Linux also has more developers working on drivers for the latest and greatest devices sold at your local computer store. Hopefully, more companies will wake up and start making drivers for Linux and not only for Windows 98. Doing so would help users a great deal, thus solving many problems that exist with unsupported hardware.

In Chapter 12, "Compiling a Kernel," you will learn how to take advantage of all these kernel improvements by recompiling the kernel, Linux's comprehensive way of upgrading itself.

Chapter 12: Compiling a Kernel

I'm sometimes asked why a Red Hat Linux user should bother to compile his system's kernel. After all, the Red Hat version installs a compiled kernel, along with the kernel modules to support many types of hardware. Wouldn't that work well enough?

The Advantages of Compiling Your Own Kernel

Red Hat's precompiled kernel may work well enough for you; that is for you to decide. Compiling your own kernel, however, yields numerous significant advantages:

- Speed
- Stability
- The addition of new features
- The ability to modify the source code and apply patches

Speed

A kernel you compile yourself will almost certainly be faster than the stock Red Hat kernel, for three basic reasons:

- By selecting support for only the hardware you have, your customized kernel will be smaller than Red Hat's generic one. This leaves more memory for programs, so your machine will swap a little less. This will be most noticeable on machines with little RAM.

- You can use a newer compiler. The compiler used on Linux (egcs, also known as gcc) tends to have a new release every several months. Sometimes these releases introduce new optimization techniques, which may slightly speed up your kernel.

- You can compile your kernel to take advantage of your particular processor's features. Red Hat's generic kernel cannot do this, because it must boot a wide range of machines. Red Hat's kernel must be widely compatible, whereas you have the option of trading some of that compatibility for speed.

Stability

Another important reason to compile your own kernel is to fix bugs in the one shipped with Red Hat. The Linux kernel tends to be very stable (I have run production

BUZZWORD

Kernel module: A piece of code that can be inserted into or removed from a running Linux kernel. Kernel modules are used to add functionality to a kernel, without taking up RAM when the functionality is not needed. Conceptually, they are similar to device drivers under Windows or extensions for the Macintosh, except they can be added and removed dynamically, meaning while the device with which they are associated is still running. You will also see them referred to as *loadable modules*, because the Linux kernel can automatically load them when they are needed.

servers on it for months on end without any problems), but if you have exotic hardware or use your computer in unusual ways, you may encounter problems. These are fixed over time, so getting the latest, most stable kernel may eliminate problems.

> Occasionally, Red Hat will release an updated, compiled kernel, typically if a serious bug is found in the shipped version. If you want to stay current with the smaller fixes, however, you will have to compile your own.

Furthermore, compiling your own kernel lets you pick and choose what parts of it you want to include. After all, the less code in your kernel (or in any piece of software), the less chance there is for problems.

Features

In theory, each patch level of the kernel should only fix bugs and perhaps improve performance. In practice, though, new features and device support do creep in along with the fixes. If a new piece of hardware is not well supported under your current kernel, try a newer one. Support may be improved.

Modifying the Source Code and Applying Patches

The last reason for compiling your own kernel cuts to the heart of Linux: You have the source code, and you can modify it however you like to better suit your needs. Perhaps you are a student studying computer science, or an entrepreneur with some slightly unusual computer needs, or simply someone who likes to tinker. The Linux source code is there for you to change. Once the source is modified, you can then just recompile the new source code in the kernel, and your changes will be implemented, for good or ill.

If you don't want to modify the source yourself, numerous patches prepared by other people are available on the Internet. A *patch* is a set of modifications to the kernel source that change the kernel's behavior in some way. For example, suppose you are short on disk space. By compiling your own kernel with a compression patch, you can have an otherwise standard system that also supports transparent file compression.

> Because this is not a programming book, this chapter focuses more on the addition of new patches to the kernel rather than user-modified source code.

Compiling the Kernel: An Overview

Compiling your Linux kernel is a fairly safe process; it is also relatively simple. First, you must get the latest kernel source. Although the kernel source is included on the Red Hat CD, you may want to download it from the Internet so that you have the latest features and bug fixes.

Next, you must install the kernel source. Optionally, you can patch the kernel source. (If you want to change the kernel, either with an official update or a third-party modification, you will need to understand the patching process.)

After the kernel source is installed (and patched, if necessary), you must configure the kernel, selecting the components to include in your kernel. Including only what you need leads to a small, reliable kernel. After you configure the kernel, you must compile it and the kernel modules. Finally, you must install your new kernel.

Obtaining the Kernel Source

You can download the kernel sources from many places on the Internet, including Red Hat's site (**ftp://ftip.rehat.com**), which provides the kernel sources in RPM format. Alternatively, you can download the kernel from the de-facto Linux kernel archive, found at **http://www.kernel.org**. Other major sites carrying the Linux kernel include **ftp://metalab.unc.edu/pub/linux/kernel/** and **ftp://ftp.tux.org/kernel/**.

> Mirrors for the **http://www.kernel.org** site exist worldwide, so you may want to download from the one closest to you to avoid getting into a download traffic jam. You can either follow the link from **http://www.kernel.org** to the mirror sites or go directly to a mirror with a URL such as **ftp://ftp.us.kernel.org/pub/linux/kernel/** (replace "us" with your own two-letter country code).

If you do not have an Internet connection—or if your connection is slow and you are impatient—you can install and use the kernel sources included on the Red Hat CD-ROM. The package name is kernel-source. Red Hat's kernel sources, however, tend to lag behind what is available on the Internet, and they cannot easily be updated via patches. If it is possible for you to get the latest sources from the Internet in tar.gz or tar.bz2 format, I strongly recommend that you do so rather than using Red Hat's RPM. The .bz2 format especially tends have better compression, resulting in shorter download times. (If you download the .bz2 archive, you'll also need the bzip2 package so that the archive can be uncompressed.)

Understanding the Kernel-Numbering System

As you've probably noticed, these sites contain hundreds of versions of the Linux kernel, all the way back to the first public version from nearly a decade ago. In order to determine which kernel you should get, you must understand the version-numbering scheme.

Versions of Linux kernels consist of three numbers separated by dots:

- The first number is the major version number, which changes very rarely.
- The second number is the minor version number. By convention, odd minor version numbers indicate a development kernel, while even numbers are used for stable kernels. Unless you intend to help the Linux kernel development effort, you should get a stable version.
- The last number indicates the patch level. This is incremented every time a set of bugs is fixed.

You may see a kernel version with a suffix, such as 2.2.16–21 (the kernel shipped with Red Hat 7) or 2.2.14pre7. Red Hat uses the first form to indicate fixes made to the named kernel. Therefore, 2.2.16–21 is somewhere between standard 2.2.16 and standard 2.2.21 kernels. The second form indicates a pre-release; bug fixes are collected in the 2.2.14pre series before the true 2.2.14 is released.

> If you are eager for a bug fix introduced in an intervening release, by all means, use that release. If you can wait, however, you should probably stick with the previous stable release until the next official version is released.

If you've installed Red Hat 7, you already have the latest 2.2 kernel, so it may be a while before you are ready to install a new kernel. For this reason, all the examples in the rest of this chapter use hypothetical kernel versions.

Installing the Kernel Source

Now that you have downloaded your kernel source (let's assume the source, the *imaginary* version 2.4.15, was contained in the hypothetical format file .tar.bz2 and resides in your /tmp directory), you must install it in the /usr/src directory:

```
$ cd /usr/src
$ tar --use=bzip2 -xf /tmp/linux-2.4.15.tar.bz2
```

If you list the directory, you'll notice that a linux subdirectory was created. Rename the linux subdirectory to reflect the kernel version number; this will help keep things straight if you compile multiple versions. You will also want to create a soft link named `linux` pointing to the new directory. That way, if you have the sources to several versions installed, you can pick which you want to compile simply by changing the soft link. Use these commands to rename the directory and create the soft link:

```
$ mv linux linux-2.4.15
$ ln -sf linux-2.4.15 linux
```

Patching the Kernel

Applying patches to your kernel is entirely optional. If you simply want to use the standard kernel you downloaded, skip to the next section. If you want to make your own kernel modifications, I suggest you get a book that discusses the internal workings of the Linux kernel. The rest of this section discusses applying kernel patches prepared by others.

Retrieving Incremental Upgrade Patches

The most common sort of patch is an incremental upgrade of your kernel sources. (You may hear these patches referred to as *diffs* because they are the difference between two kernel versions.) These patches update your sources one patch level at a time and are named according to the version you will have *after* the patch is applied. For example, suppose you downloaded and installed the hypothetical version 2.4.13 of the source from the Internet, only to later discover that 2.4.15 is the current version. Rather than starting from scratch and downloading the entire linux-2.4.15.tar.bz2 archive, you can download two files: patch-2.4.14.tar.bz2 and patch-2.4.15.tar.bz2. Such patch files should be available from the same location as the kernel you downloaded. After applying both patches, in order, you would have the 2.4.15 kernel sources installed.

Retrieving Other Patches

Other patches, which are not officially part of the Linux kernel, are also available on the Internet. Such patches usually add a feature to the kernel or support for new hardware. (These hardware patches are becoming more rare, however, and are instead usually created as separate kernel modules.) Generally, unofficial patches must be applied to a particular version of kernel sources, but it may be possible to apply a patch to different (usually newer) kernel sources if the patch is small and if it was meant for a kernel version only a few patch levels away from yours.

> Unofficial patches may not be as stable as the standard Linux kernel; they are sometimes designed for testing purposes in order to obtain user feedback. For this reason, it's a good idea to keep a bootable backup of a standard kernel when first testing a kernel compiled with an unofficial patch.

Two good places to start searching for unofficial kernel patches are **http://www.kernelnotes.org** and **http://www.linuxhq.com**. Both contain links to either local or external lists of unofficial patches.

Installing Patches

Whether your patch file is an official kernel diff or a third-party change, it is installed in the same way. This example assumes that you downloaded a hypothetical patch to upgrade 2.4.13 to 2.4.17 and saved the patch in /tmp.

Patching Your Kernel Sources

You will use the `patch` command to apply the changes contained in a patch file to your kernel source. Use these steps:

1. Change to your /usr/src directory, and issue a command similar to the following:

```
$ bzip2 -dc /tmp/patch-2.4.17.tar.bz2 | patch -p0
```

> Remember, this command will change based on the actual version numbers you are using.

> If you are updating an older kernel and must apply multiple patches, be sure to apply them in order. In other words, apply them in the order of their release.

2. If the patch was applied correctly, you should only see a number of lines reporting successful patches, like this:

```
patching file net/sunrpc/clnt.c
patching file net/sunrpc/svc.c
patching file net/sunrpc/svcsock.c
patching file net/sunrpc/xprt.c
```

The file names will, of course, differ based on your patch; the important thing is that no errors were returned.

Unfortunately, the patching process can fail in numerous ways. Some of them are due to how the patch file was made; others may be due to a problem with your installed kernel sources. Here are the common errors and their solutions.

can't find file to patch

You will almost certainly encounter this error if you try to stay on the cutting edge by applying kernel pre-patches, which are patches for the kernel that are not entirely tested for public use:

```
can't find file to patch at input line 4
Perhaps you used the wrong -p or --strip option?
The text leading up to this was:
--------------------------
|diff -u --exclude-from ../exclude --new-file --recursive linux.vanilla/CREDITS
linux.14p7/CREDITS
|-- linux.vanilla/CREDITS      Wed Oct 20 01:12:32 2000
|+++ linux.14p7/CREDITS Thu Nov 11 21:51:57 2000
--------------------------
```

If you see this error, you know the patch program can't find the file it is supposed to modify.

If you look closely at the message in this example, you will see that the program is trying to modify the file linux.vanilla/CREDITS; the file on your system, however, is linux/CREDITS. Fortunately, this is easily remedied. To do so, cancel the previous attempt by pressing Ctrl+C, and try this command instead:

```
$ cd linux
$ bzip2 -dc /tmp/patch-2.4.17.tar.bz2 | patch -p1
```

Notice that the argument to patch is -p1 rather than -p0. The number tells patch how many leading slashes to remove from the file name. Now, rather than attempting to modify linux.vanilla/CREDITS, the patch program will look for CREDITS, a file that exists within the linux directory. (This is why you issued the `# cd linux` command before the `patch` command.)

If the error persists after you fix the path, verify that the file really does exist on your system. If it does not, perhaps you accidentally deleted it, or maybe the patch was meant for a different kernel version than what you have installed. You should get a version of the patch meant for your kernel version or perhaps download the kernel version expected by the patch. Check any online documentation that was released with the patch to determine whether you have the correct one.

Reversed patch detected

Other times you may see an error similar to this:

```
patching file 'MAINTAINERS'
Reversed (or previously applied) patch detected!  Assume -R? [n]
```

This message indicates that the modification that the `patch` program was going to make had already been done. This can occur for a number of reasons:

- You have already applied the patch.
- The maker of the patch accidentally reversed the old and new versions when creating the patch, so it appears you already have the newer version when in fact you don't. This is unlikely, especially for official kernel patches, but if you think this is the problem, use the `-R` argument with `patch`.
- You are trying to update a *pre* kernel. Some of the patches you are trying to apply have already been added; others have not. It would be easiest, in this case, to download the entire 2.4.17 source.

Rejected Files

You know files have been rejected if you see an error message such as this while applying a patch

```
5 out of 5 hunks ignored -- saving rejects to MAINTAINERS.rej
```

or when you find *.rej files in the tree you patched:

```
$ find /usr/src/linux -name "*.rej" -print
```

Patches are rejected when the file you are trying to patch is significantly different from what is expected. The patch probably was not meant for the kernel version you have. Try getting a different version of the patch or a different version of your kernel sources.

Starting Fresh

If a few patching attempts fail, it is possible that your kernel sources will not cleanly accept any patch or even compile. Part of the art of patching is knowing when to reinstall the kernel sources and start over, rather than fighting a losing battle with patch.

Removing Patches

If you decide you no longer want a patch that was previously installed, thus reverting to the standard kernel, try a command like this:

```
$ bzip2 -dc /tmp/patch-2.4.17.tar.bz2 | patch -p0 -R
```

The -R parameter stands for *reverse*, not *remove*, but the effect is the same: It causes the patch program to reverse the unmodified and the modified sections of the patch file. The end result is that the patch is removed.

Configuring the Kernel

Now that your kernel sources are installed and perhaps patched, you will want to configure them—selecting what components should be compiled into the core kernel, what should be compiled as loadable modules, and what should be omitted entirely. How you configure your kernel can affect both its speed and the hardware it supports.

Installing the Required Packages

The remaining three steps—configuring, compiling, and installing the kernel—require a number of RPMs. Before continuing, you make sure the packages in Table 12.1 are installed.

To check whether a package is installed, issue a command such as this:

```
$ rpm -q make
make-3.77-6
```

If the package is installed, rpm responds with the specific version. In this example, it was make-3.77-6. If it had not been installed, rpm would have printed nothing.

Table 12.1   Required Packages

Package	Notes
binutils	Required
dev86	Required
egcs or gcc	Required
glibc-devel	Required
lilo	Required to make your kernel bootable. This is named *milo* on Alpha and *silo* on Sparc.
make	Required
modutils	Required if you enable modules
ncurses and ncurses-devel	Required for make menuconfig
tk and tkinter	Required for make xconfig

Starting the Configuration Program

There are three ways to run the configuration script:

> Before running the configuration script, change to the directory containing the sources.

- **make config.** This is the original configuration script. It asks scores of questions but gives you no options to change your mind. I don't recommend using this to customize your kernel unless you have a lot of patience and a long attention span.
- **make menuconfig.** This method contains the same configuration questions as make config, but it organizes them into groups and is accessible through a menu system.
- **make xconfig.** This method presents the same information in the same menu format, except that it uses X, so you can use your mouse.

The following tasks use make menuconfig. I recommend that you use either make menuconfig or make xconfig. The interfaces are similar, so you should be able to follow along with either.

Starting the Kernel-Configuration Utility

Start the kernel configuration process by doing the following:

1. Change to the directory that contains your kernel sources:

   ```
   $ cd /usr/src/linux
   ```

2. Start the kernel-configuration utility (either make menuconfig or make xconfig).

> Errors that happen after you type make menuconfig or make xconfig usually indicate that you have not installed all the necessary development RPMs.

Configuration Options

Once the configuration program is up and running, you'll be confronted with various configuration options. The default configuration options are usually appropriate for a networked home or work computer. You needn't carefully check and set all options, but you'll certainly want to check that the device support (IDE, SCSI, network, and sound) suits your computer.

> The options covered here are for the Intel x86, but they should apply with few exceptions to the other platforms on which Red Hat runs, such as the Alpha.

> While in the configuration program, you can choose Help for most options. Some help screens provide additional (hopefully current) information such as URLs relevant to the option. Other options are not yet documented at all.

Many options can be built as modules rather than as part of the core kernel. Building pieces of the kernel as modules saves RAM because modules can be automatically loaded when needed and unloaded when they are no longer being used. If you are short on RAM, you should build everything possible as modules. At a minimum, you should build device support and file-system support as modules.

Code Maturity Level Options

In this category, there is only one option to configure.

Prompt for Development and/or Incomplete Code/Drivers

Selecting Prompt for Development and/or Incomplete Code/Drivers causes the options for incomplete and development parts of the kernel to be displayed. Such options are noted as *experimental* in the help section. Unless you know you want such an option, do not select this.

Processor Type and Features

In this category, you will set the attributes of your processor.

Processor Family

In the Processor Family option, you can select the minimum processor needed by this kernel. Select 386, for example, to build the kernel without using any of the optimizations offered by later processors. This will allow your kernel to run on all Intel-compatible CPUs, albeit more slowly than necessary. The same rule applies to non-Intel processors: Picking the oldest or least specific processor model creates a kernel that will run on all models, but at a non-optimal speed.

> Usually you will want to pick your true processor, not an older one. (If you are unsure of the exact model of your processor, run the command `cat /proc/cpuinfo`.)

Maximum Physical Memory

This option enables you to select the tradeoff between the size of virtual memory available to programs and the size of physical memory. The 1 GB option allows you to use up to 1GB of physical memory, allowing each program 3GB of virtual memory. The 2 GB option allows the use of up to 2GB of physical memory, but programs only get a 2GB virtual address space. The vast majority of users should leave this at the default, 1 GB.

> If you need several gigabytes of physical RAM, consider using the version 2.4 kernel (when it is released) because it has support for 4GB.

Math Emulation

You must select the Math Emulation option if you do not have a math coprocessor in your computer. Because all reasonably current processors include a math coprocessor, you will most likely not need this option.

MTRR (Memory Type Range Register) Support

MTRRs are registers on some Intel-compatible processors (including Pentium Pro/II/III, AMD K6-3, and some AMD K6-2 processors) that control access to memory. When enabled, MTRRs can dramatically improve video performance.

The X server shipped with Red Hat Linux 7 (XFree86 version 4.0.1) supports the MTRRs for better video performance, but they are not automatically configured by the X server. You must do this yourself. Keep this in mind before you select it.

Symmetric Multi-Processing Support

Enable Symmetric Multi-Processing Support only if you have more than one processor. Enabling this for a single-processor machine will actually result in a slightly slower kernel.

Loadable Module Support

In this category, you choose how modules will be handled.

Enable Loadable Module Support

Loadable modules allow you to add and remove pieces of code from a running kernel. Even if you do not plan to compile parts of the kernel as modules, this is still a useful option to enable. Doing so allows you to later add modules obtained from other sources without needing to recompile anything.

Set Version Information on All Symbols for Modules

Selecting this option allows modules compiled from non-kernel sources to be safely loaded into a running kernel. You need to enable this option only if you plan to use third-party modules.

Kernel Module Loader

Selecting the Kernel Module Loader allows modules to be loaded by the kernel on demand and then unloaded when no longer needed. You enable this option unless you are not using modules at all.

General Setup

In this category, basic configuration options are listed.

Networking Support

Enable the Networking Support option even if your computer is not networked. This will keep your kernel ready to handle networking if you connect your PC to a network later.

PCI Support

Enable the PCI Support option if you have a computer with a PCI bus. Older 386 and 486 computers typically will not; Pentiums typically will, as will Alphas.

MCA Support

The MCA bus was used mainly on IBM PS/2 machines. Unless you have one of these, disable this option.

SGI Visual Workstation Support

Enable this option only if you have one of these computers. A kernel compiled for an SGI Visual Workstation will not work on any other type of machine.

System V IPC

Many programs use System V IPC, so you should include it.

BSD Process Accounting

The BSD Process Accounting option enables you to track resources, such as CPU time, used on your system. This option is useful only if you run a multi-user system. If enabled, you should also install the psacct package.

Sysctl Support

Sysctl support should usually be enabled unless you are trying to build a small kernel such as for a rescue disk.

Kernel Support for a.out Binaries

Enabling the Kernel Support for a.out Binaries option enables your kernel to run programs that are packaged in an older format called *a.out*. Despite the dire warning in the configuration utility's help, you can compile this as a module or perhaps omit it entirely because Red Hat uses the ELF format, not a.out. The only instance where you may need compatibility with the a.out format is to run older binary-only programs obtained from other sources.

Kernel Support for ELF Binaries

You should enable the Kernel Support for ELF Binaries option. Do not compile this as a module because all programs included with Red Hat are compiled as ELF.

Kernel Support for MISC Binaries

Selecting Kernel Support for MISC Binaries allows you to start interpreted programs simply by typing the name of the script. Linux will automatically start the correct interpreter. Read the file /usr/src/Linux/Documentation/binfmtmisc.txt to learn how to configure this feature.

> Even if you select this option, you should still select Kernel Support for ELF Binaries.

Parallel Port Support

Parallel port support is necessary if you want to use a device attached to the parallel port, such as a printer or a Zip drive.

Advanced Power Management BIOS Support

The Advanced Power Management BIOS Support option is most useful for laptops. Regardless of whether you include this option, you might want to install the hdparm package, which will power down inactive hard drives.

Plug and Play Support

You should enable Plug and Play support if you have Plug and Play cards installed in your system. Linux can still use such cards without this option enabled, but selecting it makes Linux better able to automatically configure some cards.

> If Plug and Play support is important to you and 2.2 kernels don't correctly configure your devices, you might want to look at the upcoming 2.4 kernels. The 2.4 kernels should have improved Plug and Play support; you will no longer need to use the isapnptools package.

Block Devices

The ways your kernel handles devices are the options here.

Normal PC Floppy Disk Support

Enable this option to allow use of the floppy drive. The util-linux package includes a number of floppy drive tools.

Enhanced IDE/MFM/RLL Disk/CDROM/Tape/Floppy Support

Unless your system has only SCSI devices, you almost certainly want to select this option.

Loopback Device Support

A loopback device allows a file to be treated as if it were a block device. This has several uses, including mounting and checking a CD image before burning it onto the CD-ROM disc. It should definitely be enabled.

> The configuration utility's help warns that you need a recent version of mount. Red Hat includes a suitable version. Although not strictly necessary, the losetup utility provides more control over loopback devices than the mount program alone.

Network Block Device Support

Enable the Network Block Device Support option to allow block devices to be transparently accessed remotely via TCP/IP. To use this, you will need the client and server software. Follow the URL listed in the configuration help to obtain this software; it is not included with Red Hat.

Multiple Devices Driver Support

Enable the Multiple Devices Driver Support option to allow multiple partitions to be combined into a RAID. If you enable this option, you will also want to install the raidtools package.

RAM Disk Support

The RAM Disk Support option enables you to create a RAM disk. This is useful only for kernels meant for installation or recovery disks.

XT Hard Disk Support

XT Hard Disk Support adds support for 8-bit hard disk controllers, found in older computers. You probably don't have one.

Parallel Port IDE Device Support

Parallel port IDE device support is required if you want to connect a drive, such as a Zip drive, to your parallel port. If you enable this option, be sure to enable both the Parallel Port Support option (listed in the General Setup menu) and the IDE Support option in the Block Devices menu.

Networking Options

Unless you have special networking needs, you can use the defaults in the Networking Options section. The options discussed here require the installation of additional packages if enabled.

Network Firewalls

If you need to provide network firewall capability on a Linux router, you should start out by installing the ipchains package.

The IPX Protocol

The IPX protocol may be useful if you want to connect to older NetWare servers or to have your Linux machine act as a NetWare server. Relevant packages are ipxutils, mars-nwe, and ncpfs.

SCSI Support

If you have SCSI hardware, this category will be of interest to you.

SCSI Disk Support

Enable SCSI disk support if you have a SCSI disk, including a removable drive such as the SCSI version of the Jaz drive.

If you plan to boot from an SCSI disk, you cannot compile this as a module.

SCSI Tape Support

This option enables support of SCSI tape drives. The mt-st package may be useful.

SCSI CD-ROM Support

You'll need this option to enable support of SCSI CD-ROM drives.

SCSI General Support

Enable the SCSI General Support option to allow use of some other type of SCSI device, such as a SCSI scanner or SCSI CD writer. sane is a basic utility to enable use of scanners (not just SCSI scanners), but Red Hat does not include it. To use a CD writer, you should also install the mkisofs and cdrecord packages.

Probe All LUNs on Each SCSI Device

You should only enable the Probe All LUNs on Each SCSI Device option if you have a SCSI device that acts as several devices, such as a CD jukebox.

SCSI Low-Level Drivers

From the SCSI Low-Level Drivers sub-menu, you can select support for your specific SCSI adapter(s). Although perhaps misplaced, this sub-menu also contains support for non-SCSI versions of Iomega's Zip drive.

Iomega Parallel Port

Select the Iomega Parallel Port option if you have a Zip drive attached to the parallel port. You do not need this option for SCSI Zip drives; instead, select the SCSI General Support option.

Network Device Support

Network options are handled in this category.

Network Device Support

Network device support should be enabled unless your computer is entirely standalone. There is support for a wide array of networking devices.

PPP (Point-to-Point) Support

To use PPP support, you must install the ppp package. The kppp graphical front-end may also be useful; it is in the kdenetwork package.

Amateur Radio Support

This option will enable you to network your computer via amateur radio. Unless you're an amateur radio enthusiast, you will not want to select this. If you are interested, however, click Help to find relevant URLs because supporting software is not included in Red Hat.

IrDA Subsystem Support

This selection allows Linux to communicate with laptops and PDAs using an infrared port. Be sure to install irda-utils if you need to use this.

ISDN Subsystem

ISDN is a type of digital phone service that allows your computer to connect to the Internet faster than you can using a standard modem while still leaving the phone available for voice. You must, of course, have an ISDN card to use this service and must install the isdn4k-utils package.

Old CD-ROM Drivers (Not SCSI, Not IDE)

You should enable this option only if you have a CD-ROM drive that doesn't use a SCSI or IDE interface. Often, these drive types will connect either to a sound card or to a proprietary card. Such drives haven't been produced in a number of years, so you should probably disable this option.

Character Devices

The sub-sections under Character Devices highlight a few options that, if enabled, require the installation of additional packages.

Mouse Support (Not Serial Mice)

A useful utility for all mice (including serial mice) is gpm. The gpm utility allows you to cut and paste with the mouse at a console. You should enable this for sure.

Video for Linux

The Video for Linux option allows a number of audio and video capture cards and FM radio cards to be used with Linux. View the configuration help for relevant URLs because Red Hat does not include supporting software.

Ftape, the Floppy Tape Device Driver

If you have a tape drive connected to your floppy controller, enable Ftape. You might also be interested in the mt-st package, which is used to control tape drives.

File Systems

In this category, the various file systems your kernel can handle are dealt with.

Quota

Quota support lets you set per-user limits on disk space usage. This is typically useful only for multi-user systems; for home, disable this option. You must install the quota package before you can take advantage of quotas.

Kernel Automounter Support

Kernel Automounter Support allows network file systems to be mounted automatically as they are needed. The supporting package autofs is required if you enable this option.

Apple Macintosh File System Support (Experimental)

If you need to read from and write to Macintosh floppy and hard disks, enable this option. You probably would also want to install the macutil package.

DOS FAT fs Support

To share floppies and hard drives with Windows, check the DOS FAT fs Support option. You will also want MSDOS fs Support and VFAT (Windows-95) fs Support.

> You probably do not want to enable the UMSDOS option. This option brings some Linux file-system features (such as links) to FAT file systems, but it also brings the problems of the FAT file system to Linux (most notably, inefficiency.)

NOTE

ISO 9660 CDROM File System Support

Select the ISO 9660 CDROM File System Support option if you have a CD-ROM drive.

Minix fs Support

Minix file-system support is rarely necessary. Because you will almost certainly not encounter the Minix file system, you should disable this option.

NTFS File System Support (Read Only)

NTFS is the file system used by Windows NT. If you dual-boot between NT and Linux, you probably want to enable this option.

It *is* possible to compile this with write support, but it's not a good idea because the write support has not been tested extensively. Writing to an NTFS partition may cause corruption, especially when writing to large files.

OS/2 HPFS File System Support (Read Only)

HPFS is the file system used by OS/2. If you have OS/2 installed on your computer or share removable disks with an OS/2 machine, you'll want to enable this option. If you want write support, look at the 2.4 series of kernels.

/proc File System Support

The /proc file system is a virtual file system; it is created on-the-fly by the kernel and does not exist on disk. It allows a number of kernel settings to be queried and changed. This is very useful, so enable the /proc File System Support option.

/dev/pts File System for Unix98 PTYs

The /dev/pts File System for Unix98 PTYs option is important if you enabled the Unix98 PTY support option in the Character Devices menu. If so, you should enable this option as well.

ROM File System Support

You need to enable the ROM File System Support option only if you are building a special-purpose kernel, such as for an installation or recovery disk. Normally, this option should be disabled.

Second Extended fs Support

You almost certainly want to include second extended fs support as part of the kernel, not as a module. This is the standard Linux file system. A relevant package is e2fsprogs, which should already be on your system from the installation.

System V and Coherent File System Support

Enable the System V and Coherent File System Support option if you need to share System V or Coherent hard disk partitions with Linux.

UFS File System Support

Enable the UFS File System Support option if you want to share BSD hard disk partitions with Linux.

Network

Additional network settings are included in this category.

Coda File System Support

Coda is an advanced network file system. The Coda client and server are not included with Red Hat. Refer to the configuration help page to obtain them. Enable this option only if you need to work with large networks.

NFS File System Support

NFS is the most common network file system for UNIX-like operating systems. If you want to use NFS as a server, install the knfsd package. If you want to use your computer as an NFS client, install the knfsd-clients package.

SMB File System Support

Enabling the SMB File System Support option allows your Linux computer to connect to Windows file servers. You will need the samba-client and samba-common packages. The samba package is only needed if you want to use Linux as a Windows file server.

NCP File System Support

The NCP file system enables Linux to act as a client to NetWare servers. If you choose this option, also install the ncpfs package. This option is not needed if you want Linux to act as a NetWare server.

Partition Types

Some of the previously mentioned file systems come with their own type of partition table. You must enable some of the partition types offered in the Partition Types menu if you want to mount a hard disk with such a file system.

Console Drivers

The text mode of Linux, known as the console, has settings that can be configured in this category.

VGA Text Console

You almost certainly want to enable the VGA Text Console option. The package SVGATextMode will allow finer control over your console.

Support for Frame Buffer Devices (Experimental)

The Support for Frame Buffer Devices option abstracts the graphics hardware, hiding some of the differences between hardware. This is optional on Intel platforms but may be needed for others. One nice feature of this driver is that it replaces the standard text virtual console with a graphical one, allowing more flexibility in fonts, font sizes, and refresh rates. The package fbset is needed to control these settings.

Sound

The Sound option lists a number of sound cards. If your precise card is not listed, you may need to determine what chipset it uses and then install support for that chipset. Regardless of what support you choose, you should install the sndconfig package. This allows you to easily configure and test your sound card.

Kernel Hacking

Do not enable anything under the Kernel Hacking menu item unless you are doing kernel development work and need to test the kernel.

Compiling the Kernel

After the kernel is configured, it is a simple matter to compile it. To build the core kernel, do the following:

```
# make dep
# make zImage
```

Usually the `make zImage` command will succeed after several minutes (or perhaps hours for a slow computer). If you have included many options in the core kernel, compilation may fail with an error message similar to this one:

```
System is 632 kB
System is too big. Try using bzImage or modules.
make[1]: *** [zImage] Error 1
make[1]: Leaving directory '/usr/src/linux-2.4.17/arch/i386/boot'
make: *** [zImage] Error 2
```

If you receive this error, you have two choices: You can reconfigure the kernel and change items previously compiled into the kernel to modules, and/or you can try to compile a big kernel with this command:

```
# make bzImage
```

Once you have successfully compiled the kernel, you can compile the modules like this:

```
# make modules
```

These should compile without errors.

Installing the Kernel

Once the kernel and modules are compiled, you are ready to install them. Issue these two commands to copy the kernel and the modules to the correct places on your system:

```
# make install
# make modules_install
```

The first command copies the kernel to /boot/vmlinuz-2.4.17, where 2.4.17 is replaced by your kernel version. It also installs the file /boot/System.map-2.4.17. (This map file lists the offsets of structures in the kernel. This is necessary for the kernel to dynamically load kernel modules.)

The second command, `make modules_install`, copies all modules into /lib/modules/ 2.4.17/. Again, 2.4.17 will reflect your actual kernel version.

As a final step, you must tell the boot loader where to find the new kernel. For Intel systems, this is done with the program lilo and its configuration file /etc/lilo.conf. Other platforms may differ—Red Hat on Alpha uses a program called milo and the /etc/milo.conf configuration file. Red Hat on Sparc uses silo and /etc/silo.conf. These programs are similar enough to lilo that you can follow the examples here, but you should read the correct manual page for your platform (man milo or man silo) for any platform-specific concerns.

Modifying LILO

LILO is short for *Linux loader*. The default LILO configuration file for a Linux-only Red Hat system looks like this:

```
boot=/dev/hda
map=/boot/map
install=/boot/boot.b
prompt
timeout=50
default=linux

image=/boot/vmlinuz-2.4.0-16
```

```
        label=linux
        initrd=/boot/initrd-2.4.0-16.img
        read-only
        root=/dev/hda1
        vga=ask
```

> From the name, it's obvious that LILO can boot Linux; it can also boot nearly any other operating system you might have on your computer. If you boot other systems with LILO, extra lines will exist in your /etc/lilo.conf file. You can ignore those lines while installing a new kernel.

The `image` line and all lines indented below describe a Linux kernel to boot. To make the new 2.4.17 kernel bootable, you need to add appropriate `image`, `label`, `read-only`, and `root` lines. Keep the original section for the 2.4.0 kernel in case something goes wrong and your new kernel is not bootable, but change the label for the 2.4.0 kernel to something else, such as `backup`. The next code example places the section for the new kernel first so that it is the default kernel; here's how the final /etc/lilo.conf file looks:

```
boot=/dev/hda
map=/boot/map
install=/boot/boot.b
prompt
timeout=50
default=linux

image=/boot/vmlinuz-2.4.17
        label=linux
        read-only
        root=/dev/hda1
image=/boot/vmlinuz-2.4.0-16
        label=backup
        initrd=/boot/initrd-2.4.0-16.img
        read-only
        root=/dev/hda1
        vga=ask
```

Once you have modified the lilo.conf file, run lilo. This causes the changes to be written to the boot sector of the disk. You should see output like this:

```
Added linux *
Added backup
```

> The asterisk marks the entry that will be booted by default.

Now, safely shut down and restart your system. The new kernel will boot. If something goes wrong, restart, press the Tab key at the LILO boot: prompt, and then select the backup kernel. Most likely, however, things will load fine, and you will be ready to enjoy your new kernel.

Conclusion

In this chapter, you learned where to download kernel sources and how to install the sources so that multiple versions can co-exist. You also learned to patch the kernel sources and how to troubleshoot errors that might occur. Finally, you learned how to configure the sources for your computer and then how to compile and install the new kernel.

Chapter 13, "Troubleshooting," offers specialized tips and tricks to help smooth away any unforeseen problems that may occur.

Troubleshooting is rarely pleasant; after all, if you need to troubleshoot your system, it means there are problems. With a little help from this chapter, however, the troubleshooting can be somewhat painless. This chapter outlines many common problems and their solutions, along with various tips on how you might be able to avoid trouble in the first place.

If you are having problems with a program, you should first look for updates or fixes on the author's Web site. Only if your search for a fix is unsuccessful should you begin the troubleshooting process.

Although Linux has no central knowledge base for solutions to common problems, many Linux users use newsgroups to ask and answer questions from other Linux users. To locate Linux newsgroups, look for those whose names begin with the prefix comp.linux. Read the messages to see whether an answer to your question is already there; if not, you can then post questions about the problems you may be facing. You should also use Web search engines to locate solutions to your questions.

Installation

When you're installing Linux, any number of situations may require you to improvise, especially when you're installing Linux on older or smaller systems. For example, the machine on which you want to install Linux might lack a CD-ROM drive and modem or may lack sufficient memory for the installation. Other problems you may face during installation include trying to dual boot with Windows NT, misplacement of LILO, misconfiguration of X, boot problems, and more.

Installing Linux on Machines Without CD-ROM Drives or Modems

Do you want to experiment with Linux using an old computer, such as a 486 system with 16MB of RAM and no CD-ROM drive or modem? If so, you'll have to figure out how to get the Red Hat Linux distribution from the CD-ROM to the old system. You might try one of the following installation methods:

- Installing Linux on a network
- Installing Linux from the hard drive
- Buying a CD-ROM drive

Installing Linux on a Network

To install Linux on a machine without a CD-ROM drive or modem, try using a network. To begin, buy two Ethernet cards (which can be found for about $20 each)—one for the machine on which you want to install Linux and one for a machine with a CD-ROM drive. Connect the two systems using a cross-over RJ45 Ethernet wire (which can be purchased for about $10).

Once you've connected the machines, you can set up a Web or FTP server on the system that contains the CD-ROM drive and create a boot floppy with the bootnet.img file. This file is used to boot the system without the CD-ROM drive. After the installation starts, you will be asked for IP information and the server name of the system with the CD-ROM drive. The installation process will then retrieve the files from the CD-ROM over your small network.

Alternatively, consider enabling a proxy on the system that contains the CD-ROM drive. Then, instruct your Linux installation to retrieve the files from the Red Hat Software public FTP site rather than setting up an FTP or Web site yourself. This would require the installation of proxy software on the system without the CD-ROM drive. One such program is called WinGate and is available at **www.wingate.com**.

Installing Linux from the Hard Drive

If you're daunted by the method described above, you'll appreciate the strategy presented here. To install Linux from the hard drive, you'll need two things:

- The hard disk on the "trial" system must be big enough to support both the uninstalled and installed packages. This means that you'll need about 2GB of unused hard disk space.
- A PC-to-PC cable to be used for file transfer is required. Such a cable is available from any local computer store for about $10. Both serial cables and parallel cables exist, any of which will do fine.

After you have the cable, you need to use DOS or Linux's fdisk program to create the partitions on your trial system. You need half of the drive partitioned as a DOS (FAT or FAT32) partition, with the remaining half reserved for Linux. Then, using the cable, transfer the files from the CD-ROM on your existing system to the DOS partition on the trial system. When you start the installation process, you can tell Linux to look on the DOS partition of trial system to get the files.

To transfer the files over the link cable, you need a special program. Many shareware programs will work, as will several applications you must purchase, such as Norton Commander, PC Anywhere, LapLink, and more. You can browse your local computer store or search the Internet for such a program.

Buying a CD-ROM Drive

This method is the easiest and does not have to be very costly. Simply buy an older CD-ROM drive and install it. Once the drive is installed, you can use your Linux CD-ROM to get the installation going.

Accommodating Limited Memory

If your system has only 4 or 8MB of RAM, the installation program may not be able to start. Depending on your system, there may be a way around this.

If you go to the BIOS setup, it typically offers a few settings for changing memory organization. For example, I have an old 386 laptop with 4MB of RAM that is divided in the BIOS into extended (XMS) and expanded (EMS) memory. If I enter the BIOS setup, I can change these settings to put all memory into XMS mode, making it accessible to the Linux installation. Be careful when you change BIOS settings, however; be sure to read your manual before attempting any change.

Swap Files and You

Staying with memory problems, many people wonder how large a swap file they should enable in their Linux installation. A good rule of thumb is that the size of the swap file should be twice the size of your system's physical memory (RAM), unless you have 128MB or more. For example, if your system has 32MB of RAM, you should allocate 64MB for the swap partition. If you don't allocate enough swap file space, you may see the Linux kernel start killing programs when they try to use too much memory. This is done to free up memory for critical uses and is a very big indicator that you need more swap space.

In some other operating systems, such as Microsoft Windows, you can select the size of your swap file. For example, in Windows 98, you can go to your Control Panel, System, Performance and set the size of the swap file space (referred to as Virtual Memory). In Linux, swap file space is kept in a separate partition, which means you must decide on the size of the swap file you want before the installation even begins. There is a way, however, to add more swap file space later without the necessity of to reinstalling the system or adding a new hard disk.

You can create a swap file in Linux and add it to your pool of memory. First, you must decide the amount of swap file space you need to add. For example, assume that you need an additional 64MB of space. You would then type this command to create the file:

```
dd if=/dev/zero of=/swapfile bs=1024 count=65536
```

Change the count size to the number of kilobytes you need. Then, you need to make that file active:

```
mkswap /swapfile 65536
sync
swapon /swapfile
```

If you use the `free` command after using these commands, you should see 64MB of space added to your swap area. If you want to add that file again the next time you reboot your system, add the swapon command to the file /etc/rc.d/rc.local.

When you start the Linux installation, you are presented with a boot prompt that displays an introductory message. There, you can press the Enter key to continue or type various other commands such as text or expert. There are many more parameters that you can add. For example, if you know your hard disk parameters, you can type them at the prompt, or you can list the amount of memory you have. The following command specifies that your system has 128MB of RAM; that your hard disk has 64 cylinders, 32 heads, and 202 sectors; and that you want to enable expert mode:

```
boot: linux mem=128M hda=64,32,202 expert
```

You can specify these options at the LILO boot prompt or you can add them to your lilo.conf file.

Dual Booting with Windows NT

As you learned in Chapter 2, "Installing Red Hat Linux 7," dual booting Linux and Windows 95 or 98 is simple. You just install both operating systems in a separate partition or disk, and you install LILO in your Master Boot Record (MBR).

Things get more complicated, however, if the other operating system is Microsoft Windows NT. Windows NT has a special loader called NTLDR, which must be placed in the MBR. This means that you cannot overwrite it with LILO, or Windows NT will refuse to boot.

To work around this limitation, install Windows NT first, so it can write its loader to the MBR. Then, when you install Linux, set the Linux partition as the active (bootable) one. When it is time to install LILO, specify that you want it installed on the Linux partition, rather than on the MBR. That way, when the system boots, the Linux partition gets loaded before NTLDR, and LILO can ask you which system you want to boot. If you select Windows NT, it will then load NTLDR, allowing both systems to coexist without problems.

LILO Won't Load Linux?

In the old days, the BIOS was unable to recognize more than 1,024 cylinders in a disk. Now, however, many large hard disks (greater than 8.6GB) have more than 1,024 cylinders—something that makes working with LILO a bit difficult. If LILO is placed after the first 1,024 cylinders, it probably won't be able to load Linux or any other system.

To resolve this, place your root partition—the one with your kernel—at the beginning of the disk. Do the same for your C: drive if you have DOS or Microsoft Windows installed. At the end of the drive, you can create some data or swap partitions. This will ensure that LILO has no problem loading any OS on your machine.

X Issues

When the Linux installation is nearly complete, it launches a program called Xconfigurator, which asks you questions about your video card and monitor in order to configure the X Window System. X, also called *X11*, is the common graphical environment in Linux and is used by nearly all Linux users; it is important, therefore, that the configuration succeeds.

In most cases, Xconfigurator detects your hardware and configures X with no problem. There may be a few instances, however, in which it fails. If this happens to you, install XF86Setup, which is included on your Linux CD-ROM. (You must also install the XVGA16 package.) Run the XF86Setup command when the installation program is finished to launch a graphical program that prompts you for information about your video and monitor hardware.

Another X problem that occurs occasionally, especially on laptops, is that graphic acceleration causes the screen to display black spots and lines. X uses acceleration for many cards in an attempt to make your graphical experience better. If you determine that this is causing a problem, it can be disabled. To disable acceleration, you need to edit the /etc/X11/XF86Config file manually. Add the following line in the [monitor] section:

```
option "noaccel"
```

Working with fstab

One file that you may want to customize when the installation is complete is /etc/ fstab. This file is responsible for many small annoyances you may encounter. For example, if you try to mount a floppy disk and you receive a message indicating that the disk has the wrong format, it may be because /etc/fstab requires floppies to be in ext2 format. Your floppy may have been formatted through DOS. Further, if you try to mount a CD-ROM or floppy as a user and find out that the system doesn't allow you to do so, it is likewise because of settings in the /etc/fstab file. If you have another operating system installed on your computer and you want it to always be mounted in /other when you boot, it is again configurable in /etc/fstab.

The fstab manual page will tell you the required syntax for the file, which is not very complicated. Unfortunately, the manual page is short and non-descriptive. The next paragraphs illustrate how to correct these common minor problems.

Drive Issues

To select the file system to be used with floppies, edit the line beginning with /dev/ fd0. The third column is the file system type. If you know you will always use DOS formatted floppies, change it to msdos. If you know your floppies will always be formatted in Linux, set the file system to ext2.

To allow any user to mount a CD-ROM drive, find the line that begins with /dev/ cdrom, and modify the user parameter, which appears in the fifth column. The line should read:

```
/dev/cdrom    /mnt/cdrom    iso9660 noauto,ro,user0 0
```

The *user* parameter is the important option here, which tells the Linux system to allow users to mount the CD drive.

Another annoyance you may face is with boot messages. Boot messages are designed to tell you whether everything was properly loaded and if all hardware devices were detected. However, you may see strange messages such as the following:

```
modprobe: cannot find net-pf-5
modprobe: cannot find char-major-14
```

These warnings are not important and do not mean that something has gone wrong in your system. They can, however, be annoying. You can turn these warning messages off by adding the two following commands to the file /etc/conf.modules:

```
alias net-pf-5 off
alias char-major-14 off
```

Getting More Stuff

Red Hat Linux comes with hundreds of programs that you can tinker with. After a while, you may want more programs. In the Linux world, there are two primary methods to get more programs. The first is from the Internet. The site, **www.freshmeat.net**, is the primary database of virtually all Linux programs available in the world. You can go there, search for something, and download the program you want. The second method to get programs is through application libraries. You can buy a set of two, four, or even six CD-ROMs for a minimal cost that contain thousands of programs. These are available at the same locations Red Hat Linux CD-ROMs are sold, such as Cheap*Bytes and the LinuxMall.

Language Concerns

When you install Linux, the installation program prompts you to select a language for your keyboard configuration. After the installation process is done, you can use the setup command to change it, but there is a much easier way to change your console keyboard locale at any time. For example, to switch a keyboard from its current U.S. configuration to Canadian French (CF), simply type:

```
loadkeys cf
```

To switch back, use the same command with the US parameter.

Play (and Work) Well with Others

When you create a file with a text editor or with any other program, it will be set to a default user access permission. That default permission is set by the umask command. If you don't like the default permission, it can be changed, although it is a bit tricky because umask works with the inverse octal number of the permission you want to set. For example, if you want to set your permission so the user has total control but no one else can read or write (a permission of 700), you can use the command:

```
umask 077
```

To set the permission so that you have all rights and everyone else can read or execute the file but not write in it (a permission of 755), you would type:

```
umask 022
```

You can add this command in the /etc/profile file so it is executed at each login.

Boot Problems

If you encounter boot problems, you may want to consider a few different culprits. Boot problems can be created when you modify scripts and configuration files in your Linux system or when you change the configuration of your physical drives.

Did You Modify Scripts or Configuration Files?

When you modify scripts and configuration files in your Linux system, you may unwittingly make your system unbootable either by setting incorrect parameters or by deleting important files. A good way to enable booting so that your mistakes can be corrected is by issuing the following command on the LILO boot prompt:

```
boot: linux init=/bin/sh
```

This command launches the Linux kernel and sets the init parameter to /bin/sh, allowing Linux to bypass the boot scripts, which may be faulty, and launch a shell as root. You are then allowed to make modifications to your system.

This can be useful for repairing problems, but it can be a big security hole. Anyone is able to use this (and many other tricks) to access your system and read your data. Physical access to your system is required, so the solution is to make sure your system is off-limits to undesirable people. You can set a BIOS password if you want a more secure system, but this still doesn't prevent someone from opening the system and removing the drive. Security is a huge subject—beyond the scope of this book—but you should be warned that anyone with physical access to a system can get data from it.

CAUTION

Did You Change the Configuration of Your Physical Drives?

Another nasty problem will occur if you change the configuration of your physical drives. For example, assume that you have a hard disk on IDE channel 0 that is set to master. You want to move the drive to IDE channel 1 because you are having problems with one of your IDE controllers. This would cause the drive reference to go from hda to hdc, making it unbootable.

The problem resides in the file /etc/fstab, which specifies where every file system is located and is currently set to hda. You must edit the file and set it to hdc. Unfortunately, you can't boot the system in such a case, even with the init=/bin/sh trick. You need to use both a Red Hat boot disk and the rescue disk created during the installation process. From there, you can manually edit the file and change the parameters.

```
Can"t mount root filesystem
```

One of the most disconcerting problems is signaled when you boot your system and receive the error message:

```
VFS: Can"t mount root filesystem
```

This means that the partition on which the Linux kernel is found could not be mounted. There are three common causes for this error:

- You recompiled your kernel and forgot to add basic features such as IDE support (and you use IDE disks).
- You forgot to include support for ext2, the Linux file system.
- The drive has failed.

In these situations, you must use the rescue disk to boot your system. You can then begin to investigate the problem.

Hardware

Hardware-related problems are often the most difficult to resolve because there are so many hardware devices using so many different protocols. Fortunately, Linux tools exist to help you deal with these problems.

Using the /proc File

The /proc file system is a wonderful place to locate useful information about your hardware and about processes that are running. If you go to that directory and list its contents, you will find two types of files and directories:

- Files such as cpuinfo, devices, ide, and scsi, which list information about your hardware.
- Directories with numbers as names, which are information directories about currently running processes.

You can change to the directories and read various files to get information about the processes, which is useful when your are debugging serious problems or performance issues.

For example, if your system has dual-processors, you need to make sure Linux sees them both. To determine whether the second processor has been detected, type the following:

```
cat /proc/cpuinfo
```

> For Linux to see both processors, you need an SMP-compatible kernel. When you install Linux, you can elect to install that version of the kernel, or you can recompile the kernel with SMP turned on.

Printer Issues

Various problems can arise with printers. For example, the printer daemon lpd may be running, but if you query it using lpq, it responds that the printer has not been found or is offline. There may be many reasons for this:

- The printer may really be offline. Be sure to check.
- The cable might be bad.
- The correct modules were not loaded. If you recompile your kernel or use some other custom kernel, make sure parallel port, PC-style port, and printer support are enabled.

Another printer problem you may encounter is when printer/system communication occurs, but the output has a staircase effect or looks totally wrong. If this happens, it means you are using the wrong filter. Use the printtool program to correct it by selecting the right printer filter.

Input Errors

The mouse is a very important piece of hardware, especially in X. Linux may have problems detecting it, however. For example, if your mouse is a serial mouse, it may be connected to one of two serial ports, and you may need to specify which one. The two serial ports in Linux, found in the /dev directory, are called ttyS0 and ttyS1. To make configuration easier, symbolic links are created to more common names. For example, the /dev/mouse file is usually a symbolic link to /dev/ttyS0. If your mouse is on ttyS1, however, you must re-do the link. Here's how:

```
rm -f /dev/mouse; ln -s /dev/ttyS1 /dev/mouse
```

Another problem you may have is with the protocol used by the mouse. For example, if you use a Logitech mouse, you may be tempted to select the Logitech C4 protocol when in fact it most likely requires a MouseMan protocol. The C4 protocol is used only with older mice; most recent mice use either the MouseMan or Microsoft protocol.

A similar protocol problem can occur with keyboards. If you have a PS/2 mouse and PS/2 keyboard, the system will refuse to work correctly if you connect them to the wrong port.

Removable Drive Problems

I have experienced problems with removable disk devices, such as Zip disks and ORBs. For example, every Castlewood ORB disk comes formatted in DOS mode, with one extended FAT partition. If you try to mount it as /dev/hdc1, it may not work because the first four partitions on any disk are considered as primary in Linux. You may have to use /dev/hdc5 to mount the drive. This should work with the ORB drive.

Networking

In the old days, networking was reserved for scientists and the military. Now, however, anyone with a computer can be linked. Conveniently, most networking problems have also been fixed. This section shows you how to resolve common networking problems.

Linux as a Proxy or Router

One common usage for Linux is as a proxy or router for an internal network. This means you need two network interface cards (NICs). Many drivers will detect only one card and will then ignore any other cards. This can be a problem if you want both cards to be detected by the kernel. My system, for example, contains two NE2000 Ethernet cards. The kernel driver used to detect these cards is ne, but the ne driver will not detect a second card unless I tell it to do so. The way to correct this problem is to edit the /etc/conf.modules file and specify the location of both cards. If the cards are at I/O ports 0x200 and 0x300, you need to add these lines:

```
alias eth0 ne
alias eth1 ne
options ne io=0x200,0x300
```

The ne module is now forced to detect both cards.

Speaking Another Protocol

You may encounter problems if you try to use the wrong protocols on the wrong network. For example, you may know your corporate LAN is an IP network, but you may not know the transport protocol. Chances are that it is either a TCP/IP or an IPX network, but you should check with your administrator to find out which protocol is used and then use the correct configuration.

You may also be away from a corporate office or a LAN and want to communicate by phone line. Three standards are common for dial-up networking: PPP, SLIP, and PLIP. If you want to communicate using a modem, you will probably connect to a PPP server and then to the Internet. Fortunately, many graphical clients exist, including kppp, gnome-ppp, and xisp.

If these clients fail to work, a problem may exist elsewhere in your system. Here are some steps you can take to troubleshoot the situation:

1. Make sure that the pppd daemon is well installed. Type the following command to locate the program:

```
whereis pppd
```

2. After you locate pppd, issue the following command to ensure that it is correctly installed:

```
ls -l /usr/sbin/pppd
```

   Assuming your pppd program is in /usr/sbin, you should see the following line:

```
-rwsr-sr-x 1 root root 120020 Apr 9 1999 /usr/sbin/pppd
```

The important part here is the two "s"es in the first part of that line. If you see x instead, you must change that parameter to s so that you can dial out as a normal user. As the root user, type the following command to enable dial-out access:

```
chmod +s /usr/sbin/pppd
```

Looking for Domains

A nice trick when networking is to specify domains in which the system would search the hosts you type. For example, if you often access various hosts on the mylan.com and privlan.net domains, you can edit the file /etc/resolv.conf and add the following line:

```
search mylan.com privlan.net
```

The next time you try to access station2, for example, the system will first look to see whether station2 exists; if not, it will search for station2.mylan.com and then for station2.privlan.net. This makes it possible to type:

```
rsh station2
```

rather than the usual:

```
rsh station2.privlan.net
```

When dealing with networking issues, it often helps to use IP addresses rather than hostnames, for two reasons. First, the name server might not be available during routing changes or if you have problems with network accesses. Second, you may not have the time to wait for completion of IP resolving as you try to solve a problem. Fortunately, many networking utilities in Linux share a common option flag. The -n flag will enable you to make the utility display IP addresses rather than host names. Here are a few examples:

```
netstat -an
traceroute 1.2.3.4 -n
arp -n -i eth0 -a proxy
```

Because these commands were all given the -n flag, they will display only IP addresses. The first command will display the list of open ports and the list of hosts connected to your system. The second will trace to the IP 1.2.3.4 but will not display the resolved host names for the various hops. The last command will list the arp entries for the host proxy.

Dealing with E-Mail

Many people use their Linux system as an e-mail server. There are two popular e-mail servers: Sendmail (which comes with your Red Hat Linux distribution) and Qmail.

If you read the documentation for Sendmail, it will suggest that you complete configuration of the entire system before building the sendmail.cf file, which contains the resulting configuration. This is a long and complex process and needs to be done with the sources of the Sendmail package. Many people find it much easier to edit the sendmail.cf file itself. In most cases, it's only necessary to edit the first part of the file to set your domain name and information about your server.

Another common problem occurs if you want to allow systems on your own LAN to send e-mail using the e-mail server for SMTP communications. You need to list every host name that will use your e-mail server for outgoing mail in the file /etc/mail/relay-domains.

The Qmail mail server can bring problems too. If you want to allow other hosts to send e-mails with your server, you will need to add the following line to the file /etc/hosts.allow:

```
tcp-env: ip1, ip2, ip3: setenv = RELAYCLIENT
```

Replace ip1, ip2, and so on with host names or IP addresses of the systems that will send e-mail via your server.

Dual Networking Concerns

If your Linux box will access two networks with two network cards, Linux must know about both networks in addition to both cards. A common problem occurs in the routing. To make sure that packets will be able to travel on both networks, you need to add a route for both of them. Here are the commands to add these routes:

```
route add -net 10.0.1.0 netmask 255.255.255.0 dev eth0
route add -net 10.0.2.0 netmask 255.255.255.0 dev eth1
```

These entries will add two routes to the two interfaces, eth0 and eth1. You may also want to add the gw parameter to these code lines. This is useful if you must access gateway servers or a default Internet route via one of these networks.

Access Issues

You can easily access files on remote UNIX or Linux systems without reconfiguring or rebooting. First, make sure the remote system is running the NFS server and is allowing you to access its files. You need to specify the remote system in /etc/exports. (A good example can be found in the exports manual page.) When the remote system has your system in its exports file, you can simply mount the remote directory like so:

```
mount -tnfs 1.2.3.4:/remote-directory /mnt/remote
```

As shown in the previous command, you specify the IP address of the remote system, and the mount command handles the rest.

Security Issues

Because security is such an important topic, additional discussion is merited to help in your attempts to keep your system safe. If possible, install ssh, the secure shell. ssh can replace—in a secure, encrypted manner—the Telnet and FTP services. Further, to connect to your system, a user must also have the ssh package.

Speed Problems

Some people have reported speed problems on PPP dial-up connections. For example, they use a 56Kbps modem but actually connect at much lower speeds. The principal program used to make a PPP dial-up connection is PPPd, which will attempt to connect at a default speed of 33,800bps. If you want a higher rate, it must be specified. Many graphical dial-up clients allow you to specify a default speed. Alternatively, by calling PPPd manually, you can specify a default speed on the command line. Note that if you specify an invalid speed, the dial-out program will go back to its default speed of 33,800bps.

Another reason for speed loss is the number of unwanted packets on the line. The Internet uses many protocols, and one of these is ICMP. This protocol is of no use to you unless you are running a server or router. You can use the ipchains command to disable it.

Specifying Name Servers

Internet host names are resolved to IP addresses via the Domain Name System (DNS). For this to work, you must have access to a DNS server. In your netcfg utility, you can specify one or more addresses for name servers, which resolve host names. You should specify more than one name server in case your primary name server goes down. You can also specify the name servers in the file /etc/resolv.conf.

Examining Open Ports

Your system probably has many Internet ports opened: one for Telnet, another for DNS, and one for the FTP service. This can be a potential security hazard that you will need to plug. To see a list of all opened ports, type the following command:

```
netstat -an
```

This command lists every open port and every host connected to your system. Ports are only numbers, however; you may see numbers you don't recognize and want to know which service is associated with that port. The fuser command will tell you that information. For example, if you want to know which service is using the UDP port number 1,024, type the following:

```
fuser -v -n udp 1024
```

fuser reports the process using that port and the user who owns the process.

PCMCIA

Other network-related problems can occur with the PCMCIA driver, which is the core driver for all laptop PC cards. It first loads itself as a module and starts a program that should detect any card in the PCMCIA slots. Sometimes, however, the driver detects the wrong type of card, especially at boot time. If this happens, a common trick is to remove the card and insert it again. Then see whether the module has detected the card properly by reading the messages in the /var/log/messages file.

Software

Software is the primary reason computers are used. Many software packages come with your Red Hat Linux distribution. This section covers a few problems that may occur when you run some of them.

Internet Concerns

A popular application under Linux is Netscape Communicator, a well-known Web browser. One nice feature of Netscape that is used by few people is its Personal Toolbar. When downloaded, Netscape includes a Personal Toolbar with buttons that you may not find useful, such as taking you to the Yahoo and Netscape home pages. Most people, therefore, either turn off the Toolbar or ignore it. The Toolbar can be a more useful tool than Bookmarks. What appears on the Personal Toolbar is simply what's listed in the Bookmarks, Personal Folder. Within the Personal Folder, you can create subfolders for news sites, Linux sites, and so on. To set up the Personal Toolbar, move your bookmarks into the Personal Folder using the Edit Bookmarks menu option. In this way, all of your frequently used bookmarks can be accessed directly from a Toolbar button.

Many Linux users use a program called Pine to get their e-mails. Pine is a console based e-mail client that has many features and is very easy to use. It is, by default, configured to access only the e-mail messages on your local system, in a standard UNIX mail format. Here's how you can use Pine both with local mail and with POP mail from your Internet provider, without first using fetchmail or some other tool to get POP mail. Start by using multiple config files:

```
pine -p localmail
pine -p popserver
```

The two configuration files specified in the last commands are identical except for the mail fetching parameters. Now, configure Pine to use your POP server. Start Pine with the popserver argument. Next, choose Setup, Config. Set your inbox-path parameter similar to:

```
{pop.server.com/pop3/user=myid}INBOX
```

The server name and user ID you should use are provided by your Internet provider. Now restart Pine. You will be prompted for your password and then connected to the remote server from where you can now use Pine just as if you were accessing local mail while continuing to use the localmail configuration file for local mail handling.

You may also want to host Web pages with your Linux system. Your system may be on a static link with a hostname, but you may want to support multiple hostnames such as www.domain1.com and www.domain2.com. The next paragraphs describe how to make virtual hosts in Apache, a popular Web server.

The common way to create a virtual host is to assign one IP for each hostname. But what if you want to host multiple hostnames on a single IP? Apache allows you to do so. The trick is a single command in the httpd.conf configuration file:

```
NameVirtualHost 1.2.3.4
```

Replace 1.2.3.4 with your real IP address to tell Apache the IP on which it should serve the virtual hostnames. You can add *virtual* commands for every hostname:

```
<VirtualHost www.domain2.com>
ServerAdmin webmaster@domain2.com
DocumentRoot /home/httpd/domain2
ServerName www.domain2.com
</VirtualHost>
```

These commands add a virtual host and specify the files that exist for that site. In the DNS database, the actual www.domain2.com hostname must point to your system. Next, update the record so that the host points to your server. You can do so yourself if you own the domain2.com domain name and control its name server. If not, ask the owner or technical representative to do it for you.

You may also want to create a secure Apache server, by adding an encryption library to the Apache sources. These sources and documentation are available from the Apache-SSL project site, **www.apache-ssl.org**. The encryption library can be a bit complex to install, so here are a few general-purpose hints. The goal is to compile the encryption module into the Apache binary file. You'll need to first uncompress them both in the same directory and then compile the library. With a provided patch, you can integrate both together. Once the compilation is done, continue installing the server as you would when installing a normal Apache Web server. Finally, you will need to create a certificate for your server. Using certificates is a complex topic, but you can create a temporary certificate in your Apache-ssl distribution until you purchase one from a company.

Productivity Applications

If you need to read documents on your Linux system that were created on other operating systems, such as Lotus 1-2-3 or Microsoft Word, you'll want to install StarOffice. The StarOffice program exists to view files from many popular formats and, in my opinion, is one of the best office suites available for Linux. You can download StarOffice from the Web site **www.sun.com/staroffice**. It is free for personal use; the instructions on how to install it are discussed in Chapter 10, "Installing Software."

Alternatively, you may have programs that you used and liked on the Microsoft Windows or other operating system platforms, but you can't find a similar Linux-based program or one that performs the same tasks as your old program. Fortunately, a number of emulation programs exist. For example, you can run the program DOSEMU on your Linux system to emulate a DOS system. You can then run various DOS applications while still in the Linux operating system. The same thing is true for Windows applications; the WINE program enables you to run many Windows 16-bit (and some 32-bit) applications while still in Linux. For example, you could run Microsoft Word for Windows in Linux using the WINE emulator.

> The WINE project is still under development and is known to fail often. If you want to run a program such as Microsoft Word through WINE, try the 16-bit version first. At this time WINE emulates 16-bit Windows applications better than it does 32-bit ones.

There are a number of other emulators, including Executor for MacOS and VMware, a commercial product that simply emulates a computer. VMware enables you to run virtually any operating system on top of Linux.

Locating Shared Libraries

One problem that may occur when you try to run a Linux program is an error message telling you that a shared library was not found. Programs use libraries to store functions that are common to, and shared by, many programs. If a program needs a library but can't find it, the program can't run. To avoid these situations, always try to install applications that are in RPM format, using the `rpm` command. RPM-format programs check your system for the existence of all necessary libraries on which the new program depends.

Removing Oddly Named Files

Some programs, unfortunately, create strange-looking file names, often as temporary files. You should be able to remove them using the `rm` command, but doing so can be difficult when strange alphanumeric characters are used. You may not always know how to reproduce the character so that you can use it in the `rm` command string. In these cases, use a file manager such as mc to list the files in the current directory and allow you to select one using your cursor or mouse. You can then delete the file.

> When you type any command (such as `rm`) that enables you to include file-name parameters, including a space will indicate to Linux that you have specified multiple files. To force Linux to look at a space-containing file name, surround the file name with quotation marks.

Working with Other File Systems

The Linux kernel supports many file systems, but they are not always compiled into the kernel itself or loaded at boot time. You may need to add the required module before you try to mount a disk with a foreign file system. For example, if the MS-DOS–based file system is not loaded and you try to mount a floppy formatted in DOS mode, you will receive an error message. To load the right module, type

```
modprobe msdos
```

Many people use Microsoft Windows 95 OSR2 or Windows 98 alongside Linux. Mounting a file system from these systems on Linux using the msdos parameter won't work. The msdos parameter worked with older Windows 95 file systems, but it will not work with newer Windows versions because the file system type has changed. DOS and Windows 95 used the FAT file system; Windows 95 OSR2 and Windows 98 use VFAT or FAT32. Mount a VFAT system this way:

```
mount -tvfat /dev/hda2 /mnt/w98
```

Formatting Floppies in ext2 Format

To select the file system to be used with floppies, edit the line in fstab beginning with /dev/fd0. The third column is the file system type. If you know you will always use DOS-formatted floppies, change it to msdos. If you know your floppies will always be formatted in Linux, set the file system to ext2.

Allowing Users to Mount CD-ROM Drives

To allow any user to mount a CD-ROM drive, find the line in fstab that begins with /dev/cdrom. Modify the user parameter (located in the fifth column) to tell the Linux system to allow users to mount the CD drive. The line should read:

```
/dev/cdrom        /mnt/cdrom        iso9660     noauto,ro,user    0 0
```

Suppressing Annoying Boot Messages

Boot messages are designed to tell you whether everything was properly loaded and whether all hardware devices were detected. You may, however, see strange messages such as the following:

```
modprobe: cannot find net-pf-5
```

```
modprobe: cannot find char-major-14
```

These warnings are not important and do not mean that something has gone wrong in your system. They can, however, be annoying. You can turn these warning messages off by adding the two following commands to the file /etc/conf.modules:

```
alias net-pf-5 off
alias char-major-14 off
```

Useful Programs

Many programs that may be useful in your everyday tasks are not production applications, but rather utilities that help you manage your files, communicate efficiently, and allow you to more easily troubleshoot problems. Some of these programs are available on your Red Hat Linux CD-ROM; all of them are listed on the Linux applications site at **www.freshmeat.net**.

Good system management brings efficiency and fewer problems, which results in more time for you to do real work. Several programs exist to help with this; including the following:

- **GProc.** This program allows you to configure and manage processes, displaying a graphical tree of all that are currently running. GProc can be a useful tool to either kill or wake up a process that refuses to terminate or that has stopped responding. It allows you to send various signals to processes and is configurable to give you the best view of them.

- **gTaskMgr.** This is similar to GProc. It provides you with additional information about the current processes and allows you to filter out some programs. It is somewhat similar to the Microsoft Windows NT task manager.

- **gUserMan.** This program is useful if you are having difficulty adding or managing users and groups. It shows you all existing users and groups and allows you to add new ones. This is particularly useful for a server, where you may have many users and groups to add.

- **gViewConfig.** This program enables you to view information about your hardware. It lists the most important information and may be useful to you when troubleshooting driver problems.

- **Kgconfig.** This program simplifies configuration of the kernel. It displays a graphical configuration screen with each kernel option and provides help for those options.

Monitoring programs help you deal with more complex problems, perhaps showing you summary information about your desktop or displaying detailed information about the inner working of Linux. Here are a few programs that can help you monitor your system:

- **Ethereal.** This is a nice graphical monitor that captures and lists network packets, giving you every detail about every packet. This is particularly useful when you are trying to solve networking problems because it helps you determine which packets get to your system.

- **gsysboard.** This small program is helpful when you are diagnosing performance problems. It displays summary information about system resources, including the CPU, RAM, and swap memory usage.

- **top.** This program displays detailed information about the CPU and memory usage of every program running on the system. It refreshes in real time to show the dynamics of the processes.

- **Printerspy.** This program monitors SNMP-enabled printers, such as some network printers. For example, Printerspy can alert you if the printer goes offline or if a paper jam occurs.

New Linux users tend to have a particularly difficult time learning how to manipulate files. Fortunately, many good file managers exist to solve problems. Here are the file managers that may help you deal with everyday problems:

- **mc.** The mc file manager is a console-based program with many options. From the main interface, you can press various function keys to activate functions on the selected files. mc includes a file viewer, a simple file editor, and a dialog box allowing you to change permissions on a file.

- **kfm.** This is the graphical file manager for KDE. It allows you to browse directories, compressed files, and even the Web. kfm includes a few options and can be set to view files as icons or as lists, with full details.

- **gnome-browser.** This is similar to kfm but works with the GNOME desktop. It performs the same functions as kfm.

Administration software allows you to manage your Linux system, even if you are not running a server. For example, you may want to connect to various networks, share files, print, or allow other users to log on to your system. Several programs can help:

- **Appletalk Configurator.** This program helps you configure an Appletalk network. From it, you can configure your network interface, printers, and files.

- **Comanche.** This graphical tool can help you input all the parameters used to configure the Apache Web server. You can use Comanche to modify various settings in the configuration area and see the currently running Apache processes.

- **GLilo.** This is used to configure LILO, the Linux boot loader. You can, for example, change which operating system is loaded by default or the amount of time left before LILO switches to the default. Using GLilo, you can set multiple operating systems and see the configuration for each of them. You can also input pre-set variables, such as the timeout setting, the place where you want to install LILO, and an optional password that will be required before booting. Extensive help is also available for each GLilo command inside of the program.

Conclusion

This chapter has offered various ways to make your troubleshooting experiences less painful. There will always be problems; that is the nature of computing. With the solutions and utilities presented in this chapter, however, you should be able to correct any problem that occurs on your system. Other tools do exist, and you should refer to the Web for more information about them.

Now that you have reached the end of the chapters in this book, I invite you to start exploring your newly installed Red Hat 7 PC and discover the great ways it can help you boost your productivity!

PART IV

Appendixes

A The Linux Primer

B Online Resources

C Hardware Compatibility Journal

D Advanced Configuration Reference

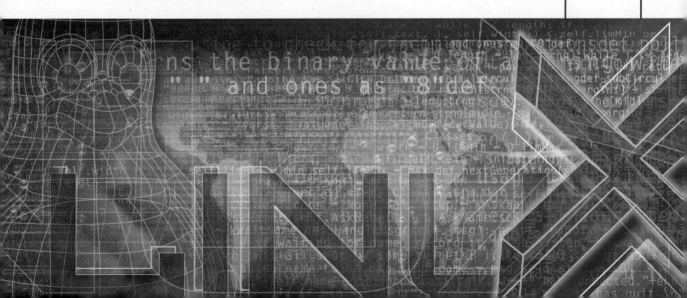

Appendix A: The Linux Primer

ow that you've successfully installed Linux on your computer, it's time to log on to your system and start getting acclimated to working in Linux. You're probably already familiar with using a GUI and can find your way around unfamiliar GUIs such as KDE or GNOME pretty easily. After all, you just experiment with pointing and clicking on icons or menus until you find one that does what you want. With a command-line interface (CLI), however, you might have a little more trouble getting around if you don't know what's going on.

Getting Started: The Login Prompt

When you start your computer and Linux has finished booting, you get a prompt to log in that looks something like this:

```
Welcome to Linux 2.4.0.
Odin Login:
```

The name in front of Login is the name you've given your computer when you set up networking. If you haven't given your computer a name (shame on you), the default is localhost.

If you've set up a regular account for yourself, type in your user name at the prompt. If you haven't set up a normal user account for yourself, however, type in **root**.

> It is a bad idea to do all your work on your system as root if you aren't very familiar with Linux. Actually, it's a bad idea to do all of your work as root even if you are very familiar with Linux. Linux is an obedient operating system—it does whatever you tell it to do if you have the proper permissions to do so. This means it is possible to delete your entire directory tree without any fuss from the system. Consider yourself warned.

Using Passwords

After you type in your user name, you are prompted to type in your password. For security reasons, your password does not display as you type. Furthermore, if your computer is exposed to other users—even if just through a dial-up Internet connection—you probably should change your password from time to time and use one that includes numbers as well as letters. Passwords made up of regular words are considered weak because they can be found in a dictionary and are therefore vulnerable to what is known as a *dictionary attack*. Don't be so clever with your password that you forget it, though—especially if you don't use Linux every day. On a dual-boot system, it's very easy to install Linux, forget about it for a while and then go back to find you've forgotten your password! There are ways to fix this, but it's easier not to worry about it in the first place.

> If you are having trouble with your password but you're sure you're typing it correctly, make sure that the caps lock key is not toggled. Linux passwords are case-sensitive. You'd be surprised how often this happens.

Now that you're logged in to the system, it's time to start getting familiar with how to navigate the Linux OS from the command line.

Getting Familiar with Multi-User Operating Systems

Linux is a multi-user operating system. That means you can have several people logged in to one Linux machine, all working simultaneously. Typical desktop operating systems are designed to handle only one user at a time. A typical Linux machine, however, can have one user logged in locally and several other users logged in remotely over a network connection.

Using Virtual Terminals

Another way to make use of Linux's multi-user functionality is to log in to multiple virtual terminals. While you're logged in to the system, press Alt+F2 to be shown another login screen. This enables you to work on several things at the command line simultaneously, just by alternating between virtual terminals.

You can be logged in to several virtual terminals at a time, which is very useful. If you find you need to do something as root, for example, you can log in to a virtual terminal and execute the commands you need to as root. After you finish with the system administrator stuff, you can log out again so you aren't tempted to work as root on everyday tasks.

Using the whoami Command

If you're logged in to five virtual terminals, some as yourself and some as root, what if you forget which is which? Easy. At the shell prompt, type in **whoami**, and the system tells you who you are logged in as at that terminal. Figure A.1 shows an example of the output of the `whoami` command.

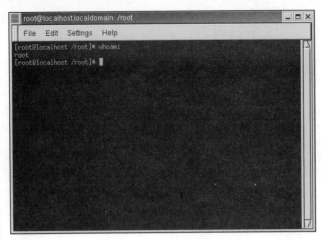

Figure A.1   *An example of the output from the* whoami *command.*

Another sign to look for is the shell prompt. Under bash, the shell prompt is a dollar sign ($) when you are logged in as a regular user. When you are logged in as root, the shell prompt is a pound sign (#) instead.

Understanding and Using File Permissions

The key difference between the root user and the typical user on a Linux system is the permissions each has on the system. As the name implies, permissions indicate what a particular user is allowed to do. If you have permission to manipulate a file, Linux lets you do so. If you do not, however, the system returns a permission denied error message.

Permissions are very important for a multi-user operating system. They prevent unauthorized users from accessing files vital to the system, and they prevent users from accessing or accidentally overwriting each other's files.

This also makes Linux a great OS for home use. When a family shares a computer, Mom, Dad, and the kids each have separate home directories where they can save their own files without worry. With legacy operating systems, such as Windows, files belonging to one family member often get misplaced or deleted by another family member who doesn't realize the files are important. This often has the effect of contributing to Dad's ulcer when his report due Monday morning has been deleted to make more room for a game Junior downloaded.

There are three types of permissions: read, write, and execute. These permissions can apply to the owner of the file (the user), the group to which the file belongs (the group), and all other users (the others). By making a file owned by a particular user and group and then setting permissions for the user, the group, and the others, you can control precisely who can access the file (see Table A.1).

Table A.1 Meanings of Permissions

Permission	File	Directory
Read	File can be read	Directory contents can be listed
Write	File can be modified	Files can be created and deleted in the directory
Execute	File can be executed	Directory can be opened

Typically, a new file is owned by the user who created it. The file has read and write permissions for that user and read access for anyone else. If you don't want anyone else to be able to read the file, be sure to remove the read option from the file for the group and for all other users. To do this, execute the following command:

```
chmod 600 file
```

Running the `chmod` (change mode) command on a file changes the mode of access to the file, depending on the arguments you pass to the file when you run it. In the preceding example, you pass the octal notation for the level of permissions allowed for that file. The first digit describes the permissions for the user, the second digit is for the group, and the last is for all other users. Also, note that no matter what permissions are set on a file, the root user can always access a file.

> The octal notation, 0–7, represents the file permissions numerically. 0 indicates no permissions, 1 indicates execute permission, 2 indicates write permission, and 4 indicates read permission. When you add the numbers together in various combinations, you have numbers between 0 and 7. So, for example, if you have read and write permission, the number would be 6. For some people it is easier to remember number schemes than the other way round.

NOTE

It's also possible to tell chmod only what permissions to change, rather than give it an entirely new set of permissions. For example, if you wanted to allow everyone in the file's group to write to it, you could use this command:

```
chmod g+w file
```

You refer to the user, group, and others with the letters u, g, and o. A plus sign sets the permissions; a minus sign clears them. The permissions themselves are indicated with r for read, w for write, and x for execute. You can specify multiple letters at once.

To find out what permissions are currently set on a file, run the ls command with the -l argument, as follows (I use my own screen name as a placeholder for these examples):

```
$ ls -l testfile
-r----------   1 BKP    users          0 Sep 26 15:28 testfile
```

The r and the next two hyphens are related to permissions; the next three are related to my (BKP) permissions; the next three are related to my group's permissions; and the final three are related to the permissions of all users. As you can see, I only have read access to the file, and no one else can read the file. If I had read, write, and execute access, the output would look like this:

```
-rwx---------  1 BKP    users          0 Sep 26 15:28 testfile
```

Files stored under MS-DOS or Microsoft Windows can also have permissions, but you'll have fewer options because those are not multi-user operating systems.

Finding Hidden Files

Unlike MS-DOS files, which can have a flag set to make them hidden, Linux files are hidden when they begin with a dot (period).

BUZZWORD

Dotfiles: Linux files that begin with a dot are hidden. These are commonly called dotfiles.

Many common configuration files are stored in dotfiles in each user's home directory. You normally don't see these files unless you ask to see them, as in this example:

```
$ ls -a
./    .Xdefaults   .bash_profile  .emacs   .mailcap   .zshrc     tmp/
../   .bash_logout  .bashrc        .kderc   .vimrc     Desktop/
```

Working at the Shell

The default command shell under Red Hat Linux is the GNU BourneAgain Shell, or bash. The shell is the command interpreter for Linux, much like command.com is for MS-DOS or its GUI equivalent, Windows Explorer, under MS Windows. The bash shell executes commands from standard input or from a script. Shell scripts under Linux are the functional equivalent of batch files under MS-DOS, except that they are much more powerful than the average batch file.

The bash shell is not the only command shell available for Linux. Three other popular shells are csh, which is similar to the Berkley UNIX C shell; the enhanced version of csh, tcsh; as well as the Z shell, zsh.

As is often the case in Linux, there is a dizzying variety of options—far too many to cover in a book concerned with brevity and simplicity. Generally, the Bourne Again Shell is probably the only shell you ever need to know. However, there are plenty of other shells available if you find you want to experiment.

You do not need to do anything to initialize the bash shell; it is available after you install Red Hat and runs whenever you log in to the computer. You can, however, configure the way bash behaves.

When you log in to Linux, bash looks for a file called /.bashrc in your home directory. If this exists, bash reads the file and executes the commands that you put in the file. Under Red Hat Linux, ~/.bashrc is not created by default. However, if you wish to customize bash, you can easily create your own /.bashrc.

> Remember, /.bashrc is not the same to Linux as bashrc. The /.bashrc file is a dot file, which means it is normally a hidden file. Most configuration files under Linux are dotfiles found in the user's home directory.

NOTE

Understanding the Linux Philosophy: Piping and Redirecting

As you continue reading this primer, you'll probably notice that I mention piping and redirecting output and input several times. This is because according to the UNIX philosophy, every command should be a filter and operate on input and output. Almost any command's output can be piped or redirected into a file, a device, or another command. Linux follows the basic idea of UNIX in this fashion. I explain a few simple ways to utilize this in this appendix, but I can barely touch the surface of the capabilities of Linux. You should experiment with redirection and pipes a little on your own; you might be surprised what kind of timesaving shortcuts you discover.

Piping Input and Output

Piping is taking the output of one command and making it input for another command. For example, to pipe the output of the `ps` command to the `grep` command to search for a process ID, issue this command:

```
ps -ax | grep netscape
```

The `|` is the pipe symbol. If there is a Netscape process running, grep outputs the lines with `netscape` in them to standard output (the monitor).

Using Direction and Redirection

You can redirect input or output with the symbols `>` and `<`. The `>` symbol redirects output to a file or device. The `<` symbol changes a command's input to come from a file or device rather than from the keyboard.

You can use the `>` symbol to create a file by redirecting output from a command to a file name. Be careful not to overwrite an existing file with this redirection. If you would rather append the output to an existing file, use `>>`, which tells the shell not to clobber the file, but instead append to it. If you want to overwrite a file, use `>|`, which tells the shell to go ahead and overwrite the file without asking. Some shells treat `>` and `>|` the same, never asking you if it is okay to overwrite the file.

> As always, be careful with redirection symbols. You can easily overwrite an important file.

Common Commands

There are quite a few common commands that you should familiarize yourself with in order to get around in Linux. Even if you plan on spending most of your time in KDE, GNOME, or one of Linux's other GUIs, you'll find using these commands in an xterm or at the console very useful. You will also find you are able to combine commands with each other to simplify everyday tasks.

Some commands have a large number of options, and they might not all be covered in this text if they aren't likely to be used in normal situations. For a complete list of options, you can consult the command's man page.

Copying Files: The cp Command

Name: `cp`

Function: To copy files and directories.

Syntax: `cp options file(s) destination`

Description: The `cp` command is similar to the MS-DOS command `copy`; it's used to copy files or directories from one place to another. You can copy one file to a new file, one file to another place, or a large number of files all at once to a new place. When you copy a file, you do not delete the original file by default. If you wish to move a file rather than make a copy of it, use the `mv` command instead.

Usage: To use the `cp` command, type **cp**, followed by any options, and then type the directory or file name(s) you want to copy, followed by the destination. If you want to copy multiple files, you can use wildcards, or you can list multiple files separated by spaces.

Options:

> `-f` **(Force).** Remove any existing files of the same name.
>
> `-i` **(Interactive).** Prompt the user if there is an existing file of the same name in the destination directory.
>
> `-p` **(Preserve).** Preserve the original file's permissions, if possible.
>
> `-R` **(Recursive).** Copy directories located under the starting directory. The default is not to copy subdirectories.

Example 1: Copying a File into Another Directory

Suppose that you download a /.tgz file called ~/program.tgz—which contains source code—into your home directory, and you want to unzip and untar it, but you don't want to do it in your home directory. You can cp the file into the /tmp directory and work with it there. To do this, type the following:

```
cp program.tgz /tmp
```

Note that you do not get an error message if the file already exists unless you use the interactive option. If the file exists, you are asked whether you want to over-write the file, like this:

```
cp -i program.tgz /tmp
cp: overwrite  /tmp/program.tgz'?
```

If you answer **y**, the file is overwritten; if **n**, the file is not overwritten.

Example 2: Copying Multiple Files into Another Directory

If you have a group of files you want to move into another directory without having to type each file name individually, you can use wildcards. If you want to copy all files in the current directory to another directory, type

```
cp * /tmp
```

This copies all files in the directory to the /tmp directory; however, it does not copy directories unless specifically told to. To copy files and directories, use the recursive option.

```
cp -R * /tmp
```

> Note that -r and -R are not equivalent. Unlike MS-DOS and Windows, Linux is case-sensitive. Be careful when typing commands under Linux, as interchanging uppercase and lowercase letters might cause unwanted and possibly disastrous results!

If you'd like to copy all files with a specific extension to another directory, you can use wildcards to selectively copy groups of files like this:

```
cp *.jpg *.gif images
```

This copies all JPEG and GIF files to the image directory, without copying any other files with them. You can also use the question-mark character (?) to match a single character rather than a group of characters.

Moving Files: The mv Command

Name: mv

Function: To move or rename files and directories.

Syntax: mv options file(s) destination

Description: The mv command can be used to move a file or files to another directory, or to rename a file or files. The mv command is similar to the MOVE command under MS-DOS, but the mv command is much more powerful than its MS-DOS equivalent. The mv command does delete the original file that is being moved, so be sure to use the command carefully. The mv command is also used to rename files under Linux, so it also takes the place of the REN command under MS-DOS.

Usage: To move a file, type **mv**, followed by any options, then the name of the file(s) or directories to be moved, and then the destination to which you want the file(s) moved. As with the cp command, you can use wildcards to move multiple files rather than typing individual file names.

Options:

-b **(Backup).** Creates a backup file of any files that would be overwritten by moving a file. By default, backup files have a tilde character (~) extension.

-f **(Force).** Removes any files of the same name when trying to move a file without prompting the user.

-i **(Interactive).** Prompts the user if moving the current file will overwrite another file. If there are no conflicting files, mv simply moves the file with no complaint.

-s **(Suffix).** Appends a suffix to any backup files. By default, the tilde suffix is applied, but you can specify any type of suffix, such as .bak or .tmp.

Example 1: Moving a File to Another Directory

To move the file index.html to another directory without making a backup or being prompted in the event of an overwrite, use the mv command, followed by the name of the file and its destination:

```
mv index.html /home/BKP/backup/
```

If you're not certain whether a file of the same name already exists, use the interactive mode of mv. If the file already exists, your output looks like this:

```
mv -i index.html /home/BKP/backup/
mv: replace /home/BKP/backup/index.html'?
```

Example 2: Moving Multiple Files to Another Directory

You can use wildcards to move more than one file to another directory. Be careful! The mv command can move directories as well as regular files. Be sure you actually want to move everything under a directory before using the wildcard (*).

If you want to move all the HTML files in the current directory to the /home/ httpd/ directory, you use this command:

```
mv *.html /home/httpd/
```

The *.html specifies that you want to move all files that end in .html to another directory. If you want to move all files in the current directory to the /home/httpd/ directory, you type

```
mv * /home/httpd/
```

This moves all files in the current directory, except any dotfiles. To move dotfiles, you have to be more explicit:

```
mv .* /home/httpd/
```

Example 3: Renaming Files with mv

Linux does not have a separate rename command, so the `mv` command is used to rename files. If you want to rename index.html to index.html.old, for instance, you use the `mv` command like this:

```
mv index.html index.html.old
```

As far as Linux is concerned, moving a file and renaming it are the same thing.

Creating Directories: The mkdir Command

Name: `mkdir`

Function: To create new directories.

Syntax: `mkdir options directory`

Description: The `mkdir` command is pretty straightforward. It behaves the same way that the MS-DOS command `MKDIR` works. The Linux command does have some additional functionality—you can set the permissions of the directory when it is created.

Usage: To create a new directory simply type **mkdir** and any options and then the name of the directory you wish to create.

Options:

   -m **(Mode).** Creates a directory with specified permissions.

Example 1: Creating a New Directory

To create a new directory called /html under the current directory, use the `mkdir` command followed by the name of the new directory:

```
mkdir html
```

Suppose you want to create a new directory called download under the /tmp directory, and you want the new directory to have read-only permissions for other users and members of your group and read and write permissions for you. To do so, use the `mkdir` command plus the proper octal mode:

```
mkdir -m 644 /tmp/download
```

This creates a directory named download under the /tmp directory. (You do not need to be in the /tmp directory to create a subdirectory for it.) If a file or directory named download already exists in the /tmp directory, you receive the following error message:

```
mkdir /tmp/download
mkdir: cannot make directory  download': File exists
```

Listing and Finding Files with ls

Name: `ls`

Function: To list the contents of a directory.

Syntax: `ls options directory` or `file(s)`

Description: The `ls` command lists the contents of a directory. This command is similar to the MS-DOS command `DIR`. In fact, typing `dir` under Linux is the same as typing `ls -c`. The `ls` command is one of the commands you use the most under Linux. You can also use the `ls` command to get information about a specific file in a directory.

Usage: To use the `ls` command, you simply type the command, followed by any options you want to invoke and any file names (including wildcards) that you want to specify.

Options:

   `-a` **(All).** Lists all files in a directory, including hidden files.

   `-A` **(Almost all).** Lists all files in a directory, except for "." and "..".

   `-i` **(Inode).** Prints inode number of each file.

   `-l` **(Long).** In addition to the file names, lists the file type, permissions, owner name, size of the file, and the last time the file was modified. Also known as the verbose mode.

   `-r` **(Reverse).** Lists the directory contents in reverse order.

   `-sk` **(Kilobytes).** Lists file sizes in kilobytes. The `s` specifies that, yes, you want to see the sizes.

   `-x` **(Extension).** Sorts files by their extension; files with no extension will be sorted first.

Example 1: Listing Files in Your Home Directory

You probably want to know what files are in your home directory from time to time, so it's a good idea to know how to check. To list the files in your home directory, type the following command:

```
ls ~
```

That's all you need to type. The ~ character is a shortcut that refers to your home directory. The output for the command looks something like Figure A.2.

> Not only are the files in the current directory listed, but they're in color. That's one of the ways Linux makes your life a little bit easier.

Example 2: Listing Hidden Files in a Directory

If you decide you want to edit resource files, you probably have to find some hidden files. To list all files in a directory, type in the following:

```
ls -a
```

When listing all of the files in your home directory, you find there are quite a few more files than you might have thought.

```
root@localhost.localdomain: /root                            _ □ ×
 File   Edit   Settings   Help
[root@localhost /root]# whoami
root
[root@localhost /root]# ls
Desktop  office52  rpms  so-5_2-ga-bin-linux-en.bin   xv-3.10a-13.i386.rpm
[root@localhost /root]# █
```

Figure A.2   *Output of the ls command.*

Example 3: Listing All Files and Their Attributes

If you want to see all of the files in a directory and their attributes, combine the -a and -l options, as follows:

```
ls -al
```

You see a list of all files in the directory, as well as their permissions, modification dates, to whom they belong, and the size of the files. The first letter indicates whether it is a file, directory, link, or other. A file is a dash (-), a directory is d, a symbolic link is an l, and a hard link is represented as a regular file. Other characters indicate it is a special type of file.

After that letter comes the permissions. There are three groups of three letters. The first set is the permissions given to the owner of the file. The next set of three is for the group of the file, and then finally is the set for the permissions for everyone else. Then you see the owner of the file, followed by the group to which the file belongs. By default, the size of each file is displayed in bytes. Next in the list is the last time the file was modified, or touched, and then the name of the file itself.

> The expression *touch* is not one I coined. On UNIX-style operating systems, a file is said to be touched when it is modified by a user in some way. A file is not touched when you just list the contents of a directory the file is in or view the contents of the file.

NOTE

Making Links

Name: ln

Function: To create a hard link or symbolic link to a file.

Syntax: ln options source linkname

Description: The ln command creates a link to a file or directory. By using the ln command, you can create either a symbolic link or a hard link. A symbolic, or soft, link is a special file that contains a path name. Hard links are actually another name for a file, rather than a pointer to that file like symbolic links.

As long as a name (that is, a hard link) for a file exists, it remains on disk. Even if you create a file, create a hard link to it, and then delete the original file, the data remains safely on disk. If you create a symbolic link pointing to a file and delete the original file, the file ceases to exist, and the soft link is left pointing to nothing.

The other major difference between symbolic links and hard links is that symbolic links can cross file systems, while hard links can point only to files on the same file system. For instance, if you have your /home directory on one hard drive partition and the /opt directory on another, you could not create a hard link from something in the /home directory to something in the /opt directory. However, you could create a symbolic link between the two with no problem.

Usage: Use the `ln` command to create symbolic or hard links to files or directories. If you do not specify the name of the link, `ln` attempts to create a link with the same name as what you're linking to.

Options:

-f **(Force).** Removes files if they already exist with the link's name.

-i **(Interactive).** Prompts the user if files exist.

-s **(Symbolic).** Makes a symbolic link rather than a hard link.

Example 1: Creating a Symbolic Link to a Directory

Let's say you do a lot of work in the /home/httpd/Webpages/uri/ directory but don't feel like typing the entire directory name each time you want to change to that directory. You can create a symbolic link to that directory in your home directory called /Web, and then you only have to type **cd Web** to change to the /home/httpd/Webpages/uri/ directory. To create that link, use the following command:

```
ln -s /home/httpd/Webpages/uri/ ~/Web
```

As long as there are no files in your home directory called /Web, you have created a symbolic link to the proper directory. This can be very useful and save quite a bit of typing!

Moving Around the Command Line Interface: cd

Name: `cd`

Function: To change the working directory.

Syntax: `cd directory`

Description: The `cd` command changes your working directory to another directory that you specify. This command is used to navigate the directory structure in Linux. Typing only **cd** returns you to your home directory. The `cd` command works similarly to the `CD` command under DOS. However, the `cd` command is a little more flexible in that it allows you shortcuts to change between your home directory and the previous working directory.

Usage: Use the `cd` command to change directories. Specifying no directory returns you to your home directory.

Options: None

Example 1: Changing to the Parent Directory of the Current Working Directory

As in DOS, the parent directory is always .. . To go up one level in the directory structure, simply type the following:

```
cd ..
```

> You must have a space between the .. and `cd`. If you type `cd..` with no space (as you might be used to doing under DOS), you get an error message telling you that the command `cd..` is not found.

If you want to go up several levels in the directory structure, you can do so by typing this:

```
cd ../../
```

This moves you up two levels from your current directory.

Example 2: Changing to a Specific Directory

To change to a specific directory, you issue the `cd` command and then the name of the directory you wish to change to. If you're working in your home directory and decide to switch to the /tmp directory, you use this command:

```
cd /tmp
```

> It is important to note that /tmp and tmp are not the same in this instance. The /tmp tells the shell you want to go to the tmp under the / (root) directory and not a tmp directory under the present working directory.

Example 3: Going Home Quickly

To get to your home directory quickly, simply use the `cd` command with no arguments, like this:

```
cd
```

If you do not specify a directory, the bash shell assumes you wish to go back to your home directory. You can also use the tilde (~) symbol to specify your home directory, as in the following example:

```
cd ~
```

Example 4: Going Back to the Previous Working Directory

If you want to quickly jump back to the directory you were last in without typing the full path name of that directory, type this shortcut:

```
cd -
```

Once you get the hang of the `cd` command and Linux's directory structure, you'll find that using the command-line interface is not as unfriendly as you might have thought when you first started using Linux. If you try using DOS after using Linux for a while, you'll really find yourself missing Linux.

Where the Heck Am I? Using pwd

Name: `pwd`

Function: To print the name of the present working directory.

Syntax: `pwd`

Description: The command `pwd` is about as straightforward as you can get. It's a one-trick pony. If you have lost track of where you are in the directory structure, you simply use `pwd` to get the shell to print the present working directory to standard out.

Usage: Use the `pwd` command to find the present working directory.

Options: None.

Example 1: Using pwd to Find the Present Working Directory

At the command shell, type in

```
pwd
```

The output is the current working directory. The `pwd` command does not take any options or arguments.

Mounting File Systems with mount

There are two commands under Linux that are pertinent to accessing file systems: mount and umount. The mount command is used to mount a file system, and not surprisingly, the umount command, discussed in the next section, is used to unmount a mounted file system.

Name: mount

Function: To make available, or mount, a file system.

Syntax: mount options device directory

Description: Unlike other operating systems you might be used to, Linux requires that you mount a file system before you can use it. Generally, most of this happens during the boot-up procedure, and you don't do it manually. CD-ROMs and floppies have to be mounted as you wish to use them and unmounted when you are finished. Normally you have to be the superuser (root) to issue the mount command. You do not normally need to specify the file-system type or the directory to mount in if the device is already listed in the /etc/fstab file. If you want to make a device mountable by a user or all users, include that information on the device line in /etc/fstab. Open your favorite text editor and put an entry in the /etc/fstab file like this:

```
/dev/hdd /cdrom iso9660 ro,user
```

From left to right, that line includes the name of the device, the directory it should be mounted under, the file-system type, an option specifying read-only, and an option specifying that non-root users can mount the device. Be sure to separate the options with commas but no spaces; otherwise, Linux doesn't understand what you're saying.

Currently mounted file systems can be found in the /etc/mtab file. Do not edit the /etc/mtab file by hand, because it is updated dynamically by your system. It is useful to be able to read the /etc/mtab file, however, to see what devices are currently available and what file systems they are mounted as.

Usage: To use the mount command, type **mount** followed by any options and then the device name you wish to mount and optionally the directory you want the device mounted under. In Red Hat Linux, the default directory for the CD-ROM is /mnt/cdrom. If you have additional devices you need to access, you can create directories for them under the /mnt directory (or wherever else you like, but the /mnt directory is the standard location).

Another nifty thing about Linux (and there are plenty!) is that it can handle quite a few file-system types. Linux can read disks in its own native format (ext2), the FAT16 and FAT32 formats used by MS-DOS and Windows 9x, the Macintosh file system HFS, the Joliet file system used by Windows 9x for CD-ROMs, and the standard ISO9660 CD-ROM format, as well as many others. I found this very handy when I was sent a Zip disk with art files in Macintosh format. Using Windows, I would have had to buy an expensive program to read files from a Mac disk; using Linux, I just had to recompile the kernel to support HFS and mount the disk like any other Zip.

Options:

-a **(Auto).** Determines file-system type automatically, if possible.

-n **(No write).** Mounts the device without writing in /etc/mtab. Useful if /etc/mtab is a read-only file.

-t **(Type).** Specifies the file-system type. The following file-system types are common:

- ext2. The native Linux file system
- msdos. FAT16 file system
- umsdos. UMSDOS file system
- vfat. The FAT32 file system
- minix. The Minix file system
- nfs. Network file system
- smbfs. SMB shares from Windows or Samba
- iso9660. Standard CD-ROM file system
- hfs. Standard Macintosh file system

-v **(Verbose).** Prints any messages to standard out.

-o **(Options).** File system-specific options are specified by -o followed by a comma-separated list of options. Note that I am listing only the most common options. Most of these apply to all file-system types, but some file systems may support additional options:

- auto. Can also be specified by -a.
- defaults. Uses the default options (rw, suid, dev, exec, auto, nouser, async).
- exec. Permits the execution of binaries on the file system.
- noexec. Does not permit the execution of binaries on the file system.

- **ro.** Mounts the file system read-only, does not allow writing to the file system
- **rw.** Mounts the file system read-write, allows writing to the file system if the user has the privileges

Example 1: Mounting a CD-ROM

To use a CD-ROM, you need to mount it. By default, Red Hat Linux comes with a /mnt/cdrom directory. To mount a typical CD-ROM, type this command:

```
mount -t iso9660 /dev/hdd /mnt/cdrom
```

This tells the system that the file-system type (-t) is iso9660, the CD-ROM standard, and that your CD-ROM is located on the fourth IDE channel (hdd). Typically, your hard drive is hda; if you have a second, it usually is hdb, and so on. On most PCs there are two IDE controllers that can each have two devices, allowing for hda through hdd. The master device on the first controller is hda; the slave device is hdb. The master device on the second controller is hdc, and the slave device is hdd. The final argument to the mount command is the directory you want the CD-ROM mounted under. Now, unless there are errors, you can access the CD-ROM from that directory.

Example 2: Mounting a Floppy

To mount an MS-DOS floppy in what would be drive A under MS-DOS, use the mount command like this:

```
mount -t msdos /dev/fd0 /floppy
```

This mounts an MS-DOS (FAT16) floppy under the /floppy directory. By default, it allows read and write access. If you do not want to allow write access to the floppy, you can specify that with the -o rw option, like this:

```
mount -t msdos -o rw /dev/fd0 /floppy
```

If your /etc/fstab file is set up correctly, you can save typing. You only have to tell the mount command what device to mount; it tries to assume the rest by reading /etc/fstab. So to mount your floppy, usually all you really need to type is this:

```
mount /dev/fd0
```

Unlike Windows, Linux does not assign drive letters to devices. Devices become part of the file system when mounted. Although this probably seems foreign to you at first, it actually tends to make more sense. For one thing, you're not limited to 26 devices on your system! Okay, you probably won't hit this limit at home, but it is a real concern in a networked environment.

Unmounting File Systems

> When I first started using Red Hat, I kept trying to unmount CD-ROMs and floppies using unmount instead of umount. It's a common mistake. I eventually started remembering that it was umount instead of unmount, but you don't have to. If you want to type a more logical command, go to the /bin directory and make a symbolic link to umount called unmount, like this: ln -s umount unmount. Then the system finds a command called unmount after all. The -s provides a symbolic link to the command umount, thus providing for those who think unmount is more logical.

Name: umount

Function: To unmount a device attached to the file system.

Syntax: umount options directory

Description: The umount command unmounts a mounted device. You probably only need to use umount on devices such as your CD-ROM drive or floppy drive, though it can also be used to unmount any device on the system that is not currently being used. It is the opposite of the mount command.

Usage: To use the umount command, type **umount** followed by any options and then the directory name the device is mounted under. You can also use the device name instead of the directory, but it's usually easier to type the directory name.

> Note that if the file system is in use, Linux does not allow you to unmount it. If you are in the /cdrom directory, for instance, it does not let you unmount a CD-ROM mounted under that directory.

Options:

-n **(No write).** Unmounts without writing in the /etc/mtab file.

-r **(Read only).** If unmounting fails, this will try to remount read-only instead.

Example 1: Unmounting the CD-ROM

To unmount a CD-ROM mounted under the /cdrom directory, type

```
umount /cdrom
```

As long as no one is currently accessing /cdrom or is in that directory, the device is unmounted with no error messages or other output.

Example 2: Unmounting the Floppy

The syntax for unmounting a floppy is the same. Type

```
umount /floppy
```

Deleting Files

Name: rm

Function: To remove files and directories.

Syntax: rm options file(s)

Description: The rm command is similar to the DEL command under MS-DOS, but it is much more powerful.

> Unlike MS-DOS, Windows, or the Mac OS, Linux assumes you know what you're doing. This means if you have the permissions to remove files, Linux lets you and it doesn't complain that it might damage the system. Be very careful when removing files under Linux; once they're gone, they're gone. There is no undelete command under Linux, so be sure to exercise this command with caution. You can wipe out your entire directory tree and Linux happily lets you. This is a good reason not to do your work when you are logged in as root. Normal users don't have the permissions to really mess up the entire system. The root user, on the other hand, can delete the entire file system with one command.

CAUTION

Usage: To remove a file, type **rm**, then any options, and then the name of the file to be removed.

Options:

-f **(Force).** Do not prompt the user for confirmation, and give no error messages for nonexisting files.

-i **(Interactive).** Ask before removing each file.

-r,-R **(Recursive).** Remove directories and their contents recursively.

-v **(Verbose).** Print the names of files being removed.

Example 1: Removing a File

To simply remove a file, use the `rm` command with no options and only one argument—the name of the file you wish to remove, like this:

```
rm file
```

This removes the file with no error message or output of any kind as long as the file does exist and you have permissions to remove it. If the file doesn't exist or you don't have permissions, `rm` produces an error message.

Example 2: Removing a Directory and All Files Under It

To remove an entire directory and any contents in the directory, use the `rm` command along with the recursive (`-r` or `-R`) option and the name of the directory, like this:

```
rm -r tmp/
```

As long as you have the proper permissions and the directory exists, there is no prompting or message; Linux simply removes the directory and all of its contents. This is a good argument for using the interactive option as well, like this:

```
rm -ri tmp/
```

As you can see from the Figure A.3, you have several chances to change your mind about removing the file under the tmp directory and removing the directory itself. Unless you are very sure of yourself, and even if you are, I recommend using the interactive option of the `rm` command. It takes a little longer, but there's less chance of deleting an important file. Granted, deleting a vital part of your system helps you build valuable troubleshooting skills, but that's probably not the way you want to build them.

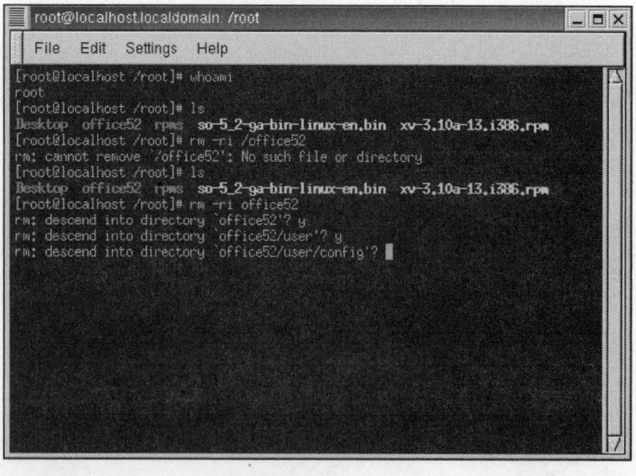

Figure A.3   *Using* rm *interactively.*

Example 3: Deleting Multiple Files with Wildcards

You can use wildcards to delete multiple files at once without having to type individual file names.

> Be very careful with wildcards. You can very easily destroy files you do not want to delete.

If you have multiple files whose names differ by only one character, you can use the ? wildcard to represent the character, like this:

```
rm -i temp?
```

That command deletes any file named temp1, temp2, and so on. It does not delete a file named temp22, stuff, or just plain temp.

The * wildcard in the next example deletes any file that begins with temp in the current directory. You can use the * wildcard to match a few files, like this:

```
rm -i temp*
```

Or you can use the * wildcard to match all files in a directory, like this:

```
rm -i *
```

> The interactive option is not necessary, but I'm putting it in the examples to encourage you to use it, at least until you're very familiar with Linux.

Example 4: Utter Insanity

If you're just fed up with your system, you can delete the entire directory tree with the following command executed as root under the / directory. Be sure you've got installation disks ready to go.

```
rm -rf *
```

Do not try this at home, and no, I haven't tried it to make sure it works.

Viewing and Manipulating Files with cat

Name: cat

Function: To concatenate files and print on standard out.

Syntax: `cat options file(s)`

Description: The `cat` command takes a file (or standard input, if you don't specify a file) and prints it to standard out. This is somewhat useful for quickly viewing files such as /etc/fstab or one of the other configuration files. The `cat` command really becomes useful in conjunction with other commands, either by piping the output of `cat` to other commands or by creating files with the output.

Usage: To concatenate a file to standard output, type **cat** followed by any options and the name of the file. Generally `cat` is used with some sort of redirection.

Options:

-b **(Number).** Number all lines that are not blank.

-s **(Squeeze).** Replace multiple blank lines with one blank line.

-n **(Number all).** Number all lines.

-v **(Show nonprinting).** Show nonprinting characters as well as regular characters.

-T **(Tabs).** Show tabs in a file.

Example 1: Concatenating a File to the Display

The simplest use of `cat` is to display the contents of a file to the screen, with no options. This can be useful to quickly view the contents of a file without opening the file in vi or Emacs. To see what file systems are currently mounted, you can cat the contents of /etc/mtab to the display (standard out) like this (see Figure A.4):

```
cat /etc/mtab
```

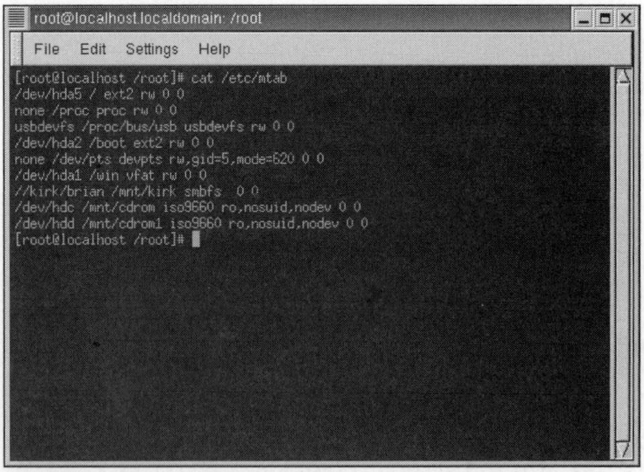

Figure A.4 *The output of* `cat /etc/mtab`.

This is somewhat useful, but `cat` becomes very useful when you redirect the output of the command to a file or another command.

Example 2: Redirecting the Output of a Concatenation

To redirect the output of `cat`, you should either pipe the output of `cat` to another command or redirect the output into a file. Here's how you redirect output from `cat` into another file.

```
cat file > file2
```

The preceding command overwrites the contents of the file if it already exists and creates the file if it doesn't exist. Basically, this is a poor man's copy.

If you want to append the contents of one file onto another without overwriting the original contents, you can use the following command:

```
cat file >> file2
```

This tells the shell to append the output of `cat` to the file rather than overwriting it.

`cat` is also used frequently in conjunction with the `less` command and the `grep` command. Say you have a text file where you save all of your friends' names, addresses, phone numbers, and email addresses, and you want to find one quickly. You can cat the file, pipe the output to grep, and use grep to search for your friend's name:

```
cat phonenumbers.txt | grep Bob
```

The preceding command outputs every line with `Bob` in it, saving you the hassle of searching through all of your friends' information in that file. You can even create a file just for Bob by redirecting the output to /Bob.txt, like this.

```
cat phonenumbers.txt | grep Bob > Bob.txt
```

Viewing Files with less

The `less` command is also useful to view files, especially longer files. It also enables you to navigate files in a way that `cat` does not.

Name: `less`

Function: To read a file (or standard input, if no file is given) to standard output. It is similar to the more command but allows forward and backward movement.

Syntax: `less options file`

Options:

-E **(End).** Tells `less` to exit when it reaches the end of a file.

-f **(Force).** Forces non-regular files to be opened. No error message is given when opening a binary file.

-i **(Ignore).** Causes searches to ignore case.

-p **(Pattern).** Starts less on the first instance of a given pattern.

-s **(Squeeze).** Displays multiple blank lines as one blank line.

-s **(Chop lines).** Truncates long lines rather than wrapping them. In other words, lines too long for the display are chopped to fit and the remainder is discarded.

-u **(Printable).** Carriage feeds and backspaces to be treated as printable characters.

Example 1: Displaying a File with less

```
less /etc/rc.d/rc.modules
```

The preceding displays the file /etc/rc.d/rc.modules and enables you to navigate the file without having to open a text editor.

To move around in less, use the following keys:

- **Enter.** Move one line forward.
- **D or Ctrl+D.** Move forward one-half screen at a time.
- **B or Ctrl+B.** Move backward one-half screen at a time.
- **Left arrow.** Move horizontally to the left.
- **Right arrow.** Move horizontally to the right.
- **Shift + F.** Scroll forward.
- **G.** Go to the beginning of the file, or if preceded by a number, go to that line.
- **Shift + G.** Go to the end of the file, or if preceded by a number, go to that line.
- **H.** Display a summary of less commands.
- **Space.** Scroll forward an entire screen.

Viewing Running Processes with ps

Name: ps

Function: To display running processes.

Syntax: ps options pid(s)

Description: The ps command displays process status to standard out. You get a static report of what processes are currently running. The top command is similar, but it provides a continually updating report of processes and their status. The ps command is useful to see what processes are running, who has created the process, and what the process statuses are.

Usage: To use ps, type **ps** followed by any options and a process ID if you want to check a specific process and know its ID. If you don't know the ID of the process, you can run ps to find out!

Options:

    -1 **(Long).** Give lots of information.

    -u **(User).** Give user name and start time of processes.

    -m **(Memory).** Give memory usage.

    -a **(All).** Show processes created by other users as well.

    -x **(Detached).** Show processes that are not associated with a terminal.

    -c **(Command).** Show processes with the given command name.

    -w **(Wide).** Don't truncate output to fit on one line; display full information.

    -r **(Running).** Only show running processes.

    pid(s) **(Process IDs).** Show only the process IDs given. If you specify several process IDs, separate them with spaces.

Example 1: Show User's Current Processes

To show your processes, use the simple ps command:

```
ps
```

This displays only processes owned by the user who runs the ps command. The ps command also appears on the list of running processes.

Example 2: Show All Processes

To display all currently running processes, use the ps command with the -a and -x options (see Figure A.5):

```
ps -ax
```

The first number in the output is the process ID (pid). The next column in the output is the terminal from which the command is being run, and the third column displays the status of the command. Processes can have a status of running (R),

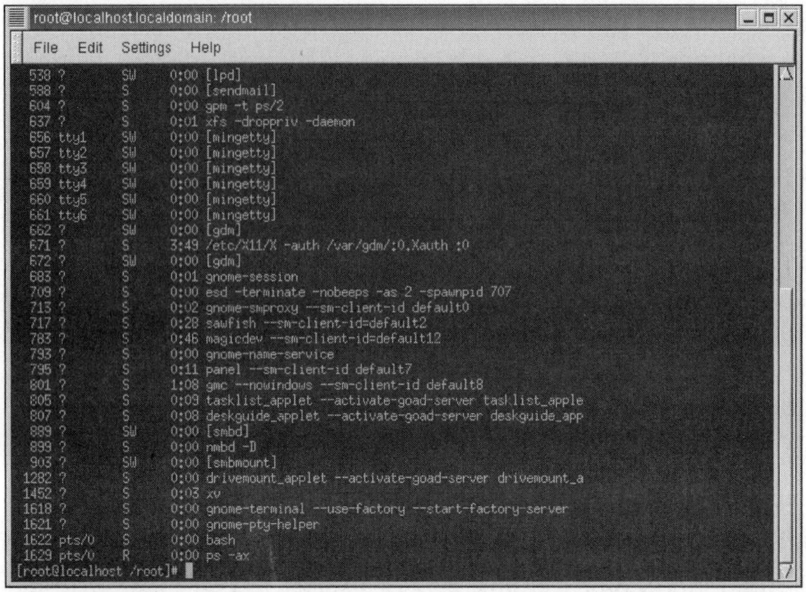

Figure A.5 *Output of* ps -ax.

sleeping (s), stopped (sw), or zombie (z). The fourth column displays the amount of time the process has been running, and the final column displays the command name.

Stopping Processes with kill

Name: kill

Function: To send a signal to a process. By default, kill sends the SIGTERM (terminate) signal.

Syntax: kill option pid(s)

Description: Generally, the kill command is used to terminate a process that does not terminate in another fashion. kill can send other signals to a process as well. The kill command can also list the signal names.

Options:

-s **(Signal).** Specifies which signal to send, which can be given as a name or number.

-p **(Print).** Tells kill not to send a signal to the process, but only to print the pid of the process.

-1 **(List).** Lists the signal names and numbers.

pid(s) **(Process IDs).** Specifies the processes to which the signal should be sent. If you want to send the signal to several processes, separate the IDs with spaces.

Example 1: Killing an Errant Process

If a process has stopped responding, you can use the `kill` command to stop the process. If the process ID you want killed is 212, the following should stop the process. Note that you can only kill a process you did not create if you are the superuser on the system.

```
kill 212
```

This tells the process to exit, but it first gives it a chance to clean up—perhaps it will save any data it has before exiting.

If the default signal sent by `kill` does not terminate the process, signal 9 (SIGKILL) should always terminate the process.

```
kill -9 212
```

You should use `kill -9` only when a normal `kill` won't do it, because this method forcefully terminates the process without giving it a chance to clean up.

> Be very careful using `kill`. If you terminate the wrong process ID while you are root, you could very easily cause problems for yourself or other users on the system.

CAUTION

Getting Help with the man Command

Name: man

Function: To display the man (manual) page for a command.

Syntax: man options command

Description: The `man` command is your friend. Really. If you learn no other Linux command—that is, commit no other command to memory—learn this one. If you know the name of a command, the man page tells you how to use it, providing the man page is installed on your system. (Hint: Don't save disk space by not installing documentation; you'll need it later!)

There are nine sections of man pages. They are:

1. **Commands.** Commands a user can execute from a shell.
2. **System calls.** System calls available from the Linux kernel. These are usually useful only to programmers.
3. **Library calls.** Functions available in libraries. These are usually useful only to programmers.
4. **Special files.** Pages for files found in /dev.
5. **File formats.** The format of files such as /etc/fstab and other useful files.
6. **Games and demonstrations.** Nuff said.
7. **Other.** Things like the man man page.
8. **System commands.** Commands only root can execute..
9. **Kernel information.** A manual section that contains information about kernel code.

Usage: Using man is simple. Just type **man** followed by the name of the command or file you want help with.

Options:

-f **(Output).** Equivalent to the whatis command.

-h **(Help).** Displays a brief help message.

1–9 **(Manual section).** Specifically names the man page section to search. Useful if the same command appears in multiple sections.

Example 1: Displaying the man Page for cp

To display cp's man page (see Figure A.6), simply type

```
man cp
```

The man pages are a bit cryptic—they're not necessarily written for non-Linux or non-geek types. However, the man pages display and explain, sometimes tersely, the options and syntax for each command. They're extremely helpful in a pinch.

Directory Structure

The directory structure under Linux is much different from the directory structure of typical desktop operating systems. Linux's directory structure is patterned after UNIX—everything is in a single directory tree. This tree includes all your files, your hardware devices, any devices you have mounted, and even dynamically generated information about your system.

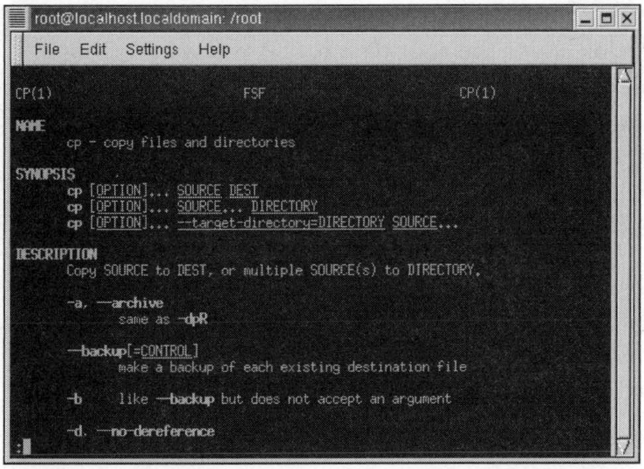

Figure A.6   *The* cp *man page.*

The / Directory

The / directory is typically called the root directory, not to be confused with /root, which is actually the home directory of the root user. All other directories fall under the root directory. Under Red Hat, this includes the following top-level directories:

- /bin
- /boot
- /cdrom
- /dev
- /etc
- /home
- /lib
- /lost+found
- /mnt
- /opt
- /proc
- /root
- /sbin
- /tmp
- /usr
- /var

> You can create other directories under the root directory if you want, although you should exercise some restraint. On systems that have Microsoft Windows or MS-DOS, I usually mount the DOS file system under /C or /Fat-C so I can use files between Linux and Windows when I need to. Remember, Linux can read FAT and FAT32 file systems, but you won't be able to see your ext2 file systems under Windows or MS-DOS.
>
> It's probably a good idea to store all of your personal files under your home directory rather than just piling them under the root directory. This helps you keep your system well organized and keeps clutter to a minimum.

The /bin Directory

The /bin directory is where the most basic binary executable files that are used systemwide are stored. As you may have guessed, /bin is short for *binary*. Executable files are often referred to as binaries on UNIX-style systems, which is probably a bit misleading. If you use WordPerfect under Linux, for example, the files are stored in a binary format, but they're not executable. Also, shell scripts are ASCII files that are flagged as an executable file, but they aren't stored in binary format.

Under the /bin directory you find most of the common commands like `ls`, `touch`, `mount`, `cd`, and other commands used by all users on the system. These fundamental commands are kept in this directory, separate from other programs (such as Emacs or games) to make it easier to recover a sick system.

The /boot Directory

Not surprisingly, the /boot directory contains files related to booting your Linux system. There is nothing very interesting in this directory, and it is probably best to leave it alone. You only modify files in this directory if you compile your own kernel.

The /dev Directory

The /dev directory is not a typical directory. It contains special files that represent devices attached to your system. Some of these are block devices, meaning they deal only in big chunks of data. Your hard drive is a block device. Others, such as your mouse, are character devices that only give and take a single character at a time. By reading and writing to and from these files, programs can communicate with your hardware. For example, the input from your mouse usually comes in to

```
Root Console                                              _ □ ×
File  Sessions  Options  Help
bash-2.03# cat /dev/mouse
```

Figure A.7 *Playing cat 'n' mouse.*

Linux from the file /dev/mouse. For a little fun, go to the /dev directory, type in **cat mouse**, and move your mouse around a bit (see Figure A.7).

```
cd /dev
cat mouse
```

> If you follow the previous steps, you start seeing a bunch of gibberish on the screen, because instead of directing your mouse input to the normal destination, you're directing it to standard output—namely your screen. Don't worry, you haven't broken your computer. Press Ctrl+C to quit sending the mouse signal to standard out. See what your computer has to put up with?
>
> If what you type is now gibberish too, blindly type **reset** and hit Enter to restore sanity.

NOTE

Your hard drive is represented in this directory. It probably is /dev/hda. You used this device when you configured partitions during installation. Advanced users might even read and write directly to these devices to make byte-for-byte copies of the hard drive.

Another popular destination under the /dev directory is /dev/null. This is basically the same as "File 13"—anything sent to /dev/null basically is being thrown away. This is sometimes useful for programmers to send output to /dev/null rather than write it to disk when there is output that has to go somewhere.

A final interesting device in this directory is /dev/zero. Like /dev/null, this isn't an actual physical piece of hardware, but Linux treats it as if it is. This device continually spits out zeroes. What good is that? For any politicians out there looking for a modern paper shredder, here's a quick way to totally blank a floppy:

```
cat /dev/zero > /dev/fd0
```

You probably don't have to worry about /dev too much, but there might be occasions when you can find use for directing input from a device to a file rather than to its normal destination—mostly for troubleshooting purposes. You also should be familiar with this directory when you are configuring new hardware.

The /etc Directory

The /etc directory, usually pronounced "etsee," contains configuration files and several other directories that contain more configuration files. Some of the more important files contained in /etc are the /XF86Config file, the /fstab and /mtab config files, and the /rc.d directory. The /XF86Config file contains the configuration information for XFree86, including which X server it should use, the refresh rate of your monitor, and information about your mouse and keyboard. You'll probably never need to edit this file directly, but it is there if you do.

The other two files, /fstab and /mtab, are short for Filesystem Table and Mount Table, respectively. The /fstab is created when you install Red Hat. If you add a hard drive or other storage device, you have to manually add a line for it to the /fstab. The /mtab is updated dynamically, depending on which devices currently are mounted on the system. For instance, if you mount a MS-DOS floppy (`mount -t msdos /dev/fd0 /floppy`), the /mtab gains a new line:

```
/dev/hda3 / ext2 rw 0 0
/dev/hdb1 /usr ext2 rw 0 0
/dev/hdb2 /opt ext2 rw 0 0
none /proc proc rw 0 0
/dev/fd0 /floppy msdos rw 0 0
```

The first entry, `/dev/hda3 / ext2 rw 0 0`, is my root partition, which is located on the third partition on my first IDE hard drive. It is an ext2 file system that is mounted with read and write enabled.

The /usr and /opt directories are actually mounted on separate physical partitions on my second IDE hard drive. They are also ext2 file systems, mounted with read and write enabled. The floppy is device /dev/fd0 mounted under /floppy, and it is an MS-DOS (FAT16) file system. If I had a second floppy drive, it would be /dev/fd1, and so on. If I unmount the floppy drive, the /mtab drops that entry. The /mtab exists for programs to read to see what devices are mounted.

The /etc/rc.d directory contains configuration scripts for the different run levels under Linux, as well as the files that control the console font, Samba, the serial port, and other fun things. You also find the ppp directory, which is where the config files for ppp are found. You might need to edit these to use ppp on your system.

The /home Directory

The /home directory contains the home directories of all users on the system (with the exception of the root user, whose home directory resides in /root). If your user name is bsmith, for example, your home directory would be /home/bsmith.

Because Linux is a multi-user system, having separate home directories for each user is a necessity. Other desktop operating systems allow users' files to be intermingled. Linux forces them to stay separate, giving you a bit of privacy and security.

The /ftp and /httpd directories are under the /home directory as well. If you are running an FTP or Web server, these directories contain the files visible to the outside world.

The /lib Directory

Under the /lib directory you find library files. Library files are files that are required when compiling or running many programs under Linux. Library files are similar to DLL files under Windows. This is another directory that it's best not to muck about in unless you need to and know what you're doing.

The /lost+found Directory

The /lost+found directory generally is empty. If your computer shuts down without properly unmounting the drives, Linux does a file system check (fsck). Any file fragments that aren't properly accounted for are put in the /lost+found directory. In general, as long as your system is healthy, this directory is unnecessary.

The /mnt Directory

Red Hat put devices such as the CD-ROM or floppy drive directories under /mnt.

The /opt Directory

The /opt directory contains optional programs—generally large programs. If you download a new version of Netscape, it might install here. The K Desktop Environment installs in the /opt directory by default as well.

The /proc Directory

The /proc directory does not contain actual files; it is generated on-the-fly by Linux. It contains information about running processes and the status of the hardware. You can get information about hardware devices or running processes by using the cat command on these files. For instance, you can find out what file systems your kernel supports by running the following command:

```
cat /proc/filesystems
```

Or, you can find out what interrupts your hardware devices are using by running this command:

```
cat /proc/interrupts
```

Generally, the /proc directory is an area for power users only, but on occasion you might be instructed to get information from the /proc directory in order to troubleshoot or configure devices.

The /root Directory

The /root directory is the home directory for the root user. When you are logged on as root, the cd command brings you to this directory. It is kept separate from the home directories in /home so that the root user can maintain the system, even if the /home directory gets destroyed.

The /sbin Directory

The /sbin directory contains more binary files. This directory is similar in purpose to /bin, except /sbin contains system binaries. Most are related to system upkeep. Typically, you must be root to use these binaries.

The /tmp Directory

The /tmp directory contains temporary files. This is a good place to stick a file you plan to delete. Many programs automatically create temporary files in the /tmp directory. KDE creates files in /tmp for the K File Manager and a few other programs while it is running, so it's a good idea not to delete anything in the /tmp directory while you're in KDE or X Windows.

The /tmp directory is a handy place to decompress and compile programs that you've downloaded. Once you've compiled and installed a program, you should be able to delete all the remaining unnecessary files from the /tmp directory. Be sure to keep an archived copy of the .tgz files you download in another area, though.

The /usr Directory

The /usr directory and its subdirectory /usr/local are often kept on separate partitions because of their size. The /usr directory is one of the larger directories, because it contains the majority of software on your system: the X11 directories, development tools, library files, and games.

The directory layout within /usr/local mimics what you see in /usr. Usually, Red Hat packages install in /usr. If you compile your own software, it goes in /usr/local.

The /var Directory

The /var directory contains variable files, mostly system logs. As a general rule, files under /var aren't of much interest unless you want to monitor the health of Linux or a Web server.

Directory structure under Linux is a bit more complex than under MS-DOS/Windows, but in the end it also makes more sense. Under DOS and Windows, directory structure tends to be a bit haphazard, and many third-party programs put program directories wherever they feel like it, with little rhyme or reason. There is actually a method to the madness under UNIX-style OSes, which should comfort you when you're getting used to the system.

Conclusion

This Linux Primer should give you a good idea of how to get around in the Linux CLI. Most users who are new to Linux and just want to use Linux as a workstation or desktop operating system probably don't need to be gurus at the shell prompt, but it never hurts to have an idea of how to get around the shell if needed. You might even find that using the CLI is better in many cases. The nice thing about Linux is that you don't need to make a choice between GUI and CLI; you can fire up KDE (or whatever your favorite window manager/desktop environment is), open several console windows, and go to town!

Appendix B: Online Resources

T hroughout this book, you have read about a lot of Linux configuration tips and tricks. Linux knowledge grows on a daily basis as more and more Internet sites are devoted to the care and feeding of this now-tame beast.

This appendix lists, by category, the Internet URLs for more Linux information and knowledge.

General Linux Information

Red Hat Linux	http://www.redhat.com
Linux	http://www.linux.org
Linux kernels	ftp://ftp.kernel.org
X Window	http://www.x.org
Prima Linux	http://www.primalinux.com
Linux Planet	http://www.linuxplanet.com
Freshmeat	http://freshmeat.net

Window Managers and Desktop Environments

GNOME	http://www.gnome.org
KDE	http://www.kde.org
Sawfish	http://sawmill.sourceforge.net
Desktop themes	http://www.themes.org

Editors

emacs	http://www.gnu.org/software/emacs
jed	http://space.mit.edu/~davis/jed.html
joe	ftp://ftp.std.com/src/editors/
Vim	http://www.vim.org

Graphics

Electric Eyes	http://www.labs.redhat.com/ee.shtml
GIMP	http://www.gimp.org
xfig xfig/	http://epb1.lbl.gov/homepages/Brian_Smith/

Internet

elm	http://www.instinct.org/elm
fwhois software.html	http://www.oxygene.500mhz.net/
gftp	http://gftp.seul.org
Lynx	http://lynx.browser.org
mutt	http://www.mutt.org
ncftp	http://www.ncftp.com
Netscape	http://www.netscape.com
pine	http://www.Washington.edu/pine/
slrn	http://space.mit.edu/~davis/slrn.html
tin	http://www.tin.org
trn	http://www.clari.net/~wayne
ytalk ytalk.html	http://www.iagora.com/~espel/ytalk/

Games

Linux Games	http://www.linuxgames.com

Appendix C: Hardware Compatibility Journal

A s you gather hardware information about your PC, feel free to fill out this form as a journal of the data you find.

CPU _____

Manufacturer _____

Model _____

Speed _____

Motherboard _____

Manufacturer _____

Model _____

Buses _____

Manufacturer _____

Model _____

Memory (RAM) _____

Size _____

Video Card _____

Manufacturer _____

Model _____

Video RAM Size _____

Monitor _____

Manufacturer _____

Model _____

Horizontal Synchronization Rate _____

Vertical Synchronization Rate _____

Hard Drive _____

Manufacturer _____

Model _____

Size _____

Type _____

   SCSI _____

   IDE _____

Network Card _____

Manufacturer _____

Model _____

CD-ROM Drive _____

Manufacturer _____

Model _____

Size _____

Floppy Drive _____

Manufacturer _____

Model _____

Size _____

Modem _____

Manufacturer _____

Model _____

Transmission Speed _____

Printer _____

Manufacturer _____

Model _____

Mouse _____

Manufacturer _____

Model _____

Type _____

   PS/2 _____

   Serial _____

Keyboard _____

Manufacturer _____

Model _____

Number of Keys _____

Language _____

SCSI Card and Devices _____

Manufacturer _____

Model _____

Type of Device Controlled _____

IDE Adapters _____

Manufacturer _____

Model _____

Type of Device Controlled _____

ZIP/JAZ Drive _____

Manufacturer _____

Model _____

Size _____

Tape Drive _____

Manufacturer _____

Model _____

Size _____

Sound Card _____

Manufacturer _____

Model _____

Scanner _____

Manufacturer _____

Model _____

Infrared Device _____

Manufacturer _____

Model _____

Type of Device Controlled _____

Joystick _____

Manufacturer _____

Model _____

Serial Device _____

Manufacturer _____

Model _____

Type of Device Controlled _____

Parallel Device _____

Manufacturer _____

Model _____

Type of Device Controlled _____

PCMCIA _____

Manufacturer _____

Model _____

Card Type _____

BIOS Settings _____

Network Settings _____

Appendix D: Advanced Configuration Reference

I n this appendix, several topics are introduced. Each topic is on the advanced side, so don't feel as if you have to tackle them at first. As you learn more and more about Linux, you can refer to this appendix to help solve some of the more sticky configuration issues you may run across.

The File System Configuration File (/etc/fstab)

An important configuration file for Linux file systems, /etc/fstab, holds all of the information necessary to mount a device. There are six fields in this file:

- `fs_spec`. Describes the device to be mounted.
- `fs_file`. Describes the mount point for the file system. Swap partitions should have `none` or `swap` in this field.
- `fs_vfstype`. Describes one of the above listed file-system types.
- `fs_mntops`. Describes the mount options, some of which are mentioned below.
- `fs_freq`. Describes whether the file system needs to be dumped with the `dump` command. A `0` indicates that the file system should not be backed up; a `1` indicates that it should be included in backups.
- `fs_passno`. Describes the order that file system checks are performed during boot. Swap partitions and devices with `noauto` in their `fs_mntops` should have `0`, the partition mounted as root should have `1`, and all other devices mounted at boot should have `2`.

The `fs_mntops` field needs some explanation. Each file-system type has its own special options, as well as options that are common to all. The options used most often in are

- `defaults`. This option sets the default options. It is equivalent to `rw`, `suid`, `dev`, `exec`, `auto`, `nouser`, and `async`.
- `user`. This option allows any user to mount and unmount the file system.
- `nouser`. This option allows only the root superuser to mount the file system.
- `ro/rw`. `ro` mounts the file system read-only. `rw` mounts the file system read-write.

NOTE

> If a device such as a CD-ROM drive that cannot be written to is mounted with the `rw` option, an error warning is displayed and the device is mounted read-only.

- **noauto.** This option disables the `mount -a` command for this file system. The file system must then be mounted explicitly.
- **auto.** This option is the opposite of `noauto`.
- **exec.** This option allows execution of binary files on this file system. This is the default.
- **noexec.** This is the opposite of `exec`.
- **suid.** This allows the set-user-identification bits to take effect.
- **nosuid.** This is the opposite of `suid`.
- **async.** This option sets all I/O to the file system as asynchronous.

In addition, one option is specific to the `ext2` file system:

- **usrquota.** This option enables user quota support. Quotas limit the amount of disk space available to a user. Group quotas are enabled by `grpquota`.

Other important options are specific to the `vfat` file system:

- **uid.** This option sets the owner of all the files in the file system to the user ID. Use `userconf` or `linuxconf` to match user IDs with user names.
- **gid.** Like `uid`, this option sets the group associated with all the files in the file system to the group ID. Use `userconf` or `linuxconf` to match group IDs to group names.
- **umask.** This option uses the octal numbering system used by `chmod` to mark the privileges denied for all files and directories in a file system. For example, `umask=002` sets rwx privileges for user and group and r-x privileges for others.

So that you can better understand how an fstab file works, I've copied mine so you can see what it looks like:

```
/dev/hda1       /C:         vfat     defaults,uid=500,gid=100,umask=2     1 2
/dev/hda2       /           ext2     defaults                            1 1
/dev/hda3       swap        swap     defaults                            0 0
/dev/hda5       /usr        ext2     defaults                            1 2
/dev/hda6       /home       ext2     defaults,rw,usrquota                1 2
/dev/hdb1       /D:         vfat     defaults,uid=500,gid=100,umask=2     1 2
/dev/hdb5       /E:         vfat     defaults,uid=500,gid=100,umask=2     1 2
/dev/hdc1       /usr/local  ext2     defaults                            1 2
/dev/cdrom      /mnt/cdrom  iso9660  noauto,owner,ro                     0 0
/dev/fd0        /mnt/floppy ext2     noauto,owner                        0 0
/dev/fd0        /mnt/A:     vfat     noauto,owner,umask=0                0 0
none            /proc       proc     defaults                            0 0
none            /dev/pts    devpts   gid=5,mode=620                      0 0
```

Notice that I have mounted some `vfat` (Windows) partitions in my root directory. This is a matter of style. Some people refuse to add anything here, preferring to keep it as bare as possible. I prefer including these file systems so that less typing is required when I need to access them. For those file systems that I must mount before accessing, I do so in the `/mnt` directory. This way, I am reminded to mount those file systems before accessing them.

I keep most of my data on my `vfat` file systems because, not only was it originally created in a `vfat` partition, I continue to access it regularly from Windows. I will probably move the data over to the Linux file system sometime in the future. An excellent freeware Windows program, called explore2fs, enables users to access ext2 file systems. It looks a little like Windows Explorer and is used to export and import files to ext2 file systems. You can get it at **http://uranus.it.swin.edu.au/~jn/linux/**.

Disk Geometry

Most of you know that hard disks can be divided into several partitions. A better understanding of disk geometry will help you install your boot loader and mount your partitions. This section gets a bit technical, but understanding the technicalities of disk geometry can help you avoid mistakes—and when they happen, make correcting them easier.

The first thing on your hard drive is the Master Boot Record (MBR); it contains some program code and a partition table of up to four partitions. The partition table stores the location of your partitions on your hard drive. Your MBR normally jumps to the first partition in the partition table marked active.

Following your MBR is one or more partitions. These partitions are either primary or extended. Primary partitions start with a partition boot sector; each file system treats its boot sector differently. DOS, for example, stores some important disk geometry information as well as the bootstrap loader, which is in the operating system (IO.SYS and MSDOS.SYS). Linux file-system types such as `minix` and `ext2` don't use the boot sector at all.

The extended partition is a special partition type designed to overcome the four-partition limit imposed in the MBR. Inside the extended partition is a chain of logical partitions. However, these partitions do not appear in the MBR's partition table. In this way, many more than four partitions can reside on a disk.

The extended partition has a boot sector, but it isn't used to boot an operating system. The partition boot sector looks like an MBR with a blank program code

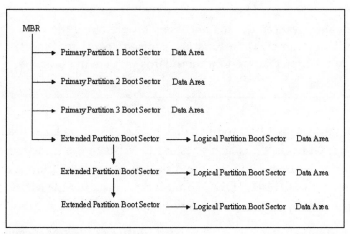

Figure D.1   *Disk-geometry map.*

area. The partition table contains a link to the first logical partition; it also points to another extended partition boot sector. This second extended partition points to a logical partition and a third extended partition boot sector.

Like primary partitions, each logical partition has its own boot sector. The file system in each logical partition uses this boot sector depending upon its needs: Linux file systems ignore the boot sector; DOS reads this sector for disk parameters and the bootstrap loader. Figure D.1 shows this relationship.

Note that the MBR sees only four of the partitions: three primary partitions and the first extended partition. Although only one extended partition is shown, you could make all the partitions extended. This can be difficult to implement, however, because most fdisk programs do not allow booting from a logical partition (you can use Linux's fdisk utility if you want to boot from a logical partition).

Size Limits

Older BIOSes impose disk size limits. There are several limit levels: 528MB, 2.1GB, 3.27GB, 8.4GB, and 137GB. Presently, the most common problem is the 8.4GB limit, which is the amount of hard drive space an older BIOS can keep track of. Possible solutions include upgrading your BIOS, which requires a *flashable* ROM. Check your manual for your motherboard or the manufacturer's Web site to determine whether your computer has this ability.

If your BIOS is upgradeable, you can get the necessary program and the code for the upgrade from the Internet. Unfortunately, it often seems that most motherboard manufacturers don't support motherboards that are more than a year or so old.

An alternative to upgrading your BIOS is to use a disk manager such as EZ-Disk or Ontrack's Disk Manager. The disk manager goes in the MBR of the first drive and, depending upon the software version, on the disk that needs help. Ontrack puts code it calls Dynamic Drive Overlay (DDO) on this drive just after the MBR. Ontrack offsets the entire disk by 63 sectors to allow space for its DDO.

Table D.1 displays my system's disk geometry. I needed Ontrack's Disk Manager to do the disk geometry translations for an old BIOS.

Table D.1   System Disk Geometry

Maxtor (6.4GB)	Quantum (12.8GB)	Seagate (1.2GB)
MBR (DM)	MBR	MBR
Boot sector	+DDO	Boot sector
1st partition	Boot sector	1st Partition
FAT32		FAT16
* Boot sector (LILO)	1st partition	
	FAT32	
2nd partition ext2	Extended partition boot sector	
Boot sector	Logical partition boot sector	
3rd partition swap	2nd partition	
	FAT32	

* = active boot partition

Linux currently has difficulty with disks larger than 33.8GB. There is a patch for this and it will probably be included in a future kernel. With this patch, Linux can see disks up to 2TB. Windows 95 OSR2 and later (Windows 98, 2000, and so on) can see disks up to 2TB as well.

Partition Types and Sizes

This section will give you some helpful advice about what sizes you should make your Linux partitions. If you typically learn as you go, this information will be equally relevant to you—for when you need to reinstall over a trashed system. It happens to everyone; call it a learning experience and count yourself a winner if you know what you did wrong. Thus are Linux gurus made.

Linux is different from many other operating systems in that it uses a special partition as swap space. Anyone familiar with Windows knows about swap files. Multitasking systems have several programs running at one. Each program requires physical memory. When this memory gets filled up, the computer puts some of the information on the hard drive. The space used for that information is called *swap space* because the computer swaps memory information in and out of this area. Linux uses a special partition type to speed up the process.

In previous versions of Linux, swap space partitions were limited to 128MB partitions. This limit is eliminated in the current kernel. You may still want to put smaller partitions on different drives, however. The speed of the heads limits the transfer rate from disk; you can optimize the transfer speed from disks to memory by running disks in parallel.

> If you are fortunate enough to have more than one drive available and one drive is faster than the other, place the swap space on the faster drive.

You can create a new swap partition quite easily. To do so, use the command `fdisk /dev/hda` where `/dev/hda` is the disk you want to partition. Some people, however, prefer to use the more user-friendly `cfdisk`.

Once the partition is created, make sure it is type 82 (Linux swap). Next, to format the swap partition, use the command `mkswap -c /dev/hda3`, changing `/dev/hda3` to your swap partition.

Next edit /etc/fstab to include the following line:

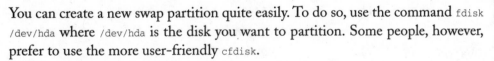

```
/dev/hda3            swap            swap    defaults    0 0
```

The new partition is ready for use. The next time Linux starts, a `swapon -a` command in your boot script will start it. For now, you can start it using the following command:

```
swapon /dev/hda3
```

With the memory requirements of X Windows and desktop environments such as GNOME, a swap space of 300MB is appropriate. If you don't plan to run X, you can get by with swap partitions of 100MB or less.

Many people install the rest of Linux on a single partition. This way you don't need to guess the future requirements of the directory tree's branches. This is usually the best choice for novices. If you plan to create another partition, it will likely be a /boot partition. /boot partitions are sometimes required to fit all of the boot files needed by LILO under BIOS's 1024-cylinder limit. /boot partitions need only be 10MB in size.

If you want to split the system up even more, Table D.2 displays my recommended partitions and sizes, in order of preference. If you mount a partition as a subdirectory, you should reduce the size of the parent.

Table D.2   Recommended Partitions

Partition	Mount Point	Memory Allotment
Workstation		
Boot partition	/boot	16MB
Swap partition	None	64MB
Root partition	/	The remainder of any unpartitioned space on the disk
Server		
Boot partition	/boot	16MB
Swap partition	None	64MB
Root partition	/	256MB
Var partition	/var	256MB
Usr partition	/usr	Half of remaining unpartitioned space on the disk
Home partition	/home	Half of remaining unpartitioned space on the disk

Some of these size recommendations numbers are very tentative. Your /home partition will have different needs depending on whether only one user is on the machine or there are a hundred users. Determining where you keep your data files also determines your needs. Don't try to use straight subtraction on the above table. For example, even with all the above listed subdirectories, your root directory will still need to be about 80MB.

If it takes so much guesswork to divide up the file system, why does anyone do it? The answer is that there are no archive bits. DOS users are familiar with archive bits; under DOS, when a file is backed up, its archive bit is cleared. Incremental backups are then quite easy. Linux's `ext2` file system does not have archive bits. If a person wants to back up only the most recent files, a more complex solution is needed. The easiest way is to back up the entire file system on a partition.

Even when backup data files are generated to allow incremental backups, you probably don't want all modified files backed up. Files in /var and /tmp are often changed, but you probably wouldn't want them backed up every time. Putting them in their own partitions separates these files from the rest of the system. It is also helpful to divide the system up so that an incremental backup can fit on one backup tape. Then the backup can be done overnight without requiring you to switch tapes.

Partitioning the system branches also makes sense for the aggressive Linux user. If you crash the system or want to do a clean install of a newer version, you can wipe the /usr partition but leave the /usr/local partition alone. This partition usually contains separately installed programs that would take a great deal of time to reinstall. Separate partitions really make that second install much easier.

If you want to go ahead with mounting a new file system, you first need to create a new partition. Use `fdisk` to create a new partition like you did for the swap partition. However, make this partition type 83.

Install the new file system using the command `mke2fs /dev/hda3`, changing `/dev/hda3` to your new partition. Next, edit your /etc/fstab file. Include a line like the following:

```
/dev/hda3        /var        ext2        defaults    1 2
```

Change `/dev/hda3` to reflect your new partition and `/var` to your mount point. You still need to copy your existing files in /var to the new file system. Rename /var to a temporary name, using the command `mv /var /var.old`. Now, create a new /var directory with the command `mkdir /var`.

Next, mount the new partition using `mount /var`. Finally, copy the directory contents from the temporary directory to the new file system using the command `cp -a /var.tmp /var`.

Remember, while using the commands listed here, to change `/var` to reflect the name of your own new mount point.

At this point, everything should be up and running okay. Keep the /var.tmp directory around for a few days in case there is a problem. If nothing is wrong, delete this directory using the command `rm -rf /var.tmp`.

LILO

LILO, the Linux Loader, has two main parts. The first part is called the *map installer*. It is the /sbin/lilo program run by the user from Linux. The second part of LILO is the boot loader, which doesn't have a name since it is only called by the system during the boot process.

The Map Installer

The easiest way to understand the map installer is to look at the configuration file, /etc/lilo.conf. Here is a simple example:

```
boot=/dev/hda2
map=/boot/map
install=/boot/boot.b
message=/boot/lilo.msg
prompt
timeout=50
single-key

image=/boot/vmlinuz
        label='Linux'
        alias=l
        root=/dev/hda2
other=/dev/hda1
        label='Win98'
        alias=w
```

Think of the configuration file as being in two parts. Those lines above `image` modify the map loader; those lines starting at `image` configure your boot images.

Modifying the Map Loader

The next few paragraphs describe each line of the part of the /etc/lilo.conf file that modifies the map loader.

boot=/dev/hda2

The `boot=/dev/hda2` line describes where the boot loader should be installed. In order of preference, the boot loader can go in a Linux partition (but not a swap partition), an extended partition (not a logical partition), or in the MBR on the first drive. (It needs to be in the first drive MBR because that is where the BIOS goes during the boot process.) The above example has the boot loader in my Linux partition—the second partition on my first drive.

If the boot loader will reside on a partition, that partition must be on one of the first two drives. Almost all BIOSes allow booting from only the first controller—that is, one of the first two disks.

If you want to run three operating systems (such as Windows 98, Windows NT, and Linux) on three disks, put Linux on the third disk. A small /boot partition on one of the first two disks will enable Linux to be booted.

map=/boot/map

The map file is the run-time configuration file for the boot installer. It contains all of the information from /etc/lilo.conf to tailor boot.b for your system, which is the file created by running the map installer, lilo.

install=/boot/boot.b

`install=/boot/boot.b` is the boot installer program code. It is called by the jump instruction residing in the MBR or partition.

message=/boot/lilo.msg

You can specify a message file to be displayed by the boot loader. It can be called anything. I find a short line listing my boot options to be convenient. For example, my message file includes a short description of my boot image alternatives:

```
(w) Windows 98 or (l) Linux
```

If you don't want this option but still want to see the choices offered at boot time, press Tab at the boot prompt.

prompt

If you want the boot loader to pause and present you with a boot prompt, use the `prompt` line. LILO will wait until you choose one of the boot images to load. An alternative is to hold down the Ctrl key while the LILO characters are displayed.

timeout=50

If you don't want the boot loader to stall while waiting for your input at the boot prompt, include a `timeout` line. It sets the maximum time (in tenths of a second) LILO will wait without any input at the boot prompt. Entering any character stops the timeout counter.

single-key

This command allows you to choose a boot image with one keystroke. For this to work, the boot image must have a label or alias of one character. No other label or alias can start with that character; in the example, I placed single quotes around the labels to work around this rule.

Other Commands

A few other commands can also be included in the configuration file.

- `default=l` **(where l is a label or alias).** If no input is received at the boot prompt, the default image is loaded. If this line isn't present, the first image in the file is considered the default.
- `linear`. If you have trouble with the boot loader, the `linear` command will probably fix the problem. Specifying the cylinders, heads, and sectors is a lot of work and probably won't solve the problem. Proceed with caution.
- `compact`. `compact` speeds up loading when booting from a floppy. This command and `linear` may conflict.

Configuring Your Boot Images

The next few paragraphs describe each line of the part of the /etc/lilo.conf file that configure your boot images. You need a different boot image for each operating system.

image=/boot/vmlinuz

Different operating systems have different requirements. The first boot image begins with the text `image=/boot/vmlinuz`. Use `image` to boot Linux from an image file. The Linux kernel's image file normally is named `/boot/vmlinuz`.

label='Linux'
alias=l

Each boot option needs a distinct name or label. I included aliases for each label for my single-key functionality, but I wanted the more verbose labels to display when the Tab key is pressed at the boot prompt. Note that the label `'Linux'` begins with a single quote so that the label and alias don't start with the same character.

root=/dev/hda2

`root` tells LILO on what partition to mount Linux as root (/).

other=/dev/hda1

If you want to boot another operating system, use the `other` command and the partition on which the other operating system resides.

Once you are satisfied with your configuration file, run lilo; it creates an up-to-date map file and places the jump instruction to the boot loader in a partition or the MBR. If you get really good and have read all the documentation, you can also use this program to change partition tables and do other neat stuff.

The Boot Loader

The boot loader is run automatically at boot time; it starts Linux, or DOS, or whatever operating system you included in the configuration file. This section examines the placement of the LILO boot loader. You can put the LILO boot loader in the program code area of the MBR, but don't do it unless you must. If you destroy the partition table in your MBR, all of the partitions on this disk are lost.

As an added safeguard, execute this bit of Linux mysticism first:

```
dd if=/dev/hda of=/fd/MBR bs=512 count=1
```

This command makes a data dump of your hard drive's entire MBR. If something bad happens and you need to restore your MBR, use the line

```
dd if=/fd/MBR of=/dev/hda bs=446 count=1
```

This command restores the MBR's program code, but leaves the partition table alone.

The placement of the referenced files is also very important. These files are usually stored together in the /boot directory. While Linux doesn't use the BIOS to access the hard drive, Linux isn't loaded yet and LILO is stuck using the BIOS Int 13 functions. These functions cannot see anything above the 1,024th cylinder. The result is that the partition containing the /boot directory must be below this limit.

If the partition containing your root directory extends above this limit, make a separate small partition just for this directory. Put this partition on one of the first two drives and completely below the 1,024 cylinder limit. The remainder of Linux can be anywhere: on higher cylinders, or on any other drives.

LOADLIN.EXE

LOADLIN is a DOS program used to boot Linux directly from DOS. It is an excellent alternative for the user who doesn't want to use LILO. It is also necessary for those Linux users who need DOS device drivers to configure their system before starting Linux. An example of this is when a sound card needs its IRQs changed in order to work properly.

To use this command, copy /boot/vmlinuz to your DOS drive. Make a batch file called LINUX.BAT. In it, have a command similar to this:

```
loadlin.exe c:/vmlinuz root=/dev/hda2
```

Include the correct paths for loadlin.exe and vmlinuz. Add LINUX.BAT's directory to your path statement in AUTOEXEC.BAT. Change the root partition to show the location of your root (/) drive.

Alternatively, this command could appear in CONFIG.SYS as part of a configuration switcher.

Viewing File-System Information

Both Linux and DOS include a `tree` command, used to see the structure of the file system. `tree` is not installed by default. Try the `tree` command; if it doesn't work, you need to install it. From the RedHat/RPMS directory on your installation CD (or hard drive subdirectory if you downloaded the release), enter the following command:

```
rpm -Uvh tree*
```

The `tree` command is simple to use and provides lots of output. For example, the command `~$ tree` yields the following:

```
.
|-- Application_Notes
|-- Daemon_Notes
|-- Desktop
|   |-- Autostart
|   |-- Printer.kdelnk
|   |-- Templates
|   |   |-- Device.kdelnk
|   |   |-- Ftpurl.kdelnk
|   |   |-- MimeType.kdelnk
|   |   |-- Program.kdelnk
|   |   |-- URL.kdelnk
|   |   '-- WWWUrl.kdelnk
|   |-- Trash
```

```
|    |-- cdrom.kdelnk
|    |-- floppy.kdelnk
|    |-- red_hat_errata.kdelnk
|    |-- red_hat_support.kdelnk
|    '-- www.redhat.com.kdelnk
|-- Disk_Notes.txt
|-- Hardware.Specs
|-- Initialization_Scripts
|-- Master ICC TOC.sdw
|-- StarOffice
|-- Startup-files
|-- dsk -> Desktop/
|-- notes.txt
'--ttt
```

```
5 directories, 22 files
```

When used with the -d switch, tree displays only directories. For example, the command ~$ tree -d yields the following:

```
.
'-- Desktop
    |-- Autostart
    |-- Templates
    '-- Trash
```

```
4 directories
```

If no directory is specified, tree displays the current directory. If you specify the root directory (/), the output will scroll for several pages.

Another very useful command is du. This command gives size of directories and files. It is particularly useful because it adds the disk used by files in subdirectories. The -s switch produces a single number for the size of the current branch. Size is measured in blocks unless you use the -h switch for more readable output. If you want to see the size of the branches off the root directory, type the following:

```
du -sh /*
```

Similar to du is the command df. This command displays the amount of total disk space, the amount used, and the amount remaining for each partition. For example, typing ~$ df -h yields the following output:

```
File system   Size   Used   Avail   Use%   Mounted on
/dev/hda2     486M   82M    379M    18%    /
/dev/hda1     4.0G   1.2G   2.8G    29%    /C:
/dev/hda5     1.1G   818M   210M    80%    /usr
/dev/hda6     329M   68M    244M    22%    /home
/dev/hdb1     7.6G   572k   7.6G    0%     /D:
/dev/hdb5     4.5G   441M   4.0G    10%    /E:
/dev/hdc1     387M   248M   119M    68%    /usr/local
```

File System Structure: A Tour

This section will take you on a tour around the Linux file system structure, starting at the root directory and then moving down through the directory layers. It will finish by introducing you to some points of interest.

- **/.** This is the root directory. It is the top of the directory tree.
- **/boot.** You have met /boot before; it contains the files necessary for LILO. /boot is often mounted on a separate partition.
- **/mnt.** I introduced you to /mnt earlier. It contains the mount points for user-mountable file systems.
- **/etc.** This directory is where most configuration files reside. Save this directory before you ever reinstall Linux.
- **/usr.** This directory holds most of the operating system. It also contains some important subdirectories.
- **/usr/doc.** This directory contains a number of documentation subdirectories. The directory name will help you decide where to go (for example, /usr/doc/lilo-0.21 for LILO).
- **/usr/doc/HOWTO.** This is a special document directory. It contains help for doing many common tasks. Look in /usr/doc/HOWTO/mini for additional, similar documents. After the man pages, this is the best place to go for help.
- **/usr/local.** This is where you usually install additional programs. I put StarOffice here, among others.
- **/usr/games.** Games usually reside in this and the /usr/local/games directory.

- **/bin.** This directory holds many of the basic Linux programs. After familiarizing yourself with the programs in this chapter, browse through this directory to improve your knowledge of Linux. Type the program followed by `--help` for a summary of the command options. Use the `man` command to see the manual on that command. If there is no manual page, try the `info` command.

- **/sbin.** This directory contains system programs.

- **/lib.** This directory contains shared libraries and modules.

- **/dev.** This directory contains references to the devices for your computer. You will refer to these devices, but rarely need to enter this directory.

- **/home.** Each user will be given a directory in this directory.

- **/root.** This is the root user's home directory. Note that /root isn't the root directory (/) and /home is never anyone's home directory. For example, /home/guest for user guest.

- **/proc.** This is a special directory; it doesn't exist. It takes up no space on your hard drive. It is, however, a convenient way to examine aspects of your operating system. You can find out some interesting things about your system by examining files in this directory. Examine cpuinfo, mounts, meminfo, and swap. There is also a very large file named kcore; this is a mirror of your kernel memory. The important thing to remember is that these files don't really exist; don't try to delete them.

- **/var.** This directory holds variables. If you try to delete files in this directory, you will probably change how some applications work. Other applications will then need to rebuild the lost variable files before running.

- **/tmp.** This directory is used to hold temporary files, such as auto-saved versions of a document. You can delete any large, old files here to free up space.

License Agreement/Notice of Limited Warranty

By opening the sealed disk container in this book, you agree to the following terms and conditions. If, upon reading the following license agreement and notice of limited warranty, you cannot agree to the terms and conditions set forth, return the unused book with unopened disk to the place where you purchased it for a refund.

License:

This book includes a copy of the Publisher's Edition of Red Hat Linux from Red Hat, Inc., which you may use in accordance with the license agreements accompanying the software. The Official Red Hat Linux, which you may purchase from Red Hat, includes the complete Official Red Hat Linux distribution, Red Hat's documentation, and may include technical support for Official Red Hat Linux. You also may purchase technical support from Red Hat. You may purchase Official Red Hat Linux and technical support from Red Hat through the company's web site (**www.redhat.com**) or its toll-free number 1.888.REDHAT1.

Notice of Limited Warranty:

The enclosed disc is warranted by Prima Publishing to be free of physical defects in materials and workmanship for a period of sixty (60) days from end user's purchase of the book/disc combination. During the sixty-day term of the limited warranty, Prima will provide a replacement disc upon the return of a defective disk.

Limited Liability:

The sole remedy for breach of this limited warranty shall consist entirely of replacement of the defective disc. IN NO EVENT SHALL PRIMA OR THE AUTHORS BE LIABLE FOR ANY other damages, including loss or corruption of data, changes in the functional characteristics of the hardware or operating system, deleterious interaction with other software, or any other special, incidental, or consequential DAMAGES that may arise, even if Prima and/or the author have previously been notified that the possibility of such damages exists.

Disclaimer of Warranties:

Prima and the authors specifically disclaim any and all other warranties, either express or implied, including warranties of merchantability, suitability to a particular task or purpose, or freedom from errors. Some states do not allow for EXCLUSION of implied warranties or limitation of incidental or consequential damages, so these limitations may not apply to you.

Other:

This Agreement is governed by the laws of the State of California without regard to choice of law principles. The United Convention of Contracts for the International Sale of Goods is specifically disclaimed. This Agreement constitutes the entire agreement between you and Prima Publishing regarding use of the software.